LIFE AND CORRESPONDENCE

OF

SAMUEL JOHNSON, D. D.

LIFE AND CORRESPONDENCE

OF

SAMUEL JOHNSON, D. D.

MISSIONARY OF THE CHURCH OF ENGLAND IN CONNECTICUT,
AND FIRST PRESIDENT OF KING'S COLLEGE,
NEW YORK.

BY

E. EDWARDS BEARDSLEY, D. D.,
RECTOR OF ST. THOMAS'S CHURCH, NEW HAVEN.

SECOND EDITION.

NEW YORK:
PUBLISHED BY HURD AND HOUGHTON.
London: Rivingtons.
1874.

RIVERSIDE, CAMBRIDGE:
STEREOTYPED AND PRINTED BY
H. O. HOUGHTON AND COMPANY.

PREFACE.

The materials for a volume of this kind are rarely accessible after the lapse of a century. Letters and papers of historic value are so often scattered and destroyed, that unless the biographer attends to his task in season, he may find it difficult to gather the information that he needs for writing with fullness and satisfaction. "If a life," said Dr. Johnson, the great name which is the pride and glory of English literature, "be delayed till interest and envy are at an end, we may hope for impartiality, but must expect little intelligence."

Though this work is published one hundred years after the death of its distinguished subject, yet I trust it will be found that besides being impartial, I have escaped the caustic criticism of giving "little intelligence." In writing the History of the Church in Connecticut, I fell upon original sources of information, which seemed never to have been carefully explored. Chandler's "Life of Johnson," brief and unsatisfactory as it may be, was very well for the day in which it appeared, and I should not have attempted an ampler biography, if I had not felt that it was now due to the memory of one of the most important names in American history.

The Johnson MSS., not a tithe of which could have passed under the inspection of Chandler, have all been kindly placed in my hands, and unless I had been familiar with them by previous acquaintance, the preparation of this work would have been much more laborious, and its publication longer delayed. As it is, the hours of leisure during a period of three years, if the busy Rector of a city parish may be supposed to have any leisure, have been devoted to it, and nothing has been overlooked which was calculated to shed any new light upon the character of Johnson, and the times in which he lived.

By introducing large portions of his correspondence with eminent men in this country, and with Bishops and leading minds in the Church of England, I have made him in a measure his own biographer, and at the same time rescued from oblivion faded manuscripts which the accidents of another generation might have put quite beyond our reach. One gets a better idea of a man from seeing him in his letters and writings than from the estimates of those who weigh him in their own scales, and describe him in their own language.

It was a remark of Bishop Jebb that "the lives of good men are an invaluable portion of a clergyman's library;" but it is to be hoped that these pages will not be limited to readers of this class. All who are interested in Yale College, its early struggles and first endowments, the gifts of Berkeley and the influence of his Philosophy, all who would know anything of the origin of King's (now Columbia) College, New York, and of the progress of liberal education in this country, and all who would thoroughly understand the efforts to secure the American Episcopate, the strange opposition to it, and the movements which led to the Revolution and the Independence of the Colonies, will find many fresh historical facts in this volume, and wonder why they were not before given to the public.

The engraving which forms the frontispiece is made from a portrait in the possession of his great grandson, Mr. William Samuel Johnson of Stratford. The painting, though there is nothing but a tradition in the family to support the statement, is without doubt from the pencil of Smibert, the artist who accompanied Dean Berkeley to America, and remained in Boston after the return of his friend and patron to England. It has the touch of Berkeley's own portrait by the same painter, which is among the treasures of Art that adorn the walls of Yale College.

New Haven, *December*, 1873.

CONTENTS.

LIFE AND CORRESPONDENCE

OF

SAMUEL JOHNSON.

CHAPTER I.

BIRTH AND PARENTAGE; EARLY EDUCATION AND STATE OF LEARNING IN THE COUNTRY; BACHELOR'S DEGREE FROM THE COLLEGE AT SAYBROOK; THE COLLEGE REMOVED TO NEW HAVEN, AND JOHNSON APPOINTED ONE OF THE TUTORS. HIS SETTLEMENT AT WEST HAVEN AND THE INFLUENCE OF A PRAYER-BOOK AND WORKS IN ENGLISH THEOLOGY.

A. D. 1696–1722.

It would not have been worth while to write the life of Samuel Johnson, had it been as barren of incident and historic interest as the lives of most clergymen. But he lived in eventful times, and the part which he bore in the literary, ecclesiastical, and educational affairs of the country will warrant the publication of fuller memorials than those hitherto given to the public.

He was born in Guilford, Connecticut, on the 14th of October, 1696, O. S., and was the great grandson of Robert Johnson, who with his wife Adaline and four sons, Robert, Thomas, John, and William, came from

Kingston upon Hull, Yorkshire, and first appeared at New Haven in 1641. Robert, the eldest of these sons, finished his academic education at Harvard College, and graduated in the class of 1645. He went to Rowley, in Massachusetts, where a brother of his father had settled, and was pursuing his studies with a view to the sacred ministry, when he sickened and died. In his will, dated "13th of the 7th mo. 1649," and probated at Ipswich "the 26th of the 1st mo. 1650," he directed his executors to distribute a portion of his goods to the poor of Rowley, and to return the remainder to his father, Robert Johnson, at New Haven. Thomas, the second son, died a bachelor. John married, and his descendants settled in Wallingford and Middletown.

William, the grandfather of Samuel Johnson, and who was twelve years old when the family emigrated from England, removed to Guilford, and became one of the leading men in that town and a deacon in the Congregational Church. He married July 2, 1651, Elizabeth Bushnell, daughter of Francis Bushnell of Saybrook, and had eight daughters and two sons — the youngest, Nathaniel, dying not long after his birth, and surviving his mother but a few weeks. Samuel, the father of the subject of this volume, was born in 1670, and at twenty-six married Mary, daughter of David Sage of Middletown, by whom he had eleven children, six sons and five daughters. He was a successor to his father in the office of a Congregational deacon at Guilford, and the distinguished son, late in life, speaking of them both, and giving some account of their character to one of his own children, said, they were "well esteemed for men of good sense and piety, but neither of them had much more of a turn for worldly wisdom than I have."

Samuel, though not the first-born of his parents, was the eldest child that lived beyond infancy, and he appears to have been a pet of his grandfather, William, who taught him to read and commit to memory not only passages of Scripture, but the Lord's Prayer and the Creed. He was very proud of his progress, and occasionally took the boy with him in visiting his neighbors, and made him repeat for their entertainment specimens of the knowledge which he had acquired. Among his earliest recollections, Samuel mentions finding in a book of his grandfather's several Hebrew words which excited his curiosity, but no one could tell him their meaning, or explain them further than to say they belonged to the original language in which the Old Testament was written. This but increased his desire for learning, and as the project of establishing a college in the colony at Saybrook, in the neighborhood of Guilford, had just then taken shape, he was marked out in the mind of the household as a future candidate for its course of instruction. Upon the death of his grandfather, however, which happened when he was six years old, the design was relinquished, and it might not have been renewed had not his fondness for books continued and the prospect of bringing him up to other business become discouraging.

In the eleventh year of his age, he was sent to a school, in his native place, kept at that time by Jared Eliot, a young man who had graduated at the new college, a son of the then recently deceased minister of Guilford, and whose affection for his pupil ripened into friendly relations in after life. But he was not long to enjoy the happiness of such an instructor. Before the year expired, Mr. Eliot relinquished the school to prepare for his settlement in the ministry at Killingworth, now Clinton, and the lad, impatient to learn, was finally sent from home and placed under the care of Joseph Smith, pastor of a newly organized church in Upper Middletown, now Cromwell. Though a graduate of Harvard College, Mr. Smith was not a scholar who inspired his pupil with much respect for his attainments, and after trying in vain for six months to make progress in his studies, he left his poorly qualified master and returned to Guilford.

Here he fell first into the hands of Daniel Chapman, another graduate of the new college, who was an improvement upon his last instructor, and with whom he continued for nearly two years. At length he found in the person of Mr. James, who had been educated in England, a respectable classical scholar, and notwithstanding some eccentricities of character, a very good teacher. Under his tuition he made rapid advancement in Latin and Greek, and by the time he had attained the age of fourteen years, he was pronounced fit to join the College at Saybrook.

There was not much to be proud of at this period in the state of learning throughout the country. The old scholars and Puritan divines of the Connecticut and Massachusetts colonies, who came with the early emigrants, had descended to their graves, and the generation that succeeded them, not having had the advantages of the Universities in England, fell behind the fathers, and was greatly deficient, if tested by a high standard of education. The course of studies prescribed in the new college was brief, for "the utmost as to classical learning that was now generally aimed at," says Johnson in his Autobiography,[1] "and indeed for twenty or thirty years after, was no more than to construe five or six of Tully's Orations, and as many books of Virgil poorly, and most of the Greek Testament," with a portion of the Hebrew Psalter. His first tutor at college was Joseph Noyes, one of the nine graduates of the institution in 1709, and afterwards for forty-five years pastor of the First Ecclesiastical Society in New Haven. His "tutorial renown" according to President Stiles, "was then great and excellent," and having some knowledge of Hebrew, he encouraged his pupil to devote the little leisure he might have, to the study of a language which he was chiefly desirous to understand, and which soon became his favorite branch of philology.

The tutor in the department of mathematics and mental and moral philosophy, was Phineas Fisk, and his instructions, like those of his colleague in the classics, had a limited range, and were confined to the imperfect systems not yet brushed away by the scientific discoveries of Descartes, Boyle, Locke, and Newton. When Johnson graduated in 1714, something had been heard of these great names, as well as of a new philosophy that was attracting attention in England, but the young men were cautioned against receiving it, and told that it would corrupt the pure religion of the country and bring in another system of divinity. Ames's "Medulla Theologiæ" and "Cases of Conscience" and "Wollebius," had been established as the standard of orthodoxy, and no variation from these was admissible. The trustees of the institution, at the

[1] MS.

outset, made a fundamental rule that special care should be taken to "ground the students well in theoretical divinity," and the Rector was forbidden to teach or allow others to teach any system contrary to their order.

It was less difficult to confine attention to the old scholastic systems, for the reason that books of learning in the land were rare, and opportunities for improvement small. The few works brought over from England by the first settlers were treatises published a century before; and Johnson early acquired a reputation for skill by making a synopsis of them, and reducing to some method all parts of learning then known,— "a curious cobweb of distributions and definitions" as he himself termed it,— "which only served to blow him up with a great conceit that he was now an adept." But his pride of opinion was afterwards thoroughly humbled. He accidentally fell in with a copy of Lord Bacon's "Instauratio Magna," or "Advancement of Learning,"— possibly the only one then in the country — and purchasing it immediately, he lost no time in devouring its contents. It opened to him a new world of thought. With an unprejudiced mind he read its pages, and considered and reconsidered the whole circle of sciences as they had been investigated and arranged by this remarkable man. He was thus led to see his own littleness in comparison with Lord Bacon's greatness, and to use his own words, he "found himself like one at once emerging out of the glimmer of twilight into the full sunshine of open day."

After completing his collegiate course and receiving the degree of Bachelor of Arts, he followed the example of Eliot, and entered upon the labor of teaching a school of the higher order in Guilford. His classmate and intimate friend, Daniel Brown, acted in the like capacity at New Haven, and the correspondence carried on between them at this period was full of affection, and bore upon theology, and questions that related to "philosophy in general and logic in particular." The concerns of the College, too, were much in their thoughts. Brown, in one of his letters dated August 3, 1716, wrote: "As to domestic affairs, please to be informed, that July 18, Mr. Moss, Hemingway, and Noyes, went to consecrate your chapel at the North Village. . . . This town hath given eight acres of land hard joining to the town plot, for the use of the College, if it comes here. Considerable of money is subscribed also."

The beginning of the institution was a contribution of about forty folio volumes, almost all theological, and given by different ministers of the colony "for founding a college in Connecticut." The next year, 1701, this library was increased by another private donation, and in 1714, Jeremiah Dummer, the agent of the colony in England, sent over a valuable collection of eight hundred volumes, some of which were his own gift, and the remainder had been obtained at his solicitation from various English gentlemen and authors. The whole number of books was now about one thousand, and among them were works of eminent writers of the Church of England, both clergymen and laymen. Johnson and his literary friends eagerly embraced opportunities of becoming acquainted with the new collection, and read for the first time the works of some of the best English divines and philosophers. The library was placed at Saybrook, where the instruction was carried on by two tutors, and where the private commencements were held. But no college building had been erected there; and as the original charter gave to the trustees the right of selecting the town in which the institution should be permanently fixed, a diversity of opinion arose on the subject, and sharp controversies sprung up which led to disorder and dissatisfaction among the students. They complained of the want of proper accommodations at Saybrook, and entertained so little respect for their tutors as to break out into open rebellion towards the end of the year 1715. Those from towns on the Connecticut River, acting under the guidance of Timothy Woodbridge and Thomas Buckingham, ministers at Hartford and trustees of the College, collected together at Wethersfield, where instruction was set up in a collegiate way by two tutors, and in which place or in Hartford these trustees wished the institution to be finally located. Other students from the sea-side towns put themselves under the care and tuition of Mr. Johnson at Guilford, while Mr. Andrew, the rector *pro tem.*, who resided at Milford, appears to have taken upon himself the instruction and oversight of the senior class.

The breach thus made in the colony could not be readily healed, and the Collegiate School, for so it was denominated at that time, continued in a disordered state till September, 1716, when a majority of the trustees, of which number was Governor Saltonstall, voted to remove it to New Haven. The sanction of the General Assembly, which met the following month, was asked and obtained for the removal, and then the trustees proceeded to elect Mr. Johnson one of the tutors; and with a view of conciliating the opposition, they chose Samuel Smith, who was of the Wethersfield party, to be the other. But the dissatisfaction was not appeased, and at Saybrook forcible resistance was made to the removal of the library, so that the Governor and Council deemed it expedient to convene there, and aid the sheriff in the performance of his duty. Besides other lawless acts, the carts provided for transporting the books were destroyed in the night time, the bridges between Saybrook and New Haven were rendered impassable, and during the week in which the library was upon the road, many valuable books and papers were lost. An attempt to supersede Governor Saltonstall at the next election, for his activity in the matter, was well-nigh successful,[1] and the feud in the government was not diminished when a subscription was set on foot in New Haven, "and in all the neighboring towns, for building a college; and one Mr. Caner of Boston was procured to undertake the work, who directly applied himself to the business."[2] Mr. Johnson, under a commission from the trustees, waited on Mr. Smith to induce him to accept the office of tutor and bring his scholars with him to New Haven, but he and his party were inexorable, and resolved to maintain their ground and carry on their design. Johnson, therefore, was obliged to enter upon the tutorship alone, and with about fifteen students from the sea-side began his course of instruction at New Haven, being assisted by Mr. Noyes, the minister of the town.

In 1718 the trustees appointed Daniel Brown to be

[1] Prof. Kingsley's *Sketch of Yale College*, p. 7.

[2] Johnson MSS.

his colleague, — the classmate whose turn of mind and thirst for knowledge not only made him an agreeable companion, but a hearty supporter of new studies in the line of philosophy and mathematics. By the autumn of that year several apartments were finished in the college building, and Johnson first lodged and set up housekeeping therein, and shortly his colleague followed his example. The institution was now gaining friends and a good reputation. The General Assembly had hitherto, for the sake of peace, connived at the faction in Wethersfield, hoping it would die out of itself; but at the October session in 1718, an act was passed requiring all the students to repair to the established college. "They made an appearance of submission, and came all at once in a caravan; but it soon appeared that they had no good intention; they found fault with everything, and made all the mischief they could, as they were doubtless instructed to do;"[1] and after six weeks they withdrew and rejoined the old faction. At the next session of the General Assembly measures were concerted to reconcile the conflicting interests, and finally the difference was compromised in this way: the scholars should return to their duty and abide at New Haven; and in case they did, the degrees which had been given at Wethersfield should be allowed good, "and a State House should be built at the public expense at Hartford." Thus the unhappy controversy — a manuscript history of which by Johnson has been preserved — was terminated, and liberal donations of money and of books by Governor Yale gave to the college a new impulse, and the name which it now

[1] Johnson MSS.

bears was then conferred on it in honor of him for his timely benefactions.

The state of the institution demanded a resident rector, and as Mr. Andrew was advanced in life and disinclined to remove from Milford, the trustees chose Timothy Cutler, who had been for ten years the pastor in Stratford and a popular preacher in the colony, to be his successor. He was a native of Charlestown in Massachusetts, and graduated at Harvard College in 1701. His learning and superior talents qualified him for the station; but the thought of his separation from them grieved his parishioners, and they resisted it for some time with much firmness. At length, however, it was accomplished, and Mr. Cutler established himself with his family at New Haven in the autumn of 1719, after which Johnson retired from the office of tutor, though not from association with his literary friends — the Rector and Mr. Brown. Theology was the study to which he had always intended to devote himself; and as the people of West Haven — a village only four miles from the college, and at that time a part of New Haven — earnestly desired him to settle among them, he yielded to their solicitations, and was ordained there in the Congregational way on the 20th of March, 1720, "having been," according to his own account, "a preacher occasionally ever since he was eighteen."[1] He might have found other fields of pastoral labor in many respects more inviting, but his desire to be near the college and the library, as well as near those for whose society he had the keenest relish, led him to forego the acceptance of better offers, and give

1 *Autobiography.*

the preference to a situation of comparatively little promise.

The books most frequently in his hands at this period were not calculated to strengthen his faith in Independency, and some time before his ordination, for the purpose of "methodizing his thoughts," and assisting his memory, he drew up a scheme of religion, embracing its doctrines and duties, and following the plan of John Scott in his "Christian Life," a work which he greatly admired and pronounced to be the best and most compendious that had yet fallen in his way. His inquisitive mind would not allow him to rest contented in hasty conclusions, and so early as 1715 he met with the discourse of Archbishop King on "the Inventions of Men in the Worship of God," — the reading of which helped to increase his dislike of extempore prayers, and to confirm him in the opinion that the use of pre-composed forms of public worship was more devotional, and showed much greater reverence for the Divine Majesty. He had been bred up in prejudice against the Church of England, but a good, religious man in Guilford placed in his hands a copy of the Book of Common Prayer, and this, with the treatise of Archbishop King, perused the year before, caused all his prejudices to vanish, and inspired him with a love of the Liturgy, which, contrary to his former belief, he found to be collected for the most part out of the Holy Scriptures.

The direction of his thoughts may be learned from the books which he read after retiring from his tutorship in the college. About the time of his settlement at West Haven he began a catalogue of those, which he perused with evident care, and curiously enough, at the head of this list stands the Liturgy of the Church of England, followed immediately by Potter on "Church Government," and Patrick's "Devotions;" and a little later, by "The Whole Duty of Man," Wall on "Infant Baptism," Echard's "Church History," and Hooker's "Ecclesiastical Polity." The shelves of the well-selected library contained other books in English theology — among them the works of such eminent divines as Barrow, Beveridge, Bull, Burnet, Hoadly, Pearson, Sharp, Sherlock, South, Taylor, Tillotson, Wake, and Whitby, and all were included in the list of those which passed under his review and consideration during the brief period of his residence at West Haven. So much was he opposed to extempore prayers in public that he provided himself with forms drawn chiefly from the Liturgy of the Church of England, and repeated them with a fervor which won the admiration not only of his own flock but of persons connected with the adjoining parishes. It was his ordinary practice to compose carefully one discourse a month; but he read attentively the sermons of Barrow and other celebrated preachers, and so charged his mind with their thoughts that, by the help of a few notes, he delivered the substance of them in language of his own, and thus acquired a facility of expression which became of service to him in after life.

It is easy to foresee the influence which such a course of reading would have upon a candid and inquiring mind like that of Johnson. It threw new light over subjects that had long embarrassed him, and he was unable to find any sufficient support for the Congregational form of church government or for the rigid

Calvinistic tenets in which he had been educated. He spoke his doubts to his literary friends, and they shared them with him; so that from first meeting in a fraternal way at the residences of each other or in the college library, and examining the doctrines and practices of the Primitive Church, they had begun to be uneasy and anxious about the form and authority of their own discipline and worship. How to conduct themselves under the circumstances was a delicate question. There were six of these earnest inquirers besides Johnson, and they occupied responsible positions in and around New Haven. Cutler and Brown carried on the college; John Hart was the minister at East Guilford, now Madison; Jared Eliot was the minister at Killingworth; Samuel Whittelsey at Wallingford; and James Wetmore at North Haven. With the exception of Cutler, all were graduates of the college, and three of them were classmates, who had been brought into very intimate association with each other. Their conferences and readings led them to the conclusion that the Church of England was the nearest to the apostolic model, and if conformity to it had been an easy thing, they would most likely have relinquished at once their positions and made the change. Johnson wrote in his private journal, on the 3d of January, 1722, these honest and touching words: —

I hoped when I was ordained that I had sufficiently satisfied myself of the validity of Presbyterian ordination under my circumstances.[1] But alas! I have ever since had growing

[1] A manuscript of Johnson "written at Westhaven, Dec. 20, A. D. 1719," entitled, "My present Thoughts of Episcopacy with what I conceive may justifie me in accepting Presbyterial Ordination," gives the state of his mind three months before he was formally set apart to the work of the ministry. In this paper he first sets down his apprehensions formed from the best light he could obtain, which were entirely favorable to Episcopacy, and then considers the circumstances under which he was called

suspicions that it is not right, and that I am an usurper in the house of God, which sometimes I must confess fills my mind with a great deal of perplexity, and I know not what to do; my case is very unhappy. Oh that I could either gain satisfaction that I may lawfully proceed in the execution of the ministerial function, or that Providence would make my way plain for the obtaining of Episcopal orders. O my God, direct my steps; lead and guide me and my friends in thy way everlasting.

The Church of England scarcely had a foothold in Connecticut at this time. The Rev. George Pigot, a Missionary of the Society for the Propagation of the Gospel in Foreign Parts, arrived at Stratford in the spring of 1722, and was as much surprised as gratified to receive from Johnson an early visit, and learn from him the direction in which some of the leading minds in the colony were drifting. He was pleased to accept an invitation to hold a private conference with the inquirers at New Haven, and the result was too good to be kept from his parishioners and from the knowledge of the Society at home. Writing to the Secretary in August, he said: "The leading people of this colony are generally prejudiced against their mother church, but yet I have great expectations of a glorious revolution of the ecclesiastics of this country, because the most distinguished gentlemen among

to proceed. Among the reasons that led him to accept Presbyterial ordination — were "the passionate entreaties of a tender mother," the effect upon the College, if he publicly declared for Episcopacy, his "want of that politeness and those qualifications which would be requisite in making such an appearance," and the not understanding sufficiently what was needed to take Episcopal orders. "Although I seem," he adds in conclusion, "tolerably well satisfied in these my thoughts of the right of Episcopacy, yet, considering the meanness of my advantages and the scantiness of my time hitherto, I have reason to be very jealous whether I have not too much precipitated into those opinions, and then finally perhaps I may in the mean time be doing some service to promote the main interest of religion, though it be not as a method so desirable."

them are resolvedly bent to promote her welfare and embrace her baptism and discipline, and if the leaders fall in, there is no doubt to be made of the people. Those gentlemen who are ordained pastors among the Independents, namely, Mr. Cutler, the president of Yale College, and five more, have held a conference with me, and are determined to declare themselves professors of the Church of England, as soon as they shall understand they will be supported at home; they complain much, both of the necessity of going home for orders, and of their inability for such an undertaking; they also surmise it to be entirely disserviceable to our church, because, if they should come to England, they must leave their flocks, and thereby give the vigilant enemy an opportunity to seize their cures and supply them with inveterate schismatics; but if a bishop could be sent us, they could secure their parishes now and hereafter, because the people here are legally qualified to choose their own ministers as often as a vacancy happens, and this would lighten the Honorable Society's expenses to a wonderful degree."[1]

Pigot read with too much hope what he regarded as the signs of the times. He had only been in the colony a few months, and his interview with these gentlemen had made him sanguine that their declaration for Episcopacy would be followed by the conversion of other ministers of less note, as well as by the conversion of large portions of their respective flocks. He had not seen how the spirit of the old Puritan opponents of the Church of England would rise up against the movement, and the "glorious

[1] *Documentary History, Conn.*, vol. i. p. 57.

revolution of the ecclesiastics," if not a picture of his imagination, was at least still in embryo. Johnson, who was the leader of the van, and the most active among them, appears to have kept his mind open to conviction, for after making an entry in the catalogue of books before referred to of the works of Cyprian, he added immediately under it these words: "Which, with other ancient and modern authors read for these three last years, have proved so convincing of the necessity of Episcopal Ordination to me and my friends, that this Commencement, September 13, 1722, we found it necessary to express our doubts to the ministers, from whom, if we receive not satisfaction, we shall be obliged to desist."

CHAPTER II.

THE DECLARATION OF JOHNSON AND HIS FRIENDS; STRUGGLE BETWEEN FEELINGS AND DUTY; DEBATE BEFORE GOVERNOR SALTONSTALL AND ITS RESULTS; EXTRACTS FROM NOTES OF DAYS; VOYAGE TO ENGLAND FOR ORDINATION; ARRIVAL AND RECEPTION; PRIVATE JOURNAL.

A. D. 1722–1723.

THE formal declaration of Johnson and his friends, made by request of the Trustees, recited that "some of them doubted the validity, and the rest were more fully persuaded of the invalidity of Presbyterian ordination in opposition to the Episcopal." They asked for "satisfaction," and time was allowed for further inquiry and consultation, in the hope that they might get rid of their scruples, or at least be quiet and contented in their positions.

Johnson entered in his Notes of Days, September 17, immediately after the Commencement, this account of his feelings: —

Being at length bro't to such scruples concerning the validity of my ordination, that I could not proceed in administration without intolerable uneasiness of mind, I have now at length (after much study and prayer to God for direction), together with my friends (Mr. T. Cutler, Mr. J. Hart, Mr. S. Whittelsey, Mr. Jared Eliot, Mr. James Wetmore, Mr. Daniel Brown), after some private conferences with ministers, this Commencement made a public declaration of my scruples and uneasiness, and am advised to suspend administration for the present. It is with great sorrow of heart that I am forced thus, by the uneasiness of my conscience, to be an occasion of so much uneasiness to my dear friends, my poor people, and indeed to the whole Colony. O God, I beseech Thee grant that I may not, by an adherence to Thy necessary truths and laws (as I profess in my conscience they seem to me) be a stumbling-block or occasion of fall to any soul. Let not our thus appearing for Thy Church be any ways accessory, though accidentally to the hurt of religion in general or any person in particular. Have mercy, Lord, have mercy on the souls of men, and pity and enlighten those that are grieved at this accident. Lead into the way of truth all those that have erred and are deceived ; and if we in this affair are misled, I beseech Thee show us our error before it be too late, that we may repair the damage. Grant us Thy illumination for Christ's sake. Amen.

The General Assembly was to meet in New Haven the ensuing October, and at the suggestion of Gurdon Saltonstall, the Governor of the Colony, a debate was held in the College Library, the day after the session commenced, for the purpose of discussing the whole subject, and disposing of questions that had created serious alarm in the public mind. "He moderated very genteely" on the occasion ; but the "gentlemen on the Dissenting side" had not directed their studies this way, and hence when they came to the debate they were not so well prepared to cope with their opponents and answer their arguments. They rested their chief objection to Episcopacy on the promiscuous use of the words *bishop* and *presbyter* in the New Testament; but this objection was met by citing such Scripture facts as the evident superintendency of Timothy over the clergy and people at Ephesus, of Titus in Crete, and of the angels of the seven churches in Asia. The history of the first and purest ages of Christianity was also appealed to, and "at length," says Johnson in his Autobiography, "an old minister got up and made an harangue against them in the declamatory way to raise an odium, but he had not gone far before Mr. Saltonstall got up and said he only designed a friendly argument, and so put an end to the conference."

Eliot, Hart, and Whittelsey were unable to withstand the alternate fury and entreaties of their friends, and leaving their scruples behind, they quietly settled back into their former relations, and continued to the end of their days in the service of the Congregational ministry.[1] But the others were more resolute, and followed their convictions. Johnson made a private record of the reasons which influenced him in the step they were about to take. They are worth producing here in full: —

Oct. 6, 1722. — In the fear of God setting myself now upon the serious consideration of the great and urgent affair now under my hand and a deliberate examination wherein my duty lies, I now set down the motives which lie before me on both sides of the question, whether I shall now go over to England and offer myself to the service of the Church?

1. That which I propound to govern myself in general in this affair is the awful account which I expect to give of all that I do in this world, before the dread tribunal of God, where the secrets of all hearts shall be disclosed, and every one shall receive according to his work.

2. Though I have been a grievous sinner, and deserve to

[1] Chandler, in his *Life of Johnson*, p. 31, says: "Amidst all the controversies in which the Church was engaged during their lives, they were never known to act or say or insinuate anything to her disadvantage."

be left of God, yet as those instances wherein I have offended bear no relation to any of these controversies, and therefore cannot be supposed to have any influence, by way of temptation, to the present undertaking, but (if anything) the contrary; so I do renounce and abhor them, judge and condemn myself for them, and humbly purpose to continue forever in watchfulness against, and war with them, — and to make business of mortification, by God's grace, imploring his pardon and mercy in Jesus Christ, and therefore I hope in God He does not, and will not abandon me to err in anything of great consequence.

3. God's glory, the good of his Church in general and the safety of precious souls in particular, are the ends I would always and particularly in the present case have in my eye.

4. Upon the most deliberate consideration I cannot find that either the frowns or applauses, the pleasures or profits of the world have any prevailing influence in the affair.

One week later, and three days before the discussion in the College Library he made another record thus: —

Oct. 13. — Now therefore to consider particularly what lies against,—

I. In the first place, and here are several particulars.

1. Some few seeming texts of Scripture and a possibility of interpreting all on the side of and in favor to Presbytery.

2. Breaking the peace of the country in general and my own people in particular, which are great things.

3. Danger of the stumbling of weak brethren and the damage of precious and immortal souls, and grieving good men. Now these considerations are indeed of great weight, and it is not a little thing should be sufficient to balance them.

II. On the other hand I consider, —

1. Sundry texts of Scripture there are which seem to me plainly to intimate that Episcopacy is of apostolical ap-

pointment, which together with the unanimous witness of the Church immediately after the Apostles' times and downward in the purest ages of Christianity, seem as much at least (if not more) to oblige my conscience to submit to Episcopacy as a divine appointment, as to observe the first day of the week, and therefore do as much oblige me to declare in favor of Episcopacy in this country as for the Lord's day, supposing I am in a seventh day country.

2. If this be therefore a divine or at least apostolical institution (as I am fully persuaded it is), fear of breaking peace should not shut up my mouth in a matter of so much consequence.

1. Considering first that this country is in such a miserable state as to church government (let whatever hypothesis will, be right), that it needs reformation and alteration in that affair.

2. The least I can say is, that I was in so much doubt whether my ordination was lawful, that it utterly hindered my devotion in administration.

3. I am indeed forced to think (comparing my case with what I find in ancient authors, and especially in S. Cyprian) that had I lived and administered without and in opposition to Episcopacy, I should have been excommunicated for a schismatic in the purest ages.

4. That peace without one of Christ's institutions is a false peace, and it is best being on the surest side.

5. There may be offense taken where there is none given. If others are damnified by my doing my duty I cannot help that, however I endeavor the contrary.

6. There may be more souls damnified for want of Episcopal government in the country and that by far at length, than by my making this appearance.

7. If I am, by what ordination I have had, consecrated to God, yet I am not on this account guilty of sacrilege for that I design yet to devote myself, my whole life to the service of Christ and his Church, and so promote the good of precious souls, and this (if I might be allowed, and so far as I am allowed) in this place [West Haven].

These considerations all laid together, it seems to be my duty to venture myself in the arms of 'Almighty Providence to cross the ocean for the sake of that excellent church, the Church of England ; and God preserve me, and if I err, God forgive me.

This transcript of his feelings is a proof that he did not expect any new light to rise from the debate in the College Library, and shine through his doubts. His convictions had settled into a definite plan of action, and the 23d day of October found him and his two friends, Cutler and Brown, on their way to Boston to embark for England. It was a slow journey, and reaching Bristol, in Rhode Island, on the 28th, he made a note thus, — "We were most kindly entertained at Bristol, at Colonel Mackintosh's. Here, being Sunday, I first went to church. How amiable are thy tabernacles, O Lord of hosts. Mr. Orem preached." Taking with them a letter from this gentleman to the Secretary of the Society for the Propagation of the Gospel in Foreign Parts, they proceeded to Boston where they were warmly welcomed by friends interested in their movement, and spent a few days before embarking in the ship *Mary,* commanded by Captain Thomas Lithered. These friends had engaged their passage in this vessel, and very kindly at their own expense they provided everything necessary for the voyage. The last day in Boston is mentioned by Johnson in his private journal as follows :—

November 4. — Sunday. Mr. Brown and I read the Earl of Nottingham against Whiston. This day, by God's grace I first communicated with the Church of England. How devout, grand, and venerable was every part of the administration, every way becoming so awful a mystery ! Mr. Cuthbert of Annapolis Royal, preached. To-morrow we venture upon the great ocean for Great Britain. God Almighty preserve us!

The voyage across the Atlantic one hundred and fifty years ago was a momentous and awful undertaking. It was not attended with as many comforts as now, and a sailing vessel was the only mode of conveying passengers. Business rather than pleasure impelled men to attempt it, and strong health was needed to bear its hardships. In these days of steam navigation, when quick passages in large floating palaces are confidently anticipated, we are apt to forget the sacrifices and trials of those, who in the close and narrow cabins of sailing ships, were tossed for weeks and months on the ocean, and entirely dependent upon favoring gales to waft them to the point of their destination. Johnson in a fine hand, which it must have required the sharpest eyesight to have written as it does now to read, kept "a journal of his voyage to, abode at, and return from England," and some idea of his perils and of the manner in which he employed his time, may be formed by liberally extracting from its pages. His entries during the outward passage are thus made: —

November 15. — We have been even ten days now upon the great ocean, and have had much contrary wind, made small progress, were once in danger. God preserved us. To whom be glory. May He send us a good and prosperous gale of wind for Christ's sake. I have just finished reading, since I came on board, the Abp. of Cambray's demonstration of the existence of God.

20*th*. — We are, through God's goodness, safe after an other grievous storm.

23d. — Just finished Mr. Kettlewell on the Sacrament, now finished Mr. Herbert's "Temple."

26th. — We are safe, by God's goodness, after a storm. Just finished Mr. Nelson's "Practice of True Devotion."

29th. — Finished Dr. Taylor's "Golden Guide, or Guide to Devotion and for the Penitent," and "Hudibras."

Dec. 3d. — Yesterday, Dec. 2, a grievous storm. Thanks to God we are yet safe! Three last week.

Finished Dr. Bray on the Baptismal Covenant.

5th. — This week tolerable weather, only the wind too southerly.

Finished Osterwald's Catechism.

12th. — This day we came to soundings.

Finished reading "The Gentleman instructed in the conduct of a virtuous and happy Life." Truly an excellent piece. Dedicated by Dr. Hicks.

14th. — This day, blessed be God, we first came in sight of land. The first we made was the Isle of Wight, having been ten days without an observation. We were marvelously conducted by the good hand of Providence through the fog thus far up the channel: *cui laus.*

Read a short answer to a Popish Catechism. Anon.

Thus ends our boisterous and uncomfortable voyage, after five weeks and four days.

N. B. — We read prayers Sundays, Wednesdays, and Fridays.

It was purely for religious purposes that they encountered such perils on the sea. A conscientious regard for what they believed to be the truth, and not ambition or the spirit of adventure, led them to great self-sacrifices. The cordiality of their reception in England, where the knowledge of their affair had preceded them, and the interest and enthusiasm with which they viewed everything connected with the strength and glory of the Church, are best shown by extracts from Johnson's private journal.

December 15.—This day we arrived safe, by God's goodness, at Ramsgate, in the Isle of Thanet, were kindly entertained at Capt. Lithered's house, whence we took horse and came to Canterbury that night, being Saturday.

16*th*.—This day, being Sunday, we went to church (Dr. Cumberland read service) at the magnificent Cathedral of Canterbury, where we heard one Mr. Archer preach on the story of the Ethiopian and St Philip. In the afternoon we were by mistake directed to a meeting. After which we viewed the ancient magnificence of the Cathedral and heard evening service there. 84 Ps. was sung.

17*th*.—This day we went to service again at the cathedral, where we had opportunity for further view of that stately building, 500 feet in length, and by 275 steps we ascended the tower of it, where we left our names. In the afternoon we waited on Dean Stanhope, who was pleased to take a very gracious and friendly notice of us. After evening service we viewed the walls of the city and other instances of ancient magnificence.

18*th*.—This day we waited on Dr. Wilkins, one of the Prebendaries,—after which we went to service; which ended, we took a further view of the city, especially the churches, walls, and Tower, then dined with Dr. Grandorgh, who showed us the Library of the Cathedral, etc. After evening service we were invited by Mr. Norris to his house, and spent the evening there in company with Mr. Hughes, Mr. Gosling, Senr and Junr, who expressed great civility and kindness.

19*th*.—This day we took coach and came to Rochester and Chatham, and there lodged.

20*th*.—This day from thence by coach we came to London.

21*st*.—This day we provided our lodgings at Mrs. Wyldman's, in Fetter Lane, after which we were at the Exchange and N. England Coffee House, after which we waited on Mr. Hay.

23*d*.—This day, being Sunday, in the forenoon we went

to service at the famous Cathedral of S[t] Paul, where we heard Mr. Bramston on 21 Mat. 9 v. Hosanna. In the afternoon we were at S[t] Mary's, Aldermary, where we heard Mr. Jno. Berriman on 1 Tim. i. 15, with whom, after service, we conversed at Mr. Buckridge's, from whence we went to Mr. Hay's.

24th. — This day we went to Mr. Hay's, where we had opportunity with Dr. Wm. Berriman, the Bishop of London's chaplain, from whom we had a letter to Dr. Ibbotson, the Abp. of Canterbury's chaplain, wherewith we went to Lambeth, but his Grace was indisposed. After which we went over from Lambeth to Westminster and viewed the Abbey and the Hall, and sundry ancient monuments.

25th. — This day, being Christmas, we went to church at S[t] Dunstan's, where we heard Dr. Jenks from 85 Ps., 10, 11, — "Mercy and Truth," etc.,—from whom we received the Holy Eucharist, after which we took coach and went to dine with Sir Edw'd Blacket (having been invited by the Lady Blacket), from whence, in our return, we were at evening service in S[t] Ann's church.

26th. — This day we conversed with Mr. Th. Coram.

27th. — This day we were at service in the morning at S[t] Andrew's, Undershaft. Dr. Wm. Berriman read service, who after prayers informed us when to wait on the Abp.

Afternoon, went to Westminster and S[t] James's.

28th. — This day we went in the morning to Westminster, where we conversed with Dr. Fr. Astry, Treasurer of S[t] Paul's, from whence we came to the N. England Coffee House, where we conferred with Mr. Bridger and others of our acquaintance. I was at Evening Prayer. S[t] Dunstan's.

30th. — This day in the morning we were at service at the Cathedral of S[t] Paul, where we heard one Mr. Seagrave from Heb. ii. 16 — not the nature of angels. In the afternoon we were at the Old Jewry, where Mr. Trapp preached from Heb. iii. 13 — of the Deceitfulness of Sin — with whom we conversed afterwards.

31st. — This day we went with Mr. Coram through S[t]

James's Park and Chelsea (where we viewed the fine Hospital) to Parsons' Green at Fulham to dine with Mr. Hall, who treated us very kindly and generously; coming home, we saw the place of K. Charles' execution.

. . . .

January 3d. — This day in the morning we were introduced by Mr. Bridger to wait on Sir William Dawes, the L'd Archbishop of York, who treated us with great kindness and condescension, and took notice of our affair. After which I went to Dr. Astry and conferred with him. In the evening Mr. Checkley (just arrived from N. England) came to our lodgings to visit us.[1]

4th. — This day I went in the morning to confer further with Dr. Astry about going to Lambeth, after which I was at Smithfield and St Andrew's, Holborn, thence home, and read the orders and papers of the Society and the Bp. of Bristol's and Carlisle's sermons.

5th. — This day in the forenoon we (attended with Mr. Bridger, Mr. Sanford, and other gentlemen) waited on Dr. W. Wake, his Grace the Archbishop of Canterbury, at his Palace at Lambeth, introduced by Dr. Ibbotson. His Grace treated us like a Father of the ch'h, very courteously, and took notice of our affair; we returned on foot round by Southwark, where we viewed the most ancient church and monastery of St Mary Overie. . . . .

6th. — This day (being Sunday) we were in the morning at St Martin-in-the-Fields, where we were entertained with a most amiable and profitable sermon by Sir Wm. Dawes, the most excellent Abp. of York, a most wonderful preacher! His text, Gen. xviii. 19, — "For I know him that he will command," etc. In the afternoon I was at the Cathedral of St Paul, where one Mr. Bowers preached. Jno. i. 14. — "Full of," etc.

7th. — This day we were at Dr. Lovel's at Westminster.

[1] Johnson wrote on the fly-leaf of his private journal thus: — "N. B. I speak in the plural number to comprehend Mr. T. Cutler and Mr. D. Brown, who were constantly my fellow-travellers; and after Mr. Brown's death, Mr. Checkley; and after his arrival, Mr. Wetmore."

8th. — This day we waited on Dr. Willis, the Bishop of Sarum. After which we were to visit Mr. Rawlins, and dined at Dr. Lovel's in company with Mr. Cummin. In the evening we received Mr. Honyman's letters, and after Evening Prayer conferred with Mr. Hay.

. . . .

11th. — This day we went in the morning to wait on Dr. Nicholson, the Bishop of Londonderry; after which we were with Mr. Humphreys, the Secretary to the Society, thence to Mr. Massey's, from thence in the afternoon we went to wait on Dr. King, the Master of the Charter House, with whom we conferred on our affairs; after which we viewed Guildhall, and spent the evening with Mr. Massey.

. . . .

15th. — This day, after walking about the city and conversing at the N. E. Coffee House with Mr. Sanford, etc., we went in the afternoon (having been invited) to visit Mr. Dommer, a Printer by Gray's Inn (which we took a view of, and of the fields and walks by the way), where were Mr. Cambel and Mr. Whiston (Arians with whom we had a great deal of talk and dispute), as also Mr. Massey and Mr. Rawlins.

. . . .

18th. — This day in the morning we were first with Dr. Astry, with whom we went (by him introduced) before the Hon. Society for the Propagation of the Gospel in Foreign Parts. Sir William Dawes, Abp. of York, was in the chair, who with the whole body of the clergy present received us with a most benign aspect, and treated us with all imaginable kindness. From thence we went with Dr. Berriman, chaplain, before Dr. Jno. Robinson, Bp. of London, who received us very graciously, and took a kind notice of our affair.

. . . .

20th. — This day (being Sunday) in the morning we were at St Bride's, where we had a charity sermon from Deut. xv. 11, 12, preached by Dr. Th. Biss; in the afternoon we were at St Mary le Bow, where we heard Mr. Smith on

Death, from Job xvii. 13; in the evening we conversed at home first with Dr. King, Master of the Chapter House (who gave us a kind visit), after that with Mr. Checkley and Dr. Jones.

21st. — This day Mr. Brown and I were with the Bishop of London, with whom we conferred further upon our affair; he treated us with great benignity; from thence we went to dine with Dr. Astry, who after dinner took coach with us and came to the Chapter House by St Paul's, where we were kindly treated by the Committee of the Society, who granted our desire; we spent the evening with Mr. Massey, Lewis, and Humphreys.

22d. — This day, alas! Mr. Cutler falling sick of the small-pox, Mr. Brown and I thought best to remove, and we took up our lodgings at Mr. Gregson's at the Two White Fryars by the Bolt and Tun in Fleet Street; after which we were at the Coffee House and Mr. More's.

23d. — This day we were in the morning with Mr. Hay for his advice, from whom we went directly to the Bp. of London to Fulham (to his Palace), where we were kindly entertained by Dr. W. Berriman, with whom we had a very free conversation.

. . . .

25th. — This day in the morning we were at Dr. Astry's, with whom and Dr. Berriman we came to wait on the Society at Bp. Tenison's Library, who granted our requests and made way for our ordination. After which we were at Mr. Bridger's and at evening service at St Paul's Cathedral.

. . . .

27th. — This day (being Sunday) we were in the morning at St Paul's, where were present, besides the Lord Mayor and Aldermen, Sir Peter King and the rest of the Judges; one Mr. Wheatly preached from 1 Tim. iii. 16. The mystery of godliness. In the afternoon we were at Westminster Abbey, where were present Sundry Bishops. One Mr. Mandevil preached from Matt. v. 8. Pure in heart, etc.

. . . .

31*st.* — This day in the morning we went to wait on Dr. Grandorgh, upon whose invitation we took coach with him and went to Westminster Hall (it being Term time), where we saw the several courts and judges sitting. We viewed likewise the Houses both of Lords and Commons. In the afternoon we, with Mr. Checkley, were in company with Mr. Hendley and Mr. Lewis, two clergymen, and Mr. Wood and others.

February 1*st.* — This day in the afternoon we were at Mr. Hay's, and spent the evening at the Sun Tavern with Messrs. Lewis, Humphrey, Vaughan, Powel, Vincent, Wait, Scullard, etc., clergymen.

. . . .

4*th.* — This day we were to dine with Mr. Hendley at Islington, in company with Mr. Lewis, Mr. Checkley, and Mr. Wood. After we came home we were in company with Philips and Calwel, and read Irene, a play.

5*th.* — This day we were at Sion College, where we had the benefit of two or three hours' use of the Library to examine commentators on our texts.

6*th.* — This day we were not out, but at the Theatre in Drury Lane in the evening, where we had a Tragedy.

7*th.* — This day in the morning we were at service at S[t] Paul's Cathedral, where Dr. Chishul preached in defense of the Trinity against the Arians from Matt. xxviii. 19, — "Go ye therefore," etc.; after which, with Mr. Checkley, we took a view of that stupendous fabric, ascended to the top of the dome by five hundred and fifty steps, which with the Cupola and Cross make four hundred feet in height. We were in the Library also, and sundry other parts; viewed the cells, etc. It is perhaps one of the finest buildings in the world — an amazing mass of stones! In the evening also we were at service there, and afterward waited on Mr. Jennings.

. . . .

9*th.* — This day in the morning we were first with Mr. Dummer, the agent; after that we went to wait on Dr. Grandorgh, who presented us from an unknown hand[1] (whom

[1] Earl Thanet.

God bless) with ten guineas apiece; in the afternoon finished reading a book called the "Scotch Presbyterian Eloquence," and after that I finished composing my sermon for probation.

10*th.* — This day, being Sunday, in the morning I heard at S[t] Mary's, Aldermary, Dr. Kennet, Bp. of Peterborough, preach from 1 Thess. iii. 11, 12, — "Now God and the Father," etc. After which I saw him ordain Mr. Usher and another man. We dined with Mr. Negus; in the afternoon we heard Dr. Watson from John i. 11, — "He came unto his own," etc.

11*th.* — This day we were not out. I read Dr. Hoadly's Sermon on the "Kingdom of Christ," and his "Preservative Against Non-jurors," with Snape's and Law's answer.

12*th.* — This day in the morning we were at service at the church of S[t] Lawrence Jewry, where Dr. Moss, Dean of Ely, preached a Lecture from Rom. iii. 8, — "Let us do evil," etc. Afternoon we were at the Coffee House N. E., and in the evening we were at the Theatre at Lincoln's Inn, where we had a Comedy — The Drummer. N. B. — This same day after dinner we visited the good people of Bedlam.

13*th.* — This day we were not out, but I read Dr. Woodward's "Young Man's Monitor," and wrote letters to my friends in N. England.

. . . .

15*th.* — This day we were at the anniversary meeting of the Society for the Propagation of the Gospel at S[t] Mary le Bow, where Dr. J. Waugh, Dean of Gloucester, preached from 1 Pet. iii. 19, 20, — The spirits in prison, etc. We were at evening service at S[t] Paul's, and in the evening I was at the Sun Tavern Club, where, besides those who were there before, were Messrs. Hill, Bridger, Lewis, and another or two.

. . . .

20*th.* — This day in the morning we were at service at Westminster Abbey, after which we went to visit Mr. More, a young clergyman, on the affair of Baptism; he was very courteous.

. . . .

24th. — This day, being Sunday, we were at service all day at St Dunstan's, West; in the morning Dr. John Wilcox, Bishop of Gloucester, preached from 1 Pet. iv. 10, — "As every man hath received," etc. Afternoon, Dr. Nath. Marshall preached on Matt. xix. 14, — "For of such," etc.

. . . .

27th. — This day (being Ash Wednesday) we were at service at St James', Clerkenwell, where Dr. Jno. Potter, Bishop of Oxford, preached from 2 Cor. i. 12, — "For our rejoicing is this," etc. We dined with Dr. Massey.

. . . .

March 2. — This day not out but to buy books. We saw a wondrous clock that performed all sorts of music.

3d. — This day (being Sunday) we were in the morning at St Andrew's, Undershaft, or St Mary Ax, where Dr. Wm. Berriman preached from Jer. xiii. 23, — "Can the Ethiopian," etc.; in the afternoon at St Martins, Ludgate, where Mr. Crow preached from Luke xiii. 5, — "I tell you, Nay; but, except," etc.

4th. — This day we heard Esquire Boyle's Lecture at St Mary le Bow preached by Dr. Burrough from Phil. iii. 8, — "Yea, doubtless, and I count," etc. After that we took a walk with Mr. Jno. Berriman, Mr. Scullard, and Mr. Wats, through Moorfields out to Ash Hospital, and so out of town through the pleasant meadows. In the evening received a visit from Mr. David Yale.

5th. — This day we went to Kensington to confer with Dr. Berriman; we were admitted to my Lord of London; there we dined; after which we drank a bottle with the Doctor and Secretary, and then viewed the Royal Palace and Gardens.

In the evening at St Paul's, at Sir Christopher Wren's funeral. Statues.

. . . .

7th. — This day we were at service at St Paul's, where Dr. Chishul preached again against the Arians in defense of the Holy Trinity from Matt. xxviii. 19. It was his fourth

Lecture. After that we waited on Dr. Knight to confer on the affair of Baptism. He treated us very kindly. We visited Buckridge.

8th. — This day in the morning we were at service at St Paul's, where one Mr. Bearcroft preached from 2 Pet. i. 10, — Calling and election, etc. I came home and read Dr. Delaune's sermon on Original Sin, Whiston's argument about the validity of ministries and the appendices, and the spirit of some late writers about the Bishop of Rochester's commitment.

9th. — This day we were at service in the morning at Westminster Abbey with Mr. Checkley, with whom afterwards we went to confer with Dr. Knight on the affair of Baptism, and (nobis tribus an legitimum sit apud Presbyterianos Baptisma susceptum graviter dubitantibus) hora 4 pomeridianâ in ecclesia Sancti Sepulchri, Testibus Dom. Johanne Jones, Isaaco Cardel, et Dom. Dorothea Nightingale et ministrante Jeremiâ Nicholsono, Doctori Knight curato, privatum, Baptisma hypotheticum recepimus. Si rectum hoc, Deus agnoscat, et si alitercum sit simpliciter actum ignoscat.[1]

. . . .

11th. — This day we heard Mr. Usher at St. Antholin's, after which Mr. Lazingby invited us to his house with Mr. Oliver and Mr. Scullard, etc., clergymen; then we with Mr. Checkley took coach and went to Hampstead to wait on Mr. Cutler home, who (I thank God) is recovered. We walked about to view that town, and then returned and went to the Theatre at Lincoln's Inn, where we had the comedy of the Merchant.

. . . .

13th. — This day we went to Mr. Bridger's, and from thence to Kensington to confer with my Lord of London on

[1] We three, having grave doubts whether Baptism received among the Presbyterians is valid, at 4 o'clock P. M. in the church of St. Sepulchre — Mr. John Jones, Isaac Cardel, and Mrs. Dorothy Nightingale being witnesses, and Jeremiah Nicholson, curate to Dr. Knight, ministering — received private hypothetical baptism. If this be right, may God approve it; and if otherwise than sincerely done, may He pardon it.

the affair of ordination. We drank a bottle with Dr. Berriman, Mr. Sherlock, etc., and had letters to the Archbishop of Canterbury; in our return were in the Royal Gardens.

14th. — This day in the morning we first waited on Governor Shute and then on the Earl of Clarendon at Somerset House. After that we were at prayers at St Stephen's, Coleman Street, where Mr. Hay catechised and preached a lecture on the Catechism; in the afternoon we were at Mr. Bowyer's, the Bookseller, with whom we drank a bottle; after that we went up to the top of the glorious Cathedral of St Paul and viewed the town.

. . . .

18th. — This day I was at Kensington to confer with Dr. Berriman on the affair of ordination, by whose application to the Bishop of London, and by order from William, Lord Apb. of Canterbury, we had letters dimissory to Thomas, Lord Bp. of Norwich. In the evening I read the "Modern Protestant."

19th. — This day in the morning we went to wait on the Right Reverend Dr. Thomas Green, the Bishop of Norwich, for ordination, who received us favorably. Thence we went to see Mr. Rawlins and Lady Blacket. After that we were at the N. England Coffee House.

20th. — This day in the morning we were to wait on Mr. Jennings to discourse on our affairs; from thence we went to wait on the Bishop of Norwich, who examined us in order for ordination, which also did Mr. Ellotson, the gentleman who is to present us; then we signed the Articles. Afternoon we were at St Sepulchre, where Mr. Brown and I with Mrs. Dorothy were witnesses for Mr. Cutler at his baptism. After that we were about town to provide robes, etc., for ordination.

21st. — This day we were before the Society at the Archbishop's Library at St Martin's upon our affairs, and were in the evening at the Half-moon Tavern, Cheapside, with the gentlemen of the club before mentioned, besides whom were others. . . . .

22*d.* — This day in the morning, 10 of the clock, we waited on the Right Rev[d] Thomas, Lord Bishop of Norwich, and at the parish church of S[t] Martin-in-the-Fields, after morning Prayer, we were first confirmed and then ordained Deacons. In the afternoon I was at Prayers at S[t] Paul's, and then at Mr. Jonah Bowyer's, Bookseller.

. . . .

24*th.* — This day (being Sunday) we were all day at S[t] James's Church, where in the morning Dr. Samuel Clark preached from Heb. xii. 16, 17, — of Esau's selling his birthright. Afternoon, Dr. Ibbotson preached from Luke ix. 23, — "Let him deny himself," etc. In the evening I finished Abp. Dawes, etc., sermons.

. . . .

26*th.* — This day we had the honor to dine again with Dr. Francis Astry, and spent the afternoon at his house, with Mr. Carter, a clergyman, our benefactor. After that we waited on Dr. Nath. Marshall, with whom we drank a bottle in company with Dr. Grey and Mr. Wheatly, clergymen, and Mr. Martin and Dr. Walker, in both which conversations we had great kindness.

. . . .

28*th.* — This day we were in the morning to wait on the Bishop of Norwich. Afternoon we were at Clerkenwell; from thence we went with Mr. Checkley to see the Tower, where we viewed the armory, both horse and foot, the artillery and regalia, and the trophies of Sir Francis Drake, and everything to be seen there; after that we ascended the monument, one hundred and two feet high, by three hundred and forty-five steps. Glorious things!

29*th.* — This day in the morning I was at service at S[t] Clement Danes, where Mr. R. Leybourn preached from Job vii. 16, — "I would not live alway," etc. Otherwise not out.

30*th.* — This day in the morning we were to wait on the Bishop of Norwich, whose chaplain, Mr. Clark, examined us. The Bishop gave us his fatherly advice, and we subscribed the XXXIX. Articles, in order for ordination. We dined and spent the day with Mr. Dummer in company with Mr. Massey and Mr. Low.

31*st.* — This day at 6 in the morning, Sunday, at the church of S[t] Martin-in-the-Fields, at the continued appointment and desire of William, Lord Abp. of Canterbury, and John, Lord Bishop of London, we were ordained Priests most gravely by the Right Rev[d] Thomas, Lord Bp. of Norwich, who afterwards preached an excellent sermon from Rom. ii. 4, — "Or despisest thou," etc. I dined with Mr. Massey in company with Mr. Godly and Mr. Bull, clergymen. Afternoon I preached for Mr. Massey at S[t] Alban's, Wood Street, on Phil. i. 27. We all spent the evening with Mr. Low.

April 1. — This day in the morning we were at the Bishop of Norwich's house with the Secretary for our orders. Afternoon we were at S[t] Paul's Chapter House and the Chapter Coffee House.

. . . .

3*d.* — This day we dined with Mr. Carter (our benefactor), with whom we took coach and came into town. We spent the evening at Mr. Massey's with Mr. Price.

The errand on which Johnson and his associates appeared in England served as an introduction to remarkable persons and places. Wherever they went they were sure to be welcomed; and the interest evinced in their entertainment was only exceeded by the desire to send them back to their country prepared to meet the new responsibilities laid upon them, and to engage in a struggle which they could hardly hope to avoid with the steady foes of Episcopacy.

CHAPTER III.

SICKNESS AND DEATH OF MR. BROWN; FURTHER EXTRACTS FROM PRIVATE JOURNAL; VISITS TO OXFORD AND CAMBRIDGE; ARRIVAL OF MR. WETMORE; DEPARTURE FROM ENGLAND, AND VOYAGE HOME; SETTLEMENT AT STRATFORD; LETTERS TO THE BISHOP OF LONDON; MARRIAGE.

A. D. 1723–1727.

THE dreadful malady from which Mr. Cutler had just recovered now fell upon another member of the party. On Thursday, the 4th of April, Brown complained of being ill; and two days later his disease was pronounced to be the small-pox. "God grant him," entered Johnson in his diary, "a safe deliverance;" and the same day he removed his own quarters to an apothecary in the next door. He does not appear to have thought it imprudent to remain so near, or he was so anxious to learn each day the progress of the disease, and the signs of its yielding to treatment, that he could not think of being at a distance from his friend. Edward Jenner was not yet born, and hence his great discovery of vaccination as a preventive of the small-pox was unknown to the medical profession. Individuals were then subject to it in its worst form in the natural way, and inoculation was sometimes resorted to as a means of escaping its virulence, and securing a more speedy and perfect recovery.

For nearly a week Johnson went in and out of his new quarters visiting noted places, and mingling with his clerical friends. On the 7th of April, it being Palm Sunday, he was at the Royal Chapel, St James's Palace, where he saw the King, George the Prince, the Princess, and sundry bishops and persons of the nobility. Dr. W. Wake, Abp. of Canterbury, preached from Luke xiii. 6–9, — The barren fig-tree. He applied it to the present state of the nation. It is evident that the symptoms in the case of Brown had not become alarming. A few quotations from the journal of Johnson will best tell the story: —

April 9. — This day I was first at Child's Coffee House. We dined at the Cross Keys in Holborn with Mr. Hammond, in company with Mr. Massey and thirty English gentlemen. I wrote to my friends in the evening.

10*th*. — This day we were at St James's, Clerkenwell, where we heard Dr. Sherlock, Dean of Chichester, preach from Isaiah liii. 3, on "Christ's sufferings." Afternoon I was at the N. E. Coffee House with Mr. Sandford, and spent the evening (after evening service at St Foster's) [1] with Mr. Berriman and Mr. Scullard at Coach Makers' Hall.

11*th*. — This day we were at Whitehall Chapel at service, to see the ceremony of washing the disciples' feet performed, being Maundy Thursday. Afterwards we met Mr. Oliver at the New England Coffee House, who went with us to wait on Mr. Tryon, the Treasurer, where we saw Mr. More. In the evening I removed my lodgings to Mr. Skinner's.

12*th*. — This day being Good Friday, we were at service at the Royal Chapel at St James's, where Dr. Stanhope, Dean of Canterbury, preached an excellent sermon from John i. 29, — "Behold the Lamb of God," etc. I was at evening prayers at St Martin's, Ludgate.

[1] In another place Johnson speaks of "St Foster's, alias Vedast." The reference is to St Vedast's Church, Foster Lane, built by Wren, with a three storied spire, and still in use as a parish church.

13th. — This day, thinking Mr. Brown a little better, Mr. Cutler, Mr. Manning, and I, went to Greenwich, where we were on board the Royal Carolina; there viewed the glorious Hospital, then the Palace, the Park, and Royal Observatory, and after that Mr. Crawley's Iron Ware House. But woe is me! alas! alas! on our return we are accosted with the sorrowful news of Mr. Brown's death. O Father, not my will, but thine be done! O my grief! I have lost in him the best friend in the world, — a fine scholar, and a brave Christian. It is thy will, O God; let me be silent, and shut my mouth. But my flesh trembles for fear of Thee, and I am afraid of thy righteous judgments. O give me grace to be resigned, and to get good by it. O prepare his friends for the news, and comfort them. O save and spare me, if it may be thy will, for Christ's sake.

14th. — This day being Easter Sunday, Mr. Checkley and I were at St Paul's Cathedral, where we had a sermon from Rev. i. 17–18, — "I am he that was dead, and am alive," etc. We received the Holy Communion from the hands of Dean Younger, Mr. Baker, and Mr. Carleton. Afternoon we were at St Alban's, Wood Street, where Mr. Massey preached from Is. liii. 10, — "When thou shalt make his soul an offering," etc. With him we went home, and there I lodged that night.

15th. — This day I was at service at St John's Chapel, Clerkenwell; thence to Lady Blaket's and Dr. Astry's. After that I went to Mr. Berriman's, who with Mr. Scullard, and Mr. Wats and other lay gentlemen, went with me to divert me out into the fields and meadows to the new burying place, where I saw Mr. Nelson's tomb; thence to Dr. Marshall's and Dr. Astry's; thence to Whitehall, whence we went by water to Mr. Scullard's, where we spent the evening. There I lodged.

16th. — This morning Mr. Scullard went with me to see the wine vaults and water works. After that I was at St Bride's to hear the Spital sermon preached by Dean Waugh from 1 Cor. xiii. 13, — The greatest, charity. The children sang wonderfully. This evening my dear friend, Mr. Brown, was interred in S[t] Dunstan in the West, attended by about thirty of the clergy of the town.

These extracts show the depth of Johnson's sorrow at the death of his classmate and companion. The constantly changing scenes through which he passed could not put it from his mind. It was the one great disappointment of his journey, and he often referred to it afterwards with feelings of affectionate sadness. When human props fall from under us it is a comfort to be able to lean upon divine supports, and to do what is imposed upon us with increased faith and diligence. This was the privilege of the survivor who mourned so deeply the loss of his gentle and loving friend.

The private journal of Johnson carries us back a century and a half, and brings to view now and then manners and customs which seem strange to many at the present day. The frequent gathering of clergymen at coffee houses and clubs was among the social habits of the time, and as little was thought of acquaintances meeting at the "Vine Tavern" for a literary feast, as would now be thought of a party of travellers stopping at an inn and asking for refreshment and lodgings for the night. The reader will be glad to have introduced more of the notes of the subject of this volume. They are brief, and written without any attempt at rhetoric or fine description; but the simple words are graphic, and present a lively picture of what the writer saw and heard: —

April 21. — This day being Sunday I preached my probation sermon on Phil. i. 27, at S[t] Dionis Back Church, in Fenchurch Street, before Dr. Smith and Mr. Hay, members of the Society. We dined at Mr. Bridger's with the clergyman, his brother. After dinner we took coach to Trinity Chapel, in Hanover Square, where I preached the same before sundry persons of quality. We spent the evening at the Dean of Ely's, Dr. Moss, with the two Finches, Mr. Finch and the Dean of York, and Mr. Massey and Mr. Collens.

22*d.* — This day I read Morning Prayers for Dr. Polling at St Ann's; in the afternoon we walked in Lincoln's Inn Fields, were a considerable time in the Library, and at Evening Prayers in the Chapel, and after that at St Foster's; thence to Moorfields, where we saw a remarkable gun which went off eleven times in a minute; spent the evening with Mr. Wheatly, Berriman, Scullard, and the other company, at Mr. Kodden's.

23*d.* — This day in the morning we went to drink a dish of tea with Mr. Collens, a very worthy clergyman; after that we were at Lincoln's Inn, thence to John's Coffee House in Swithin's Lane, with sundry clergymen; then at N. England Coffee House with Mr. Harrison; after that we waited on Dr. Barrowby, a worthy gentleman, our physician; we spent the evening at the Vine Tavern with Messrs. Berriman, Lewis, Scullard, Higgot, Champion, Brigen, Wait, Vaughan, Rice, and Bp. Bradford's son.

24*th.* — This day in the morning we visited Mrs. Kitty Lockwood, and then Mr. Rawden; after that we were at Morning Prayers at Lincoln's Inn; thence we took a walk in St James's Park, and dined with Dr. Astry. We were at Evening Prayers at St Foster's, and spent the evening at Mr. Jno. Berriman's with Mr. Wheatly, Mr. Wait, and the other gentlemen.

. . . .

29*th.* — This day in the morning we waited on Dr. Edmund Gibson, Lord Bishop of London, lately advanced, who treated us very kindly; thence we were at Court. . . . .

30*th.* — This morning we were at Westminster Abbey, where we viewed the cloisters and monuments, and by Mr. Church's means saw the school and dormitory, as also Abp. Laud's own handwriting, and the original names and warrant of the Regicides. We dined with Mr. Truby and Mr.

Bowyer; then we were at Mr. Downing's, thence to wait on Dr. Bennet, with whom we spent the evening.

May 1.— This day in the morning we were at Mr. Scullard's, with whom we went to Mr. Clondon's, who conducted us to Gresham College to Dr. Woodward's, thence to the work house, thence we went to prayers at St Mildred's, Poultry. Mr. Scullard read prayers. Thence we went to John's Coffee House in company with sundry clergymen. We dined at Mr. Tryon's; after that we were at Mr. Bowyer's with Dr. Snape and Dr. Colebatch, and waited on Sub-Dean Gosling; were at Chapter Coffee House with Dr. Grey and Mr. Wheatly. Supped at the Old Devil Tavern with Mr. Manning and Mr. Wood.

2d. — This day I was at Mr. Checkley's; then we were all at Dr. Grey's and Dr. Marshall's, with whom we spent the evening. Read Dr. Woodward's remarks on the ancient and present state of London.

3d. — This day we dined with Dr. Woodward at Gresham College, who showed us his fine collection of rarities, of animals, minerals, antediluvian shells, Roman urns, and other antiquities of 2 or 3000 years. After that Mr. Wilmer showed us his collection of plants. We spent the evening at Mr. Berriman's; I finished Dr. Berriman's sermon at Induction.

4th. — This day I was at my Lord Mayor's with Messrs. Rawden, Chapman, and Pope, thence to St Mary-le-Bow, at the confirmation of Dr. Edmund Gibson, Bp. of London; we dined at Mr. Carter's with Dr. Moss, Dean of Ely, who took us into his coach and brought us to Holborn, and thence we went to Mr. Jenks', with whom we conversed, and after that with Mr. Middleton.

5th. — This day being Sunday I read prayers at St Michael, Queenhithe. Mr. Estwick preached from 1 Pet. ii. 21, on "Christ's example." I assisted in the administration of the Sacrament. We dined at Mr. Scullard's; for him I preached at St Antholin's; afterwards we were . . . . at Dr. Baile's; thence we went to St Ann's, where Mr. Cutler preached for Mr. Wheatly on Eccl. xii. 13, 14,—"Fear God," etc. With him we dined.

6th.—This day I was at Mr. Bowyer's, where I saw the Bishop of Rochester as he came from the Tower to the House of Lords; thence we went to Dr. Grey's, and we dined with Mr. Rawden in company with Mr. Abbot and Mr. Jenner.

7th.—This day we heard Dr. Roderick preach a Latin sermon at Sion College from these words: "He that endureth to the end shall be saved." After which we dined there in company with about fifty of the clergy convened on that occasion. After that we went over the river with Mr. Scullard and viewed S[t] Saviour's Church, *i. e.* S[t] Mary Overie's, and then the water works, and spent the evening at the Vine with our former acquaintances.

8th.—This day we took horses and went in company with Mr. Waterman to Harrow-on-the-Hill, to wait on Mr. Cox, with whom we dined, and after that we went to Eton and Windsor.

9th.—This day we visited the Castle and Palace at Windsor, and after that we went to Hampton Court, and saw the fine palaces there, in both which glorious places we saw everything curious, magnificent, or entertaining, and then returned this evening to London.

. . . .

11th.—This day we were first at Mr. Bowyer's to see the Bishop of Rochester go by; thence we went to Court, thence to Dr. Grey's, and spent the evening with Mr. Berriman, Scullard, East, etc.

12th.—This day, Sunday, I heard Dr. Thomas Wilson, the Bishop of Sodor and Man, preach from Mar. xii. 32–34,—Of the love of God,—at S[t] Vedast Foster's. We dined at Mr. Scate's. Afternoon I preached before that Bishop for Mr. Berriman at S[t] Mary's, Aldermary. After service we were at Mr. Scate's again with the Bishop. After that Mr. Berriman and I went to the Tower, and we spent the evening at Mrs. Parker's.

13th.—This day we went with Dr. Grey to view Sion

College Library, where we saw John Wickliff's Bible, original manuscript, then we went to Moorfields. After dinner we were at 'Change, we were at the Chapter House and Coffee House with Dr. Lang and Mr. Oliver, we spent the evening in visiting Walter Newbury, a Quaker countryman; finished Mr. Wheatly's Tract of "Bidding Prayer."

14*th.* — This day we heard Dr. Moss, Dean of Ely, at St Lawrence Jewry, preach on the Eternity of Hell Torments, — Matt. xxv. ult., — with whom and about twenty clergymen we were at the Coffee House afterwards; we spent the afternoon at Mr. Truby's with Mr. Oliver, Dr. Jones, and one or two clergymen.

15*th.* — This day we were first to wait on Dr. Marshall, who (being the King's chaplain) introduced us into the Palace of St James, where we were at prayers with the young Princesses, and had the honor to kiss their hands. We dined there with the King's chaplain, and after that went home with Dr. Marshall, and waited on the Dean of Ely and Dr. Grey.

16*th.* — This day we were at St Paul's Cathedral, at the Installation of Edmund, Bishop of London, performed by Dr. Bowers, Bp. of Chichester, and the whole chapter. Afternoon we were there again at service, after that with Mr. Negus, after that at St Foster's, and went with Mr. Berriman to the Tower, and spent the evening with him and Mr. Garden.

17*th.* — This day in the morning we waited on Dr. Astry; thence we went to Tyburn to see Counselor Layer hanged.

. . . .

19*th.* — This day I read prayers in the morning at St Magnus for Mr. Scullard, with whom I dined. Afternoon I preached before Dr. Waddington [afterwards Bishop of Chichester] at All Hallows the Great for Dr. Berriman. After service we were at Mr. Shaler's with Mr. Berriman and Mr. Scullard; thence to Mr. Checkley's, and spent the evening with Mr. Webster.

20*th.* — This day we took coach and came to Oxford, and lodged at the Angel Inn.

21st. — This day first we waited on Dr. Shippen, the Vice-Chancellor at Brasen Nose College; thence we went to Trinity College, where Mr. Stockwell showed us the fine gardens and Chapel of the College. We dined with Dr. Shippen, V. C., and thence we waited on Mr. Trognair, Green, and Atkinson of Queen's College, with whom and the rest of the Fellows we supped in the Hall and saw the Chapel and Library, and spent the rest of the evening.

22d. — This day we went first to Pembroke College to wait on Dr. Painting and Mr. Lockton, who showed us the gardens; thence we went to Magdalen College, where we dined with Mr. Warton (and the Fellows), who after a little conversation went with us to the famous Bodleyan Library, which we viewed, and the Antiquity and Picture Galleries; thence to the glorious Theatre and Printing House; thence to Trinity College to wait on Dr. Dobson, Mr. Ball, and Mr. Stockwell; here we were at Evening Prayers; thence we went to Corpus Christi College to wait on Mr. Bar. Smith, who showed us the gardens, library, manuscripts, and chapel of that College; after, removed lodgings to Mr. Barnes.

23d. — This day (being Ascension day) we went to wait on Mr. Conybeare of Exeter College, who went with us to Christ Church, the Cathedral, where Mr. Wyat preached before the University.

. . . .

24th. — This day we were first at Queen's College with Mr. Trognair; thence we went to Merton to wait on Mr. Moseley; thence to Trinity College to dine with Dr. Dobson, President, who brought us into the schools where Dr. Potter, Bp. of Oxford, was Moderator to a Theological Dispute on Baptism and Prayers for the Dead; thence we went with Mr. Atkinson to the Printing House and the Museum, where we saw all the curiosities of the air-pump and other engines, the skeletons, mummies, medals, jewels, antiquities, etc. . . . .

. . . .

25th. — This day in the morning we were at prayers at

Queen's College; thence, accompanied by Mr. Smith of S[t] John's, we went first to Oriel College, thence to Corpus Christi, thence to Christ's Church, where we saw the ancient monuments, painting on the glass, etc.

. . . .

26*th.* — This day (being Sunday) we were at service at Queen's College Chapel, and thence to S[t] Mary's Church, where Mr. Owen preached on Christ's Ascension, — S[t] Mar. ult., — "He was received up into heaven," etc. We dined at Dr. Shippen's, V. Ch., with Dr. Delaune and Mr. Leybourne, etc., where we received our Diplomas for the Degrees. After that we walked in the fields, and were at evening service at S[t] John's College, where cxxxix. Ps. was sung. We spent the evening at Corpus Christi College in company with Mr. Smith, Aylmer, Burton, etc.

27*th.* — This day we went with Mr. B. Smith to see the Bodleyan Library, the medals and antiquities, the manuscripts and curiosities of that glorious structure; thence we went to the Vice-Chancellor's, whence we had the honor to ride in his coach in company with Dr. Delaune, President of S[t] John's College, and Dr. Dobson, President of Trinity, to Cuddesdon, to wait on Dr. Jno. Potter, Bishop of Oxford, who treated us with the utmost civility. With him we had the honor to dine and spend the afternoon, and after our return we spent the evening with Dr. Delaune.

28*th.* — This day we first waited on Dr. Francis Gastrel, Bp. of Chester; then we dined with Mr. Conybeare at Exeter College; thence we took horses and rode out to see the famous seat of the Duke of Marlborough at Blenheim, in company with Mr. Burton and Mr. Greenaway — a most magnificent structure, gardens, and bridge. We spent the evening with Burton.

29*th.* — This day being Restauration, we were at church at S[t] Mary's, where Dr. Felton, Principal of Edmund Hall, preached on Ps. 50, — Offer unto God thanksgiving, — an excellent sermon; then we had the honor to dine with Dr. Gastrel, Bp. of Chester. Afternoon we were with our acquaintance at Corpus Christi, where we supped with the Fellows in the Hall; with them we walked in the fields, and spent the evening with Mr. Greenaway at Hart Hall, having been before at Queen's.

30th. — This day we went first to wait on the learned Mr. Sam[l] Parker; thence to S[t] M. Magdalene, where Mr. Dudley Woodbridge showed us the Park, President's garden, ... etc.; thence we went to Edmund Hall and took our leave of Dr. Felton; thence to the public Schools and Convocation House, where was a congregation, and the Vice-Chancellor gave degrees to some gentlemen; we dined with the Fellows of Queen's College and took our leave of them; then of Dr. Dobson and the Fellows of Trinity, then of the Vice-Chancellor, and then of Dr. Delaune and Dr. Haywood at S[t] John's. We spent our evening with sundry gentlemen at Mr. Blathwait's, and thus we take our leave of Oxford.

31st. — This day we took coach and came to London.

Their return to the metropolis, after an absence of ten days, was followed by the renewal of civilities to their friends, and preparations for a visit to Cambridge.

June 3. — This day we were first at Westminster to wait on Edmund, Bp. of London, who treated us very kindly; thence at Whitehall, now Banqueting House; thence I went to Mr. Downing's, thence to N. E. Coffee House and wrote home. We dined with Mrs. Cardel, were at Evening Prayers at S[t] Foster's, and spent the evening at the Queen's Head with Messrs. Wheatly, Ryan, Berriman, Jebb, and Wagstaff a nonjuring clergyman.

. . . .

6th. — This day (being Thursday in Whitsun week) we first drank a dish of tea with Mr. Berriman, with whom we went to Gresham College, where the charity children meet, whence, in company with a great number of the clergy, we went in procession before the children to S[t] Sepulchre's, where there was a sermon preached on the occasion by Dr.

Waterland, from Prov. xxii. 7, — "Train up," etc. The children, to the number of 4 or 5,000, sung gloriously — the finest emblem of heaven in the world.

7th. — This day we took coach and came to Cambridge.

Here the same kind attentions were bestowed upon them as in Oxford. They first paid their respects to the heads of several of the colleges, and visited King Henry's Chapel and the Library of Trinity. Johnson continues his notes: —

9th. — This day (being Trinity Sunday) we were in the morning to drink a dish of tea with Dr. Laney at Pembroke, with whom we went to service at St Mary's Church, where Mr. Trotter preached from Luke xxi. 15, — "Give a mouth and wisdom," etc. We dined with Dr. Ashton at Jesus College, were afternoon at St Mary's again, where Mr. Pearce preached from St John xiv. 16, — "I will pray," etc. W were at evening service at Trinity College Chapel, where was fine music; we supped at Trinity Hall. . . . .

10th. — This day we first drank a dish of tea with Dr. R. Jenkins, Master of St John's College; after that we were to see the Pictures, Library, and curiosities there; thence we waited on Dr. Middleton, Prof. bibliothecarum, who showed us the Royal Library given by K. George; thence we went to dine with Dr. Dickens, in company with Dr. Warren, Mr. Oldsworth, and Dr. Berriman; thence we all went to Emanuel College, were there at evening service, and in the gallery and library and gardens. We supped and spent the evening with Mr. Marshall.

11th. — This day we went in the morning to wait on Mr. Mickleborough of Bennet or Corpus Christi, whence we went to church at St Mary's, where Mr. Fosset preached a Latin sermon on Church discipline from 1 Cor. v. 2. We went to the congregation where the Vice-chancellor, Dr. Cross (in the room of Dr. Snape, absent), with the rest of the Doctors and Masters sat, and we with others received our Degrees, *pro forma.* After that we dined with the Vice-chancellor

4

in company with Dr. Laney, the two Proctors, and Mr Beadle; thence we were at congregation again, where sundry others were graduated. After that we went to Trinity College, and were there at evening service and in the Library, and waited on Mr. Pilgrim, Greek Professor; we spent the evening at Jesus College with Mr. Lucas and Harding.

12*th.* — This day we went first to Bennet College Library, where we saw Abp. Parker's donation to that College, his plate, ancient manuscripts, and particularly the instrument of his consecration and the handwriting of the first Reformers, etc. We dined at S[t] John's with Dr. Jenkins, and then went to Caius College to wait on Mr. Symson, and conversed there with sundry gentlemen; saw the Chapel and library; thence we went to the Coffee House, and conversed with Mr. Baker and Dr. Middleton, etc. We spent the evening at Mr. Symson's in company with Mr. Burroughs and Mr. Sanderson, the Blind Mathematical Professor — a prodigy.

. . . .

14*th.* — This day we went in the morning to C. C. C. C. to drink a dish of tea with Mr. Mickleborough, thence to church to S[t] Mary's, where we had a sermon in Latin by Dr. Hall on the text, — "The disciples were first called Christians," etc. We dined at Jesus with Mr. Harding; thence we went to Magdalen and Peterhouse, and to wait on Mr. Marshall at Emanuel, and to take our leave of Dr. Laney, Dr. Cross, Mr. Pilgrim, and Mr. Lawson, and spent the evening with Dr. Dickens, Dr. Warren, Mr. Nichols, and Mr. Marshall, and thus we take our leave of Cambridge.

15*th.* — This day we took coach and came up to London in company with Dr. Bentley.

The journeys to Oxford and Cambridge were the longest which they made out of London, after their arrival in that city. It was no part of their plan to travel into other counties of England, and they saw nothing of Scotland or Ireland. Besides the four days at Canterbury, the ten at Oxford, and the seven at Cambridge, the whole time of their sojourn was passed in London. The little book of private notes is nearly ended, and the entries now begin to show preparations for the homeward voyage.

June 16*th*. — This day (being Sunday) we were in the morning at S[t] Foster's, where the Bp. of Man preached on Mar. xii. 32–3, — "The love of our neighbor." Afternoon I was at S[t] Austin's.

. . . .

17*th*. — This day we waited first on the Bp. of London, then after dinner took a walk to Islington with Mr. Clendon, Berriman, and Champion; on our return we went to see the great fire that happened that day, and spent the evening with Mr. Wheatly.

18*th*. — This day we first waited on Dr. Snape, Vice-chancellor of Cambridge; then on Dr. Knight. We spent the afternoon with Mr. Phillips in seeing Sir John Parsons' Brewhouse and the Tower, and in company with Capt. Ruggles and Mr. Hooper at N. E. Coffee House. N. B. — I lodge now at Mr. Manning's — apothecary.

19*th*. — This day we were first to drink a dish of tea with Dr. Berriman and his brother, then about sundry private affairs, and at John's Coffee House with sundry clergymen.

. . . .

21*st*. — This day we were first to wait on Mr. Jennings, then before the Society de Propaganda at S[t] Martin's Library, then before the Bp. of London with Dr. Berriman. We spent the evening with the good Dean of Ely and Dr. Grey.

22*d*. — . . . . . I moved lodgings to Mr. Budd's, the Rising Sun, on Fleet Street. We spent our evening with Dr. Bennet after Evening Prayers at S[t] Giles'.

23*d*. — This day being Sunday I was in the morning at S[t] Paul's. Dr. Skirret preached from Matt. vii. 21, — "Not every one," etc. There I received the communion. Dean

Godolphin, Dean Younger, and Sub-dean Gosling administered. Afternoon I heard Mr. Oliver from Rom. xii. 2,—"Be not conformed," etc. It was at St Austin's. After that I was at Chapter Coffee House with Mr. Higgot and Mr. Norton. Spent the evening with Mrs. Humphreys and another pretty gentlewoman.

. . . .

26th.—This day we went in the morning to wait on Edmund Bp. of London, who gave us his License certificate and benediction by imposition of hands. Then we waited on Dr. Lovel. We dined with Dr. Grey, where were Dr. Marshall and Mr. Hains. We spent the evening at Dr. Bennet's; were at service there.

. . . .

30th.—This day being Sunday I preached at St Nicholas, Cole Abbey, in the morning, from Phil. i. 27,—"Only let your conversation be," etc. We dined at Dr. Bennet's with sundry gentlemen. Afternoon I preached the same sermon at the Cathedral Church of St Paul, for Dean Younger, with whom I went home, and he was very kind. We spent the evening with Dr. King, master of the Charter House, in company with the Bishop of Man, etc.

. . . .

July 4.—This morning we were first surprised with the arrival of our friend Mr. Wetmore from New England.[1] We went with him to Westminster; thence at Morning Service at Lincoln's Inn, and waited on Dr. Lupton; thence at sundry places, and at Evening Service at St Foster's with Mr. Berriman.

5th.—This day we went to Dr. Berriman's and Mr. Oliver's, then to Westminster; waited on Mr. Sherlock, and dined with Dr. Lovel. Then came to Evening Service at St Foster's, and Dr. Cutler and I stood witnesses for Mr. Wetmore at the font. We spent the evening at Mr. Truby's with Dr. Dawson, Mr. Oliver, Newhouse, etc.

[1] Dr. Chandler, in his *Life of Johnson*, p. 37, states that Mr. Wetmore accompanied them in the tour" to Cambridge; but this is a mistake, as it was made prior to his arrival in England.

6th. — This day I was first to wait on Dr. King, Master of the Charter House; after that at St John's, then at Mrs. Cardel's, then we were at Mr. Hay's, and spent the evening at Pratt's with Dr. and Mr. Berriman.

7th. — This day I preached and assisted in administering the Sacrament for Mr. Wheatly at St Swithin, and afternoon for Dr. Berriman at All Hallows the Great. We spent the evening with Mr. Newman.

. . . .

11th. — This day we were at Lambeth to take our leave of the Abp. of Canterbury, who after sundry civilities gave us his solemn Apostolical Benediction by imposition of hands. We spent the evening at Mr. Manning's.

. . . .

14th. — This day I heard Mr. Barrel (formerly a Papist) at St Bottolph's, Aldergate, on "Charity." Afternoon I heard Mr. Vernon at St. Paul's, — "God and Mammon." We spent the evening with Mr. Newman at the Temple.

. . . .

18th. — This day we were at the Abbey at Westminster at the Bp. of Man's Tryal, and spent the afternoon with Mr. Jones, Salmon, and Yale.

19th. — This day we were at service at Westminster Abbey, then at the Treasury, took our leave of sundry friends, and spent the evening with Mr. Oliver and Dr. Warren.

. . . .

25th. — This day I was at service at the Royal Chapel, at St James's, at Mr. Wetmore's ordination, and received the Sacrament of the Bp. of London; the rest of the day spent in taking leave of our friends.

26th. — This day we took our leave of London and came down to Gravesend, Mr. Manning and Mr. Wetmore with us.

They sailed down the river Thames on the 28th, and were ashore at Deal, and afterwards in "a bad storm." Being windbound they had an opportunity of landing at Cowes on the Isle of Wight, and went to Newport and Carisbrook Castle — the latter places associated with the memory of the unfortunate King Charles I. "Farewell to England!" said Johnson as the vessel carried them out of sight of land. They encountered storm after storm on the passage, in one of which a man was washed overboard and lost. On the 22d of September he wrote in his journal:— "This day finished Father le Compte's 'History of China,' and Dr. Goodman's 'Winter Evening Confessions,' and (God be praised) this day, after 8 weeks from London and above 6 from the Lizard, we made Piscataqua, and landed there. And so ends my voyage for England. We go hence for Boston by land."

He was now to be separated from the companionship of Dr. Cutler, though for many years afterwards they had frequent interviews and a constant correspondence. He passed a few days with Mr. Honyman in Rhode Island, and then proceeded to the paternal roof in Guilford from which he had been so long absent. His arrival at Stratford in the beginning of November was joyfully welcomed by his little flock; and Mr. Pigot, who had been waiting to be relieved, hastened to his new charge in Providence.

Johnson felt the responsibility of his situation, and was alive with the work of organizing and settling the Church of England in Connecticut. At this time there was no house of public worship for Episcopalians in the Colony, but one had been commenced in Stratford, and was opened for religious services on Christmas Day, nearly fourteen months after his establishment in that town. His predecessor had communicated to the Society that he would "find it a most difficult task to answer the expectations of the towns around him, there being work enough for Sunday laborers in the Lord's harvest;" and his own letters to the Bishop of London and others, written after a cursory survey of the field, are full of solicitude for the "necessitous state" of the Church. Their replies are equally earnest. One dated February 17, 1725, from the Rev. J. Berriman, so frequently mentioned in his private journal, contains the first intimation which Johnson received of the scheme of Berkeley: —

Dear Sir, — I received yours of October last, and cannot let slip the present opportunity of writing, though I have little time to write in, and less business to write about.

I am glad you continue to remember me among your other friends in these parts, though you are so far removed from us. You may assure yourself nothing will ever blot you out of my remembrance, and as I shall always find a peculiar pleasure in reading your letters, so I shall be diligent in answering you, if it will give you any satisfaction.

It is with regret I hear of the difficulties Dr. Cutler labors under, and the hard usage Mr. Checkley has met with. May it please God to make it all turn to the benefit of yours and of the whole Church in general, and I beseech Him to succeed your labors, and to send more laborers into your harvest. A very pious Dean in Ireland is quitting his preferment there to go and settle in the Bermuda Islands, where he proposes to erect a College — to bring up the natives of America to do the office of Missionaries, etc. Several friends of his go with him upon this expedition.

We hear of two Nonjuring Bishops (Dr. Welton for one) who are gone into America; and it is said the Bishop of London will send one or more of a different stamp as an antidote against them. God Almighty prevent the bad effects of the one, and in his due time accomplish the other, and furnish you with a plentiful supply for all your wants.

The good Bishop of Man continues to be persecuted by those stiff-necked rulers that have given him so much disturbance. The Deputy-governor lately put a man into a captain's commission who was under the censure of the Church on purpose to affront and provoke the Bishop, and throw contempt upon his authority, pretending the Bishop has nothing to do with military men. It is hoped and expected the insults he daily meets with will occasion some good law to be made to curb the exorbitant and almost independent power of the King of Man.

Dr. Waddington is made Bp. of Chichester, Dr. Clavering of Landaff, Dr. Bradshaw of Bristol, etc. My brother is married, and I am moved to his lodgings in Bow Lane, and Mr. Scullard boards with us. Mr. Chas. Wheatly has buried his wife. Lord Chancellor is turned out of office and fallen into great disgrace.

I am your very affectionate friend and serv't.

Johnson urged the importance of bishops in this country, not only to ordain the men who were inclined to the Episcopal ministry, but to exercise proper supervision in ecclesiastical matters. In a letter written twelve months after his arrival at Stratford, he said to Dr. Gibson, the Bishop of London: — "It is a great satisfaction to us to understand that one of your Lordship's powerful interest and influence is engaged in so good a work as that of sending bishops into America, and that there is nothing you desire more or would be at greater pains to compass. This gives us the greatest hopes that by your Lordship's pious endeavors, under the blessing of God and the benign influence of our most gracious King, it may at length be accomplished. And we humbly hope that the address and representation of the state of religion here which we have lately presumed to offer, may, in your Lordship's hands, be of some service in this affair. I pray God give it success."

The position of Johnson now made him influential among the friends of the Church throughout New England. He was the only Episcopal clergyman in Connecticut, and had strong adversaries around him in those from whose fellowship he had withdrawn. They did much in conformity with the narrow spirit of the age to thwart his plans, and drive him from the Colony, by rendering his situation uncomfortable and embarrassing. But he had prepared himself for all such opposition, and nothing helped more to wear off its edge and win for him the respect and confidence of many who were at first suspicious of the purity of his motives, than his constantly cheerful and benevolent temper, and the frankness and courtesy with which he defended his opinions.

For nearly two years he had lived among his poor people and been content with such provision as their humble circumstances allowed. But on the 26th of September, 1725, he married Mrs. Charity Nicoll, widow of Benjamin Nicoll, Esq., and daughter of Colonel Richard Floyd[1] of Brookhaven, Long Island. She had three children by her former husband — two sons and a daughter — and no sooner had the step-father established himself in his own house than he

[1] Writing to his son in 1757, Johnson gave this account to him of his mother's ancestors: — "*Floyd* is doubtless originally *Lloyd*, Ll being pronounced in Wales, whence they came, like Fl. All I can learn is that your grandfather was born at New Castle on the Delaware, that his father and mother came from Wales, and that when he came and settled at Long Island they came with him, and lived to be old. His wife was *Margaret Woodhull*, whose father was an English gentleman of a considerable family, cousin-german by his mother to *Lord Carew*, father to the late *Bishop of Durham*, whose niece was mother to the present *Earl of Wallgrave* or *Waldgrave*."

undertook to instruct the sons in a preliminary course of education, and prepare them for Yale College, where they both graduated in 1734. The father of Johnson wrote him a congratulatory letter on his happy marriage, and informed him at the same time that his mother was in a languishing condition, with little prospect of recovery. Her death, which occurred in the succeeding March, preceded a sickness of his own that brought him nigh to the grave, and of which he made this entry in his private journal, under date of June 13, 1726: "Blessed be thy goodness, adored be thy kindness, patience, and forbearance, O good and gracious God, who hast preserved me from the danger I have been exposed to in my late sickness at *Boston*, and granted me so successful, so speedy a relief and recovery from so dangerous a distemper. What shall I render to the Lord for all his benefits? Let my soul praise Thee while I live, and all that is within me bless his holy name. Thou forgivest all my iniquities, and healest all my diseases. Thou savest my life from destruction, and crownest me with loving-kindness and tender mercy. May I never forget thy benefits! but remember my recovery from this sickness as a fresh motive to lay out the life and powers which are yet lent and continued to me, with greater zeal and engagedness for God's glory, the advancement of his Church, and the good of the souls of men; and may it be as a warning to me to walk with more watchfulness and circumspection all my days, that I may be ready to depart whenever my last summons shall arrive."

Before the year had rolled round, another severe

affliction befell him in the decease of his father,—"a man remarkable for a friendly temper, and delighting much in hospitality to strangers." According to the son's account, he was favorably impressed with the Church of England, "entirely brought off from most of the fanatical and predestination principles, ... and would have communicated with us, if he had lived." The bitter and uncharitable spirit of the times had served to deter him from this, and he was not so thoroughly persuaded as to "think it necessary to leave the Dissenting Communion."

CHAPTER IV.

POLEMICS AND INFIDELITY; BIRTH OF A SON; PERSONAL ACQUAINTANCE WITH DEAN BERKELEY; VISITS TO HIM AT NEWPORT, AND A CONVERT TO HIS VIEWS; ALCIPHRON, OR THE MINUTE PHILOSOPHER; RETURN OF BERKELEY TO ENGLAND, AND BENEFACTIONS TO YALE COLLEGE; RELIGIOUS CONTROVERSY, AND PUBLICATION OF PAMPHLETS.

A. D. 1727–1736.

THE inquiring mind of Johnson led him to seek the society of scholars, and his thirst for knowledge was so great that he neglected no opportunity of intellectual improvement. William Burnet was now the Governor of New York, "a very bookish man, and much of a scholar," as the subject of this memoir described him, who had a large library, and whose taste for learning might have come from his father, for he was the eldest son of Gilbert Burnet, Bishop of Salisbury, and the celebrated historian of "His Own Time."

Johnson, in his frequent visits to New York, cultivated the friendship of Governor Burnet, with whom he became a great favorite. He was furnished with some of the best books that his library contained, and in this way was drawn into the thorny thicket of the Bangorian controversy, which involved the doctrine of the Trinity, and questions of ecclesiastical authority, and the proper province of the civil magistrate. The Governor was a zealous champion on the side of Clark, Whiston, and Hoadly, and attempted dexterously to bring over his young friend to his own views.

Here is one of the letters which he wrote to him: —

New York, *August* 14, 1727.

Reverend Sir, — It is so rare a thing in this country to find one that reads books with care and impartiality, that you need no apology for borrowing, but you give me pleasure in doing it. I hate to have them lie idle upon a shelf; but when I lend them to such readers, I reckon they bring me in good interest.

There is no need in reading a controversy to be of one side of the question — it is rather better to be of neither; and, in points which are not capable of demonstration, perhaps those who never entirely determine, but still are in some suspense, act most rationally. Candor and temper are sufficient bonds of unity, without sameness of opinion.

The thing that always hung most in my mind out of Dr. Clark's book was, that there were but three possible opinions upon the subject, and that whoever has any opinion fixed, has one of the three, and that all other opinions are mere self-delusion and mere nothing, however plausibly disguised. As to the style and decency of writing which you commend in the Doctor, it is certainly very taking; and it is commonly the lot of the most unpopular to write so, whereas those who are backed by numbers are apt to swagger. I remember my father was called a Socinian, because in one of his books he commends the serious, modest way of controversy. But this is no proof of people's being right; and accordingly, I remember an able member of the House of Commons, speaking of a very rising young member, said, what a pity he had not been of the side of the minority, for then he would have had a complete finishing, but as he was on the winning side, it was a great chance but he would be spoiled. So much a better school is adversity than prosperity in every stage and profession of life. As to the three opinions, I take the fashionable one to be Sabellianism, as I have often found by conversation, of which Socinianism ought to be a consequence, though seldom drawn, and therefore not fairly chargeable; the most uncommon one Tritheism, which people are oftener driven to by dispute than that they choose it; and the most obvious one that of the inequality, which would be more universal if it did not seem to lead to Polytheism, though not so much as Tritheism does. I send the books, and am, sir,

Your most humble servant,

W. Burnet.

To this Johnson replied: —

May it please your Excellency, — Dr. Clark's writings are so very agreeable and instructive that I cannot presently be disengaged from them, when I have once got them under my eye; however, I now at last return those of them which I had last, with my humble thanks for them and those kind lines which accompanied them from your Excellency, full of very wise and true observations.

But as to the last of them, relating to the three opinions: if Sabellianism do indeed necessarily include and infer Socinianism; and if, at the same time, the common orthodoxy were not really different from Sabellianism, provided there were but three possible opinions on this subject, I should readily enough subscribe to that of the inequality; for I cannot conceive how a great many texts of Scripture can be fairly accounted for upon the Socinian hypothesis; and as for Tritheism, that is demonstrably and utterly inconsistent with reason as well as Scripture. But that of the inequality, though reasonable and intelligible enough, and very well accounting for most texts of Scripture relating to this subject, yet there are some texts which I wish I could, but cannot find reconcilable to it, without too great a violence done to them, and too great a deviation from the most obvious sense and meaning of them. It seems to me, therefore, there must be a fourth hypothesis possible, though it may not be comprehensible or explicable; and yet, so far as it is discovered to us, it is intelligible, and because it is divinely revealed, must be credible. But I shall gladly embrace any further light on this subject.

If your Excellency removes to Boston, as the people there will no doubt think themselves very happy, so I shall be very glad in particular that you remove no further from us, and that it will yet remain practicable for me to enjoy the advantages of that condescending goodness you have hitherto expressed towards me. And therefore, if I may yet presume, I shall be very much obliged to your Excellency if you will please to lend me any other good book, and particularly an Italian Grammar, after the manner of Boyer for the French, for I have a curiosity to look into the nature of that language.

I am,

May it please your Excellency,

Your most humble, etc.,

S. J.

Thus he found him indisposed to adopt conclusions until he had examined and approved the basis on which they rested. The cause of truth demanded an impartial study of the matters in dispute, and therefore Johnson turned to the writings of those who had arrayed themselves in opposition to the principles of these men, — to such authors as Bull, Pearson and Waterland, Sherlock, Snape and Law, — and very soon he was more convinced than ever that the *modus* of the Trinity was not to be accounted for on any philosophical hypothesis; that it is beyond the reach of our faculties, and to be received as taught in the Scriptures, and believed in the Church for ages immediately succeeding the Apostolic. Thus he rejected human speculation in Divine things, and settled down in the conviction, as he himself states in his autobiography, — "That we must be content chiefly, if not only, both in nature and revelation, with the knowledge of facts and their design and connections, without speculating much further; that one great end of all God's discoveries, both in nature and grace, is to mortify our pride and self-sufficiency, to make us deeply sensible of our entire dependence, and chiefly to engage us to live by *faith and not by sight.*"

A club of free-thinkers in England about this time startled the nation with their bold attacks on Christianity. Included in the members of this club were Anthony Collins, Thomas Woolston, and Matthew Tindall, all of whom, as if by concert, openly engaged in an effort to bring discredit upon the religion of the Bible, and weaken the faith of the disciples of Christ. They issued their publications in succession, and attacked Christianity from different points, claiming, among other things, that the miracles of Christ were susceptible of a mystical interpretation, and at the same time asserting that they were never actually wrought.

These infidel writers were attended and followed by others in the same abandoned cause, so that, as Johnson says, "it seemed as if hell itself was broke loose at once to undermine and demolish Christianity." He read very carefully the books that were prepared in defense of the truth and in confutation of the principles of the free-thinkers, and thus became a scholar armed and ready to do battle in his Master's service. "I remember," says Chandler in his Life,[1] "to have heard him in conversation give an account of the various attacks upon revelation, and of the

[1] P. 143.

defenses which they occasioned, similar to that given by Leland in his 'View of the Deistical Writers,'" and this too before that valuable work was published.

The loss of his parents, referred to in the previous chapter, was supplied to him in a measure by the birth of a child. On the 14th day of October, 1727, he made an entry in his private journal in these words, — "This day I am 31 years old, and this sevennight (October 7) it hath pleased God of his goodness to give me the great blessing of a very likely son, for which, and in my wife's comfortable deliverance, I adore his goodness.

"Thus I am no sooner deprived of a father but I am provided for with a son to supply the demands of our mortal condition in this world. My only hope in Thee, O God, who hast been my father's God, and who art my God, is, that Thou wilt be his God and portion in the land of the living, and forever. I have dedicated him to Thee; sanctify him by thy grace, that he may be serviceable unto Thee in the world, and be fitted for and made partaker of thy glory."

The pleasant letters which follow touch upon his domestic relations, and revive the recollection of friendships formed while he was sojourning in London: —

BOW LANE, *Sept.* 25, 1727.

REV. SIR, — I have a long time wished and hoped for a letter from you, but not being so happy as to receive one, I am resolved to force myself into your acquaintance, hoping the distance cannot hinder our good wishes to each other. I heard from Dr. Cutler success attends your labors in the ministry. I pray God continue health to you, and prosperity to your endeavors. I cannot but wish you all happiness in the change of your condition, and doubt not a

5

man of your zeal and goodness will meet with all the blessings a married estate can allow. I should be pleased to divert you with a little news, but we have none fresher than the death of the good Bp. of Bath and Wells, and hope to have some good man his successor. Our new King seems everybody's favorite, and his Government so equitable that we flatter ourselves all things will be managed to universal satisfaction.

I am, dear sir, your affectionate brother,
And very humble servant,
J. SCULLARD.

Dr. Waterland is made a Prebend of Windsor.

Immediately on its reception Johnson replied to this letter as follows: —

REV. SIR, — I have received yours of the 25th of September, and am very much obliged to you for retaining me still in your remembrance, and for this kind testimony of it, for indeed I was almost afraid you had quite forgot me. But I am surprised if you never received any letter from me, for I have written to you once and again, and I was afraid I should never have the happiness of receiving one from you. But the distance makes correspondence uncertain; however, I shall be glad, and not only esteem it an happiness but an honor, to receive now and then a letter from you, and you may depend upon it that I shall not be wanting on my part.

I thank you for your kind congratulations upon my new condition, not so new now indeed, but that I have a son, I thank God, as well as a wife. I hope I shall have occasion before long to congratulate you upon the like occasion, and that you will be as happy in such a state as you can wish me, and as happy, I thank heaven, I am as this fading world and this poor country will admit of.

I am glad to hear you are all so well pleased with our new King, and that we have so good a prospect of the welfare of the Church under his auspicious reign. I pray God we may feel the benign influences of it in these distant regions. I am glad so good a man as Dr. Waterland is taken notice of, and sorry for the good Bp. of Bath and Wells' death. I shall be glad to be informed who succeeds, and what other alterations and preferments occur. In hopes of which, my humble and affectionate regards to Mr. Berriman, Wheatly, and all friends.

I remain your most humble brother,

S. JOHNSON.

I have not heard who is the Rector since good Mr. Lazinby's death.

One of the most interesting portions of Johnson's life was from the beginning of 1729 to the autumn of 1731, — the period covered by the residence of Dean Berkeley at Newport in Rhode Island. Before that dignitary came to America, he had read his "Principles of Human Knowledge," and had not only formed a high estimate of the ability and character of the author, but had become in a measure a convert to his metaphysical opinions. Desirous of conversing with so extraordinary a genius and so distinguished a scholar, he made a visit to Newport soon after his arrival, and through his friend, the Rev. Mr. Honyman, Missionary of the Church of England in that place, he was introduced to the Dean, and admitted to a free and full discussion of his philosophical works, and of the benevolent scheme which brought him to this country. It was gratifying to Johnson that in this first interview he was received with such marked kindness and confidence, besides being presented with those of the Dean's publications which had not fallen under his eye. The personal acquaintance thus begun laid the foundation of a lifelong friendship and correspondence between two great thinkers.

There are glimpses of Berkeley among the wits of the Court of Queen Anne, and he was intimate with Steele and Addison, and a companion of Swift and Pope. He had been Senior Fellow of Trinity College, Dublin, in official employment as Lecturer in Divinity, and preacher for the University, but resigned his Fellowship in 1724 on being preferred to the Deanery of Derry, — an important living in the Irish Church, with an annual income of about eleven hundred pounds. A romance connected with Dean Swift caused him to be remembered in the will of a lady of Dutch descent (Miss Vanhomrigh),[1] but as he was an "absolute philosopher in regard to money, titles, and power," the fortune which came to him so unexpectedly appears to have only ripened his conception of the plan of erecting a college at Bermuda for better supplying the plantations with clergymen, and converting the savage Americans to Christianity.

It was about this time that he published a tract in defense of the enterprise. It had taken such shape in his mind, that he pleaded for it with wonderful power, and was resolved to dedicate his life and fortune and energies to its prosecution. An extract from the humorous letter of Dean Swift to Carteret, Lord Lieutenant of Ireland, dated September 3, 1724, may furnish the best account of his enthusiasm: —

For three years past he has been struck with a notion of founding a University at Bermudas by a charter from the Crown. He has seduced several of the hopefullest young clergymen and others here, many of them well provided for, and all in the fairest way of preferment; but in England his conquests are greater, and I doubt will spread very far this

[1] See Fraser's *Life and Letters of Berkeley*, Oxford, 1871, ch. iv.

winter. He showed me a little Tract which he designs to publish, and there your Excellency will see his whole scheme of a life academico-philosophical (I shall make you remember what you were) of a college founded for Indian scholars and missionaries, where he most exorbitantly proposes a whole hundred pounds a year for himself, forty pounds for a Fellow, and ten for a Student. His heart will break if his Deanery be not taken from him and left to your Excellency's disposal. I discouraged him by the coldness of courts and ministers who will interpret all this as impossible and a vision; but nothing will do. And, therefore, I humbly entreat your Excellency either to use such persuasions as will keep one of the first men in the kingdom for learning and virtue quiet at home, or assist him by your credit to compass his romantic design.[1]

No discouragements checked the efforts of Berkeley. By his persuasive eloquence he converted ridiculers into friends and supporters, and obtained towards the furtherance of his object private subscriptions of more than five thousand pounds. He approached the throne for a charter, which was finally granted, and then his influence at Court secured the promise of an endowment of £20,000 — a fraction of the value of certain lands which the French, by the treaty of Utrecht in 1713, had ceded to the British Crown, and the proceeds of which, to the amount of £80,000, the good Queen Anne had designed as a fund for the support of four bishops in America. Her death, the next year, prevented the execution of her charitable design, and Berkeley felt that he had a moral claim upon it for his own kindred scheme.

Preparations for his voyage across the Atlantic

[1] *Works*, vol. xvi. p. 469.

were at last completed, and a business letter to his friend, Thomas Prior, dated Gravesend, September 5, 1728, opens with a paragraph which has fixed historically several matters, — "To-morrow, with God's blessing, I set sail for Rhode Island with my wife and a friend of hers, my Lady Handcock's daughter, who bears us company. I am married since I saw you to Miss Forster, daughter of the late Chief Justice,[1] whose humor and turn of mind pleases me beyond anything that I know in her whole sex. Mr. James, Mr. Dalton, and Mr. Smibert go with us on this voyage. We are now altogether at Gravesend, and are engaged in one view."

Berkeley was in middle life when he landed at Newport on the 23d of January, nearly five months after sailing from Gravesend, and "was ushered into the town with a great number of gentlemen, to whom he behaved himself after a very complaisant manner." Here he rested to think over, under new circumstances, the romantic enterprise which had absorbed his energies for seven long years, and purchasing a tract of land in a sequestered spot, he built a commodious house, which, in loyal remembrance of the English palace, he named Whitehall, and waited the tardy movements of Sir Robert Walpole, the prime minister, to send him the funds which had been promised by the Government.

It was in this retreat that he continued his philosophical investigations, and received the successive visits of Johnson. The date of the first personal interview between them has not been discovered, but

[1] John Forster, also Recorder of Dublin, and Speaker of the Irish House of Commons. The marriage took place August 1, 1728.

as early as June 25, 1729, Berkeley wrote to him at much length, in answer to objections or inquiries which he had been moved to make in reference to his Philosophy. Judging from its tenor it is thought to have been his first letter to Johnson. He began thus: —

REV. SIR, — The ingenious letter you favored me with found me very much indisposed with a gathering or imposthumation in my head which confined me several weeks, and is now, I thank God, relieved. The objections of a candid thinking man to what I have written will always be welcome, and I shall not fail to give all the satisfaction I am able, not without hopes either of convincing or being convinced. It is a common fault for men to hate opposition, and be too much wedded to their own opinions. I am so sensible of this in others that I could not pardon it to myself, if I considered mine any further than they seem to me to be true, which I shall the better be able to judge of when they have passed the scrutiny of persons so well qualified to examine them as you and your friends appear to be, to whom my illness must be an apology for not sending this answer sooner.

He proceeded briefly to explain or defend under eleven heads the philosophic ideas which he had published, and then closed his letter with words which show his high respect for the intellectual force and clearness of Johnson: —

And now, Sir, I submit these hints (which I have hastily thrown together as soon as my illness gave me leave) to your own maturer thoughts, which after all you will find the best instructors. What you have seen of mine was published when I was very young, and without doubt hath many defects. For though the notions should be true (as I verily think they are), yet it is difficult to express them clearly and consistently, language being framed to common use and received prejudices. I do not therefore pretend that my books can teach truth. All I hope for is that they may be an occasion to inquisitive men of discovering truth by consulting their own minds and looking into their own thoughts. As to the Second part of my treatise concerning the principles of Human Knowledge, the fact is that I had made a considerable progress in it, but the manuscript was lost about fourteen years ago during my travels in Italy; and I never had leisure since to do so disagreeable a thing as writing twice on the same subject.

Objections passing through your hands have their full force and clearness. I like them the better. This intercourse with a man of parts and a philosophic genius is very agreeable. I sincerely wish we were nearer neighbors.[1] In the mean time whenever either you or your friends favor me with your thoughts, you may be sure of a punctual correspondence on my part. Before I have done I will venture to recommend three points: 1. To consider well the answers I have already given in my books to several objections. 2. To consider whether any new objection that shall occur doth not suppose the doctrine of abstract general ideas. 3. Whether the difficulties proposed in objection to my scheme can be solved by the contrary, for if they cannot, it is plain they can be no objection to mine.

I know not whether you have got my treatise concerning the principles of Human Knowledge. I intend to send it with my tract De Motu. If you know of a safe hand favor me with a line, and I will make use of that opportunity to send them. My humble service to your friends, to whom I understand myself indebted for some part of your letter.

I am, your very faithful, humble serv't,

GEOR. BERKELEY.

The correspondence thus begun was continued, and the following letter, written after Berkeley was well settled in his own house, indicates that the two had

[1] The distance from Stratford to Newport is about 120 miles.

been brought face to face in the discussion of great metaphysical questions, and that further conversation was needed to "set several things in a fuller and clearer light:"—

REV. SIR,—Yours of Feb. 5th came not to my hands before yesterday; and this afternoon being informed that a sloop is ready to sail towards your town, I would not let slip the opportunity of returning you an answer, though wrote in a hurry.

1. I have no objection against calling the ideas in the mind of God, archetypes of ours. But I object against those archetypes by philosophers supposed to be real things, and to have an absolute rational existence distinct from their being perceived by any mind whatsoever, it being the opinion of all materialists that an ideal existence in the divine mind is one thing, and the real existence of material things another.

2. As to space, I have no notion of any but that which is relative. I know some late philosophers have attributed extension to God, particularly mathematicians; one of whom, in a treatise *de Spatio reali*, pretends to find out fifteen of the incommunicable attributes of God in space. But it seems to me that, they being all negative, he might as well have found them in nothing; and that it would have been as justly inferred from space being impassive, increated, indivisible, etc., that it was nothing, as that it was God.

Sir Isaac Newton supposeth an absolute space different from relative, and consequent thereto, absolute motion different from relative motion; and with all other mathematicians, he supposeth the infinite divisibility of the finite parts of this absolute space; he also supposeth material bodies to drift therein. Now, though I do acknowledge Sir Isaac to have been an extraordinary man, and most profound mathematician, yet I cannot agree with him in these particulars. I make no scruple to use the word space, as well as all other words in common use, but I do not mean thereby a distinct absolute being. For my meaning I refer you to what I have published.

By the τὸ νῦν I suppose to be implied that all things past and to come are actually present to the mind of God, and that there is in Him no change, variation, or succession. A succession of ideas I take to constitute time, and not to be only the sensible measure thereof, as Mr. Locke and others think. But in these matters every man is to think for himself, and speak as he finds. One of my earliest inquiries was about time, which led me into several paradoxes that I did not think fit or necessary to publish, particularly into the notion that the resurrection follows next moment to death. We are confounded and perplexed about time. (1.) Supposing a succession in God. (2.) Conceiving that we have an abstract idea of time. (3.) Supposing that the time in one mind is to be measured by the succession of ideas in another. (4.) Not considering the true use and end of words, which as often terminate in the will as the understanding, being employed rather to excite, influence, and direct action than to produce clear and distinct ideas.

3. That the soul of man is passive as well as active I make no doubt. Abstract general ideas was a notion that Mr. Locke held in common with the Schoolmen, and I think all other philosophers; it runs through his whole book of Human Understanding. He holds an abstract idea of existence exclusive of perceiving and being perceived. I cannot find I have any such idea, and this is my reason against it. Descartes proceeds upon other principles. One square foot of snow is as white as one thousand yards; one single perception is as truly a perception as one hundred. Now any degree of perception being sufficient to existence, it will not follow that we should say one existed more at one time than another, any more than we should say one thousand yards of snow are whiter than one yard. But after all, this comes to a verbal dispute. I think it might prevent a good deal of obscurity and dispute to examine well what I have said about abstraction, and about the true use of sense and significancy of words, in several parts of these things that I have published, though much remains to be said on that subject.

You say you agree with me that there is nothing within your mind but God and other spirits, with the attributes or properties belonging to them, and the ideas contained in them. This is a principle or main point from which, and from what I had laid down about abstract ideas, much may be deduced. But if in every inference we should not agree, so long as the main points are settled and well understood, I should be less solicitous about particular conjectures. I could wish that all the things I have published on these philosophical subjects were read in the order wherein I published them, once to take the design and connection of them, and a second time with a critical eye, adding your own thought and observation upon every part as you went along. I send you herewith ten bound books and one unbound. You will take yourself what you have not already. You will give the principles, the theory, the dialogue, one of each, with my service to the gentleman who is Fellow of New Haven College, whose compliments you brought to me. What remains you will give as you please.

If at any time your affairs should draw you into these parts, you shall be very welcome to pass as many days as you can spend at my house. Four or five days' conversation would set several things in a fuller and clearer light than writing could do in as many months. In the mean time I shall be glad to hear from you or your friends whenever you please to favor, Rev. Sir,

Your very humble serv't,

GEOR. BERKELEY.

Pray let me know whether they would admit the writings of Hooker and Chillingworth into the library of the College in New Haven.

RHODE ISLAND, *March* 24, 1729–30.

Johnson was at Newport and preached November 1, 1730, and he may have taken an earlier opportunity for the "four or five days' conversation." Whenever the interview was held, other subjects besides philosophy must have entered into their discussions. For Berkeley had already begun to realize the painful uncertainty which hung over his prospects, and to feel that the crisis of the Bermuda College was approaching. The money promised by the Government had not been sent, and he wrote a letter to Prior on the 7th of May, 1730, manifesting much solicitude about the Ministerial delays, and intimating that he had no intention of continuing in these parts, if the grant of £20,000 was in the end to be positively refused. At one time he entertained the thought of applying for permission to change the original plan and transfer the College to Rhode Island, where he had expended largely for lands and buildings, and where the chief objections raised against placing it in Bermuda would be obviated. But he quickly relinquished this idea, and at length his hopes were entirely crushed when the conclusive answer came from Walpole, "advising him by all means to return home to Europe, and give up his present expectations." He bore his great disappointment like a philosopher, and a good picture of his feelings is given in the work [1] which he wrote "in this distant retreat, far beyond the verge of that great whirlpool of business, faction, and pleasure, which is called the world:" —

I flattered myself, Theages, that before this time I might have been able to have sent you an agreeable account of the success of the affair which brought me into this remote corner of the country. But instead of this, I should now give you the detail of its miscarriage, if I did not rather choose to entertain you with some amusing incidents which have

[1] *Alciphron; or, the Minute Philosopher, in Seven Dialogues.* Two vols. Printed in London, 1732. A second edition appeared in the same year.

helped to make me easy under a circumstance I could neither obviate nor foresee. Events are not in our power; but it always is, to make a good use even of the very worst. And I must needs own, the course and event of this affair gave opportunity for reflections that make me some amends for a great loss of time, pains, and expense. A life of action, which takes its issue from the counsels, passions, and views of other men, if it doth not draw a man to imitate, will at least teach him to observe. And a mind at liberty to reflect on its own observations, if it produce nothing useful to the world, seldom fails of entertainment to itself.[1]

It is due to Johnson that the self-sacrificing and missionary enterprise of Berkeley was not wholly a failure, or rather that his name was held in grateful remembrance in America after his return to England. When it had been decided to break up and leave Whitehall and the country, he paid him a final visit and received from him many valuable books, and to use his own words, they "parted very affectionately." Nor was this all. Both were deeply interested in the cause of learning, and Johnson took the liberty of commending to his friendly notice the institution where he had himself been educated, notwithstanding the continued hostility of the authorities to the Church of England. He was in Rhode Island, July, 1731, and on the 4th day of that month, according to his own note, preached "before the Dean," a sermon from the text,—"For in Christ Jesus neither circumcision availeth anything, nor uncircumcision, but a new creature." This was undoubtedly his final visit when they "agreed" together about the books, and discussed the matters of the College; but letters passed between them afterwards, and Berkeley, on the

[1] P. 2, vol. i. 2d ed.

eve of his departure, wrote his great American friend as follows: —

REV. SIR, — I am now upon the point of setting out for Boston in order to embark for England. But the hurry I am in could not excuse my neglecting to acknowledge the favor of your letter. In answer to the obliging things in it, I can only say I wish I might deserve them.

My endeavors shall not be wanting, some way or other, to be useful; and I should be very glad to be so in particular to the College at New Haven, and the more as you were once a member of it, and have still an influence there. Pray return my service to those gentlemen who sent their compliments by you.

I have left a box of books with Mr. Kay, to be given away by you, — the small English books where they may be most serviceable among the people, the others as we agreed together. The Greek and Latin books I would have given to such lads as you think will make the best use of them in the College, or to the school at New Haven.

I pray God to bless you and your endeavors to promote religion and learning in this uncultivated part of the world, and desire you to accept mine and my wife's best wishes and services, being very truly, Rev. Sir,

Your most humble servant,

GEOR. BERKELEY.

RHODE ISLAND, *Sept.* 7, 1731.

Berkeley's gifts to Yale College were through the agency of Johnson. To him was transmitted from England the instrument by which he conveyed to the corporation his farm at Whitehall of ninety-six acres, — the annual proceeds to be used for the purpose of encouraging Greek and Latin scholarship: and he so interested some of his Bermuda subscribers in the American College, that with their assistance he was enabled to send over in 1733 a donation to the library of nearly one thousand volumes, valued at about £500 : "The finest collection of books" according to President Clap, "which had then ever been brought to America."

The letter to Johnson which accompanied "the instrument of conveyance," has not been published, or even referred to in any sketch of his life and benefactions; and that to Rector Williams is not to be found among the archives of Yale College. A little doubt has been raised about Johnson's sole agency in the matter, and the motive which actuated him and the Dean ;[1] but this letter removes it, and at the same time shows the singleness of the donor's intentions and the forecast of his mind as to a course after graduation. He appears to have been the first to suggest its advantages : —

LONDON, *July* 25, 1732.

REV. SIR, — Some part of the benefactions to the College of Bermuda, which I could not return, the benefactors being deceased, joined with the assistance of some living friends,

[1] President Stiles, in his Diary, says Johnson "persuaded the Dean to believe that Yale College would soon become Episcopal, and that they had received his immaterial philosophy. This or some other motive influenced the Dean to make a donation of his Rhode Island farm, ninety-six acres, with a library of about a thousand volumes, to Yale College, in 1733. This donation was certainly procured very much through the instrumentality of Rev. Dr. Jared Eliot and Rev. Dr. Johnson."

The latter writing to Abp. Secker, March, 1759, and referring to efforts of the Congregational ministers to depreciate the work of the missionaries, said : "I maintained all along a very friendly correspondence with the chief men among them, and endeavored to do them all the good offices I could, and in particular I procured a noble donation from Bishop Berkeley for their College in land and books to the value of nigh £2,000 sterling. But behold the gratitude of these men. At the same time that I was doing them these good offices, they were contriving and did send to the Bishop of London a long letter, full of gross falsehoods and misrepresentations, of complaint against us with a view to get all the church people deprived of their ministers, and then of their subsistence, which he laid before the Society, and which I believe your Grace may find among papers of the year 1735. In reply to which the Society gave them leave to produce evidence to make good their complaints against us, which they endeavored to do, but could make nothing of it."

has enabled me without any great loss to myself, to dispose of my farm in Rhode Island in favor of the College in Connecticut. It is my opinion that as human learning and the improvements of Reason are of no small use in Religion, so it would very much forward those ends, if some of your students were enabled to subsist longer at their studies, and if by a public tryal and premium an Emulation were inspired into all. This method of encouragement hath been found useful in other learned societies, and I think it cannot fail of being so in one where a person so well qualified as yourself has such influence, and will bear a share in the elections. I have been a long time indisposed with a great disorder in my head ; this makes any application hurtful to me, which must excuse my not writing a longer letter on this occasion.

The letter you sent by Mr. Beach[1] I received and did him all the service I could with the Bishop of London and the Society. He promised to call on me before his return, but have not heard of him, so am obliged to recommend this pacquet to Mr. Newman's care. It contains the instrument of conveyance[2] in form of law, together with a let-

[1] Rev. John Beach of Newtown.

[2] The farm contained ninety-six acres more or less, and was worth at the time, one hundred pounds sterling. It was leased March 25th, 1763, to John Whiting for nine hundred and ninety-nine years. The President and Fellows of Yale College recited in the agreement, that they had "found upon the experience of thirty years past that by leasing said farm on short leases, the housing and fences have greatly gone to decay, the wood destroyed, and the farm not improved to so good an advantage as land cultivated by freeholders, which is likely to be the case for some centuries while land is so plenty in this country ; upon mature consideration whereof and the advice of Rev. George Berkeley, the son of the generous donor, and sundry other gentlemen learned in the law, and skilled in the best economy," the annual rent, from March 25th, 1763, to March 25th, 1769, was fixed at 72 ounces of silver money, besides requiring about 300 rods of stone wall to be made upon the premises ; from 1769 to 1810, 144 ounces of silver money ; and from 1810, to the termination of the lease 240 bushels of good merchantable wheat or its value.

Whiting assigned his lease to other parties, and subsequently a new one was given for the remainder of the period, fixing the annual rent from 1769 to 1789 at 100 ounces of silver money ; from 1789 to 1810 at 126 ounces of silver money ; and after 1810 at 210 bushels of wheat.

A party wishing to buy the lease, wrote March 2d, 1799, that the rent was too great after 1810 ; and the corporation therefore voted the next year that the tenant should pay $130 annually for ten years, and after that $140.

The latest lease was executed May 18th, 1801, by Timothy Dwight, President of

ter for Mr. President Williams, which you will deliver to him. I shall make it my endeavor to procure a benefaction of books for the College library, and am not without hopes of success. There hath of late been published here a treatise against those who are called Free Thinkers, which I intended to have sent to you and some other friends in those parts, but on second thoughts suspect it might do mischief to have it known in that part of the world what pernicious opinions are boldly espoused here at home. My little family, I thank God, are well. My best wishes attend you and yours. My wife joins her services with mine. I shall be glad to hear from you by the first opportunity after this hath come to your hands. Direct your letter to Lord Percival, at his house in Pall-Mall, London, and it will be sure to find me wherever I am. On all occasions I shall be glad to show that I am very truly, Rev. Sir,

Your faithful humble serv^{t}.,

GEOR. BERKELEY.

Johnson, in his autobiography, mentions that "the Trustees, though they made an appearance of much thankfulness, were almost afraid to accept the noble donation," — suspecting a proselytizing design, and remembering the effect in previous years of Anglican divinity upon the minds of some of their leading scholars. But wiser counsels prevailed, the books and lands were received, and Berkeley maintained a friendly correspondence with the authorities of the College to the end of his life.

His well-known philosophical work, published the year after his return to England, attracted the attention of learned men, and while many rejected his

Yale College, in favor of Paul Wightman, his heirs and assigns forever, fixing the rent at $140 per annum from March 25th, 1810, to March 25th, 2761. *See Records of Y. C.*

The Farm is now estimated to be worth $100,000, and if it had been kept in possession of the College, Berkeley's gift would have been a vastly greater stimulus to classical scholarship.

speculative spirit, none denied the greatness of his intellect and the purity of his Christian character. It was some compensation for the disappointment of his cherished hopes that so far from being overlooked at Court, he was promoted to the See of Cloyne, — a secluded bishopric in the southern part of his native Ireland, to which he was consecrated on Sunday, the 19th of May, 1734. In this retired spot, where he was almost as much out of the world as he had been at Newport, he found leisure to pursue his favorite studies, and to keep up by letter a tolerably frequent intercourse with his congenial friend on this side of the Atlantic.

Johnson became a thorough convert to his system, and owned his obligations to Berkeley in removing many difficulties that had hitherto attended his philosophical and theological inquiries. As he himself says in his autobiography, "he found the Dean's way of thinking and explaining things, utterly precluded skepticism, and left no room for endless doubts and uncertainties. His denying *matter* at first seemed shocking; but it was only for the want of giving a thorough attention to his meaning. It was only the unintelligible scholastic notion of matter he disputed, and not anything either sensible, imaginable, or intelligible; and it was attended with this vast advantage, that it not only gave new incontestible proofs of a Deity, but moreover, the most striking apprehensions of his constant presence with us and inspection over us, and of our entire dependence on Him and infinite obligations to his most wise and almighty benevolence."

The history of philosophic thought was blended to

some extent with the infidelity of the times, but Berkeley went a great deal deeper and wider than those who treated his theories roughly and pronounced them fallacious and bewildering. It was his design in "Alciphron; or, the Minute Philosopher," to vindicate the Christian religion, and overcome the various objections of atheists, fatalists, enthusiasts, libertines, scorners, critics, metaphysicians, and skeptics. Years before, while present at one of the deistical clubs in London, he had heard a "noted writer [1] against Christianity declare that he had found out a demonstration against the being of a God;" and though the thing was palpably false, he was ready to disprove it, and thereby to encourage a religious faith in the constancy of a Divine and superintending Power. Johnson was doubly careful to guard the truth, for he had under his eye at this time, and directed in their theological studies, young men, who, having finished their collegiate course, declared for Episcopacy, and were preparing to proceed to England for ordination. The following letter, otherwise interesting, mentions two, Isaac Browne and John Pierson, graduates of Yale Collge in 1729: —

Dear Sir, — I am obliged to you for introducing me into the company of such worthy gentlemen as Mr. Browne and Mr. Pierson, and doubt not but they will ever be a credit to their Tutor, and a light and ornament to the Church in your parts; and I hope their success will prove an encouragement to others.

I might now send you a long account of the bustle we have had here about laying an excise on wine and tobacco, which has put the whole nation in a flame that will not presently be quenched, — of the divided state we have been in as to peace and war, by the affairs of Poland, where we

[1] Anthony Collins.

suppose a king is chosen by this time, but as yet know not who is the person, — of the death of that infamous author Tindal, etc., etc., — but you will have a better and more particular account by word of mouth, to which therefore I refer you, and am

Your hearty friend and servant,

J. Berriman.

Scotch Yard, *August* 31, 1733.

Another letter from the same clergyman, written six months later, reveals the uneasiness which was then felt about the nomination to a vacant see of one who was accused of unsound theology, especially of Arianism, and of giving to portions of the Old Testament an allegorical interpretation: —

Dear Sir, — . . . . Dean Berkeley was lately made a bishop in Ireland. There is a great bustle with us about the nomination of a new bishop to the See of Gloucester, the like to which I know not whether any history can parallel. There is one Dr. Rundle named by our new Lord Chancellor, son to the late Bishop of Durham (Talbot), to whom the Doctor was Chaplain. The Bishop of London makes a vigorous stand against him, and it is said twenty of the bishops have declared they will have no hand in his consecration. It is objected against him, that he has said these words, or to this effect, that Abraham was an old dotard, and that no man in his senses could believe that God would command him to sacrifice his son. There are two clergymen, one of which is (Dr. Stebbing) preacher at Gray's Inn, and chaplain to the King, who will make good this charge against him upon oath, to prevent his confirmation; though if the court will have it so, we reckon all opposition will be in vain. This matter has been a good while in suspense, and God only knows how it will end. He knows how to bring good out of evil, and may He order all for good.

I am very heartily, yours, etc.,

Feb. 15, 1734. J. Berriman.

And Johnson replied as follows: —

August 18, 1734.

DEAR SIR, — I very thankfully received yours of February 15, and am deeply affected with the story you tell me about Dr. Rundle. It seems the enemies of Christianity are resolved to leave no stone unturned in order to demolish it. This contrivance of endeavoring to furnish out the bench of bishops with infidels, is a notable step, which I doubt not but they will further pursue as the times will bear it. I conclude the favorite doctor is consecrated before now, for I have since heard that all the foundation of the outcry against him, was only that he said there were some allegories in the Old Testament, and that he was horridly abused, and so it was likely to be hushed up. I shall be much obliged to you to let me know what is the true event of this affair, and who succeeds at York and Winchester, and is likely to succeed at Canterbury; and what other events occur; especially about the progress of infidelity, which, with many other things, seems to have a most ominous aspect on our poor Church and nation. Notwithstanding infidelity, I hope the Church of England will yet more and more take root downward, and bear fruit upward in these American parts, where several dissenting ministers are, and many people have been hastening into her bosom. A worthy gentleman, one Mr. Arnold, has lately left them and come over to us; he had been my successor; he only wants to be encouraged by the Society (with whom things at present, I perceive, run pretty low) to come over for ordination; in the mean time will do all the good he can in a lay capacity. My very humble service to the Doctor, Mr. Scullard, and all friends.

I am, dear Sir,

Your most affectionate friend and humble servant,

S. J.

A second letter from his friend touching the case of Dr. Rundle gives a fuller explanation of it, and has a postscript which shows the extent to which an infidel moralist in that age dared to proceed: —

Dear Sir, — Yours of Aug. last came safely to me by the post; and since that I have had a packet from Dr. Cutler, in which came your second letter to a Dissenter, which I read over with great pleasure, and for which I now return you many thanks. You have had, I find, wrong accounts of Dr. Rundle's promotion, though before this you may have been set right by the public news. He did not get the Bishopric of Gloucester, at last, but since that dispute has got one of more than three times the value of that, which is Londonderry, Ireland. The great Sir R—— said he could not do without the Ch —l— r, and he must be obliged. I forgot whether I told you that Dr. R. had been charged with saying that Abraham was an old dotard and that no man could believe God should command him to sacrifice his son, and that Dr. Stebbing, chaplain to the King, and Mr. Venn, minister of S[t] Antholin's, were his accusers; but besides this, the opposition he met with from the Bishop of London was grounded on strong suspicions of his being in the Arian scheme.

The Abp. of York (Dr. Blackburn) is still living. Bp. Hoadly is translated from Sarum to Winchester, and 'tis thought as matters now stand, if Abp. Wake should die, the Bp. of London will go to Canterbury, though an alteration at Court may possibly give Dr. Sherlock the advantage. Dr. Benson is promoted to the See of Gloucester, and Dr. Secker, who succeeded Dr. Clark at St. James's, is made Bp. of Bristol, the late Bp. Herring being translated to Bangor in the room of Bp. Sherlock, translated to Salisbury, and Dr. Fleming, late Dean of Carlisle, is made Bp. of that See in the room of Bp. Waugh, deceased. Benson and Secker were Prebendaries of Durham, and both ('tis said) promoted to appease the Ch —l — r, but nothing would do till Rundle was made a bishop.

I am, dear Sir,

Your affectionate friend and humble servant,

J. Berriman.

Scotch Yard, *Apr.* 5, 1735.

There has been lately published a book here which strikes a note higher in the scheme of infidel morality than perhaps you ever heard of, and that is to show fornication to be a necessary duty. Increase and multiply is the duty; and adultery itself is justified to promote this end, but besides all this the book is wrote in the grave way with prayers and praises and other instances of blasphemy. The bookseller is taken up by the King's messenger. The author is said in the title page to be a clergyman. I hear he is one of the Kirk of Scotland.

The Church of England in Connecticut was surrounded from the beginning with bitter opponents. By this time others had followed the example of Johnson in leaving the Congregational ministry and conforming to Episcopacy, and among the people a spirit of religious inquiry had been awakened which it was not easy to check. The case of John Beach, born in Stratford and graduated at Yale College in 1721, attracted much attention. For eight years he had been settled over the Independents or Congregationalists at Newtown, about twenty miles distant from the place of his nativity, and was a "popular and insinuating young man," but early in 1732, he publicly informed his people of a change in his views, and declared his determination to cross the Atlantic and receive holy orders in the Church of England. At the instance of his friends, he was sent back by the Society for the Propagation of the Gospel with the appointment of a missionary in the town and vicinity where he had lately ministered and was so well known, beloved, and respected. The following extract from a letter of Johnson to the Bishop of London dated April 5, 1732, refers to his character and conversion: —

. . . . My Lord, as the Church here has been very unfortunate in the defeat of the noble design of the Reverend the Dean of Londonderry, which, especially if it had been executed on the Continent, would have been of great advantage to the interest of religion and learning in America, so it has, on the other hand, been happy since in the conversion (besides a number of other good people) of the worthy persons who have all had a public education in the neighboring College, and two of them have been dissenting teachers; two of them will go into other business, and one of them is Mr. Beach, the bearer hereof, whom I know, by long experience of him (he having been heretofore my pupil, and ever since my neighbor) to be a very ingenuous and studious person, and a truly serious and conscientious Christian; but I forbear to say anything further of his case, and refer your Lordship to our joint recommendation of him.

The conformity of Mr. Beach to Episcopacy, notwithstanding the admitted excellence of his character, stirred up his "congregationalist neighbors" more than any former defections from their ranks, and a sharp controversy arose which reached on through many years. There was much in the prevalent teaching of the day that savored of bigotry. The sin of covenant breaking was charged upon those who left the Congregational order, and Johnson drew up and published, partly at the instance of William Beach, a brother of the above named clergyman, a tract to meet this charge, and give plain reasons for conforming to the Church. He was answered by John Graham, a Presbyterian minister in Southbury, and a reply and rejoinder followed. The tracts of Johnson were in the form of "Letters from a Minister of the Church of England to his Dissenting Parishioners," and he wrote three of them, the second of which he began with paragraphs that outline the history of the movement: —

My writing my former letter to take off the aspersions which have been injuriously cast upon the Church, was principally occasioned by this very J. G., who, without any manner of provocation, had (as some of his friends have owned) written a scurrilous paper or verses which did most abominably misrepresent and abuse the Church, and tend to beget in people a very wrong notion of it, and a bitter uncharitable temper towards it; and now, in spite of all the caution and tenderness wherewith I endeavored to conduct myself, both in my conversation and letter, is still resolved to go on reproaching and misrepresenting us, and setting us in all the odious and ridiculous lights he can invent. For my part, I sincerely aimed at reconciling the difference between you and us, and composing our spirits as far as I was able, that if possible we might come at a right understanding of each other, and a good agreement; or at least if we could not attain to think alike, that we might not think hardly, censoriously, or injuriously of each other, and might live in tolerable good peace and charity one with another. But this man is resolved to set and keep us still at variance, and to blow up the fire of contention and uncharitableness, and all, forsooth, under the pretense of doing justice! though you will find by what follows, that his remarks are in truth one continued piece of injustice.

As Johnson was the leading spirit among the Episcopal clergy in the New England and northern colonies, the defense of the Church fell to his pen, and it is surprising that he found time with all his missionary duties to write so much and so ably. The people read the publications with avidity, and many who had hitherto believed the Church to be full of "Popery, Arminianism, and the inventions of men," became acquainted with the Liturgy, and were so persuaded of its Scriptural character, that they withdrew from their former connections and attached themselves to the Anglican Communion. His ability as a controversialist was early recognized on the other side, and the following curious letter from one of his friends pays him a compliment and gives a scrap of history worth preserving: —

ETON COLLEGE, *Sept.* 29, 1735.

DEAR SIR, — Dr. Cutler lately communicated to me your 2d controversial letter, for which I am obliged to him and the author. It were to be wished, that a clergyman's attention were not called off from the work of the ministry by the opposition of unreasonable men; but I am glad the cause has found so able a defender.

I send these lines by my friends who accompany Mr. Oglethorpe to Georgia; they go purely out of a religious motive; a circumstance not so common among our American Missionaries. They all are members of the University of Oxford, men of piety, learning, and zeal. Mr. John Wesley, Fellow of Lincoln College, Mr. Charles Wesley, student of Ch. Ch., Mr. Hall of Lincoln, and Mr. Salmon of Brasenose — all clergymen. We promise to ourselves much good from their pious endeavors under the assistance and influence of Mr. Oglethorpe, and that with regard both [to] the Indians to whom two of them go as missionaries, and to the colony itself. Your good offices in corresponding with them, and advising and assisting them in any respect, would be kindly accepted by them and me.

I continue still a member of the University, though not Fellow of C. C. C. I am Fellow of Eton Coll: near Windsor, and have a good living between that place and Oxford. If in any respect I can be serviceable to you, my best offices are at your command.

Your affectionate friend.

JOHN BURTON.

In answering this letter which reached him about a year after its date, Johnson said it would be "a mighty pleasure" to him, indeed, if he were so situated as to converse or hold any correspondence with "gentlemen of so worthy a character;" but as the distance from New England to Georgia was not much short of a thousand miles, and no trade as yet settled between the colonies, there was little prospect that he could render them essential service. He added at the close of his letter: "I thank you also for the candor you express towards the poor performance Dr. Cutler sent you. Controversy is what I have neither talents nor inclination for, but the most abusive misrepresentations of the Church which our adversaries disseminate among the people has made something of this kind in a manner necessary."

CHAPTER V.

FOREIGN CORRESPONDENCE; MEMORIAL TO THE GENERAL ASSEMBLY OF CONNECTICUT; LETTERS TO BERKELEY; WHITEFIELD IN NEW ENGLAND AND RELIGIOUS ENTHUSIASM; COMPLAINT TO THE COMMISSARY; THE CLERGY OF CONNECTICUT PETITIONING FOR A RESIDENT COMMISSARY, AND ASKING THAT JOHNSON BE APPOINTED; DOCTOR'S DEGREE FROM THE UNIVERSITY OF OXFORD.

A. D. 1736–1743.

BESIDES his extensive correspondence in this country, upon Johnson devolved the chief duty of communicating with friends at home, and keeping them informed of everything here that concerned the general prosperity of the Church. His letters[1] to the Bishops and to the Secretary of the Society for the Propagation of the Gospel are numerous, and, for that period, minute in their details. He watched every movement that bore hardly upon the labors of the missionaries, and promptly suggested means of redress and encouragement. He advocated without ceasing the appointment of bishops for America, as the best plan of settling the Church upon a sure foundation, and saving it from the reproach of enemies. This thought was so constantly in his mind that he sometimes felt obliged to apologize for referring to it, as the following letter from the Bishop of Gloucester will show, written under date of —

[1] See *Church Documents, Connecticut*, vols. i. and ii., and author's *History of Episcopal Church in Connecticut*, vol. i.

LONDON, *March* 9, 173$\frac{5}{6}$.

SIR, — You needed no apology for any application you could make to me in relation to anything wherein you might think me capable of serving the Church in America. I wish my capacity were equal to my desire of doing it. No one is more sensible of the difficulties in general you labor under in those parts, and in particular of those you complain of for want of a bishop residing among you. My own interest to be sure is inconsiderable; but the united interests of the bishops here is not powerful enough to effect so reasonable and right a thing as the sending some bishops into America. The person whom you have sent hither to be ordained is a very sensible, and seems to be a serious man, and it is plain that he came over with no view to his private interests; his only motive could be to embrace what he thought to be right, and his only desire now seems to be to be rendered as serviceable as possible to the Church of Christ. I wish we could have sent him back to you in a post and with a salary better suited to his deserts; but however small the salary may seem, the income of the Society is so very low at present, that we were forced to break through some of our rules and regulations to allot this salary small as it is. I wrote a letter to the Vice-Chancellor of Oxford to recommend these gentlemen [1] to the University for the favor of a Degree, and I have since received a letter from him to acquaint me that the degree of Master of Arts is by Diploma conferred upon each of them. I wish Mr. Caner, who has the character from you and every one of a very deserving man, might acquire a better state of health by his journey hither.

The Bishop of Cloyne has for some time been in a very bad state of health, but by a letter I have just received from him I have the pleasure to hear he is better than he was.

I am, Sir,

Your faithful servant and affectionate Brother,

M. GLOUCESTER.

[1] Jonathan Arnold and Rev. Henry Caner.

The plea was early set up, and it had its influence with the home government, that the establishment of bishops in America would lead to an independence of the Colonies. Allusion is made to this, and the idea spurned in a letter of Johnson to the Bishop of London, written —

Nov. 3, 1738.

MY LORD, — I most humbly thank your Lordship for your kind letter of February 3d, and in answer to it can only lament the unhappiness of the times, and that it is not even in your Lordship's power to do those great and good services to the Church in general and here in America in particular, which you would gladly and have faithfully labored to do. All I can say is, that though it is a most unaccountable way of reasoning to conclude in us Americans any disposition towards an independency on our mother country from our general desire of bishops to preside over us, — the reverse of which is the truth, — yet since it is thus (and doubtless there are many more instances as strange as this in the reasoning of this desperate age), we must patiently submit and wait upon Providence till it shall please God to enlighten the minds of men, and send us better times. I have delayed the longer to acknowledge your Lordship's kind letter, because I was willing to wait the issue of an affair that has been in agitation among us, which I expected to have given your Lordship an account of myself, but since Mr. Arnold[1] is obliged to go home this fall on that

[1] Jonathan Arnold, the successor of Samuel Johnson in the Congregational ministry at West Haven, conformed to Episcopacy in 1734, and afterwards went to England where he received holy orders, as may be learned from the Bishop of Gloucester's letter on the preceding page. He was not lost, as has been sometimes stated, on a second voyage to England in 1739. He did not go home on the "affairs" referred to above, but removed to Staten Island, N. Y., where he became the Society's missionary in charge of St. Andrew's Church. See *History of Episcopal Church in Connecticut*, vol. i. c. viii. Complaints against Mr. Arnold by the wardens and vestrymen were transmitted to the Society, and by an order bearing date June 21, 1745, he was "dismissed from being their missionary to the Church of St. Andrew." The Rev. T. B. Chandler writing to the Rev. Dr. Johnson from Elizabethtown, February 26, 1753, said: "I had the pleasure of receiving your favor of January 29, and am sorry to tell you that Mr. Arnold did nothing in his will for his children in New England. Mrs. Arnold was left sole executrix, and everything her hus-

and some other affairs, I beg leave to refer your Lordship to our joint address to your Lordship, and remain — may it please your Lordship — yours, etc., S. J.

Any letter from Johnson to a friend in London, was sure to be welcomed, and few young men went over for holy orders, who did not deem it necessary to take from him a note of introduction. His old associate in the first struggle for Episcopacy in Connecticut — Dr. Cutler — solicited his good offices, when he was about to send his son, a graduate of Harvard College in 1732, on the same errand which had carried them to England many years before. The answer which one of his correspondents returned is a matter of historic interest: —

Dear Sir, — I had the favor of yours of September last by Mr. Cutler; who intends to make a longer stay with us than you thought of. He has had the good fortune to get a curacy of £50 per annum in Essex, about 30 miles from London, where he may live cheap and save money to buy books, and he will have a very great advantage in conversing a good part of the year with his Rector, Dr. Walker, a very ingenious and learned man, who will assist him vastly in critical learning, and furnish him for the present with all sorts of books he has occasion for. Dr. MacSparran has been honored with a Degree by the University of Oxford, and might to be sure go on it *ad eundem* at Cambridge, but I believe he will scarce have time to go thither. I hear with much pleasure that he has prevailed with the Bp. of London to appoint Mr. Checkley a missionary, and hope we shall soon see him here in London.

band died possessed of was left to her disposal. However, she says she is willing that his children in New England should come in for shares with her own child in whatsoever he left in your parts; and I believe she will not recall it. As to the temper of mind in which Mr. Arnold left the world, I find that he had his reason for some months before his death, which he retained to the last. But I have not heard what remarks or reflections he made on his past life, and what was the moral disposition of his mind." — *MS. Letter.*

Your good friend the Bp. of Oxford is translated to Canterbury, to the universal satisfaction of almost everybody. Dr. Lisle at Bow might have succeeded him, but declined it, and the general expectation is that Dr. Secker, Bp. of Bristol, will be removed to Oxford, to make way for Dr. Gooch to go to Bristol, who (according to custom) could not be Bp. of Oxford as being a Cambridge man. Dr. Gooch is brother-in-law to Bp. Sherlock (of Salisbury), whom now in conjunction with the Abp. of Canterbury we reckon to be at the head of ecclesiastical affairs, — perhaps I should add here with us, for with you to be sure the Bp. of London is and must be at the head.

I am, dear Sir,

Your assured friend and humble servant.

J. Berriman.

Scotch Yard, *Apr.* 14, 1737.

Johnson was a great reader, and no new publication of any merit appeared in England which he did not immediately send for. In one of his letters to Mr. Berriman he said: "I am particularly thankful for the intelligence you have given me about books, a subject I shall always be glad our correspondence may turn upon, for I want very much to know what passes among the learned world." Intelligent people at that period read solid works, and he was ever ready to lend anything that he possessed to those who were earnest seekers of the truth. In the following note to Mr. Berriman, there is an allusion for the first time to one whose movements in this country were soon to fill him with watchfulness and anxiety: —

Sept. 10, 1739.

Dear Sir, — Your kind letter of January 10, 1739, came not to my hands till some time this summer. I am very much obliged to you for it, and for your care in procuring and sending Parker's "Eusebius," which I desired Mr. Cutler to get for me to make up my set, having had the first volume burnt in a house where I had lent it.

I have not seen Mr. Checkley [1] since his arrival, but hear he is like to be very useful at Providence. I have nothing remarkable to tell you from hence. Though the Church here is very ill-treated by these dissenting governments, yet it daily increases. I should be glad to know from you what is the general sense of the clergy about Mr. Whitefield and his proceedings, of which our newspapers are generally filled.

[1] John Checkley, born of English parents in the city of Boston, 1680, finished his studies at the University of Oxford, and afterwards travelled over the greatest part of Europe. As the reader has already seen, he was with Johnson in London in 1723, and upon returning to this country published a pamphlet entitled: *A Modest Proof of the Order and Government settled by Christ and his Apostles in the Church.*" It was the forerunner of the controversy upon Episcopacy on this continent, and undoubtedly had the approval and encouragement of Cutler and Johnson. The author of a reply, Rev. Jonathan Dickinson, observed that it was said to be *reprinted* at Boston, but he did not remember that he had ever seen any former edition.

A second edition of the reply together with an appendix, called, *Remarks on some part of Mr. P. Barclay's Persuasive*, soon appeared. The latter was by the Rev. Thomas Foxcroft, a Presbyterian divine of Boston, who invited Johnson to a friendly discussion of the claims of Episcopacy, and wrote him two long letters, one in June and the other in August, 1726, besides sending him books and a pamphlet, entitled *A Vindication*, etc. Careful answers were returned to these letters, and in one of them, referring to the *Vindication*, Johnson said: "If you could not be satisfied without seeing some remarks upon this performance, — there is a gentleman in your neighborhood, far more able than I am, who if he were addressed in that gentlemanly and friendly Christian manner, wherewith you seem to aim at treating me, would, I doubt not, do it to your satisfaction, and with as much Christian friendly temper, moderation, and forbearance, as you can wish for from me; notwithstanding that he is so injuriously dressed up like a morose furioso, in the imaginations of your people, and notwithstanding the ungentlemanly, unchristian treatment he meets with among you."

The pamphlet, *A Modest Proof*, etc., was followed by a republication of Leslie's "*Short and Easy Method with the Deists, to which was annexed a Discourse concerning Episcopacy, sold by John Checkley.*" For this he was arrested as a libeler, tried before a jury, and mulcted in fifty pounds to the king, and costs of prosecution, with securities for his good behavior for six months. Checkley reprinted his *Discourse Concerning Episcopacy* in 1728, in London, whither he went for holy orders — but obstacles were thrown in his way, and he returned without accomplishing his purpose. His desire to serve God in the ministry of the Church was unquenched, and again, when he was on the verge of threescore years, he crossed the ocean, and was ordained by the Bishop of Exeter, and appointed a missionary to Providence, R. I., where he officiated till his death, which occurred in 1753. His son John graduated at Harvard College, in 1738, and went to England for ordination; but fell a victim to the small-pox, and died during his sojourn abroad, in 1743.

There has been very much such a stir among the Dissenters in some parts of this country as he makes in England.

I am, sir, yours, etc.

S. J.

The members and professors of the Church of England living in Connecticut were aggrieved by an act of the Colonial legislature, whereby the proceeds arising from the sale of certain lands were designated for the sole benefit of the Congregational ministers and people. They complained of the injustice of denying them a share in the public moneys for the support of their ministers, and a memorial was sent to the General Assembly, signed by nearly seven hundred males attached to the Church of England, and asking for themselves equal privileges and protection. This memorial, which carefully recited no less than seven reasons why the legislative action should be amended, was drawn up by Johnson as were all similar memorials prepared during his lifetime, and having reference to the rights of Churchmen in Connecticut. He apprised his friends in England of these movements, and sought their advice whenever he was in any perplexity. The College at New Haven continued to interest him, and not only his affection for it, but his agency in securing important donations, led him to watch its progress and attend the public examinations in Greek and Latin, to which he was invited as the senior Episcopal Missionary in the colony, according to the terms of Berkeley's gift. So early as 1735, the Bishop of Cloyne wrote him, expressing great pleasure to find that a member of his own family, Benjamin Nicoll, had won distinction as a "scholar of the house," and he added a few words to indicate something of his design in founding the scholarship: "One principal end proposed by me was to promote a better understanding with the Dissenters, and so by degrees to lessen their dislike to our communion; to which end methought the improving their minds with liberal studies might greatly conduce, as I am very sensible that your own discreet behavior and manner of living towards them, hath very much forwarded the same effect." The subject of the memorial was the "affair" upon which the Connecticut Clergy jointly addressed the Bishop of London; and Johnson wrote to Berkeley about it, and about the treatment of Mr. Arnold, more pointedly, when in the following letter he reported "a good struggle for the scholarship:" —

May 14, 1739.

MAY IT PLEASE YOUR LORDSHIP, — I humbly thank your Lordship for your very obliging letter of May 11, 1738, which came not to my hands till precisely that day twelve months after it was written, and in the very interim when (having lately attended on the examination of the scholars at Yale College for your Lordship's premium) I was meditating to write to your Lordship and give you some account of the condition of things among us; which is as follows: We had a good struggle this year for the scholarship, and it is very agreeable to see to what perfection classical learning is advanced in comparison with what it was before your Lordship's donation to this College, though I cannot say it has much increased for these two years past, and I doubt it is got to something of a stand. Another son of Mr. Williams has got it this year, who had manifestly the advantage of the rest; but I think none have ever performed to so great perfection as one Whittelsey last year, who is son of a neighboring minister, whose performance was very extraordinary, not only for the scholarship, but also for books purchased with some money that had been forfeited by the resignation of Leonard.

I am very sorry to tell your Lordship how ungrateful New Haven people have been to the Church after so many benefactions their College hath received from that quarter, in raising a mob and keeping Mr. Arnold *vi et armis* from taking possession of the land, which, as I told your Lordship in my last, one Mr. Gregson of London had given him to build a church on near the College.[1]

Another instance of injurious treatment the Church has lately met with from this ungrateful country has been in the General Assembly denying a most reasonable petition as laid before them last year. The case was this: all the lands within the bounds of this Government [Connecticut] were by charter alike granted to all the inhabitants, without limitation to those of any particular denomination in matters of religion. Now of these lands there remained a sufficient quantity for seven new townships, which were lately laid out and ordered to be sold, and the money (amounting to about £70,000) to be considered as the common right of the whole community. When it was considered how to dispose of it, it was at length concluded that it should be divided proportionally to each town, according to their estates, for the support of dissenting teachers; whereby the Church people, who had manifestly a right to their proportion of it, were excluded. Whereupon we presented our humble address to the Assembly, signed by every male of the Church in the Government

[1] In a pamphlet entitled *A Vindication of the Bishop of Landaff's Sermon from the Gross Misrepresentations and Abusive Reflections contained in Mr. Wm. Livingston's Letter to his Lordship*, published in 1768, the author, after speaking, page 40, of the treatment of the Society's Missionaries in New England, says: "Perhaps *Mr. Livingston* may remember some instances of this himself; once especially in a gallant exploit performed by the students of *Yale College*, in which he was *more* than a *spectator*. The scene of this *noble* action was a lot of ground in the town of *New Haven*, which had been bequeathed to the CHURCH for the use of a missionary. There these magnanimous champions signalized themselves; for once upon a time, quitting soft dalliance with the *muses*, they roughened into sons of *Mars*, and issuing forth in deep and firm array, with courage bold and undaunted, they not only attacked, but bravely routed a YOKE OF OXEN and a poor *Plowman*, which had been sent by the then Missionary of *New Haven*, to occupy and plow up the said lot of ground. An exploit truly worthy of the renowned *Hudibras* himself!" The pamphlet, though published anonymously, was written by Dr. Inglis of New York, afterwards first Lord Bishop of Nova Scotia.

above sixteen, to the number of about seven hundred, praying we might have our proportion in these public moneys. But they were pleased to pass a negative upon it; and I should be very thankful for your Lordship's advice whether it be worth our while to apply to the King and Council on this affair.

I heartily rejoice with your Lordship in the health and prosperity of your lady and family, and am no less grieved for the illness you labor under, in your own person. I sincerely pray, God remove it, and give you health.

Good Dr. Cutler is in great grief, having lately lost a very hopeful son, nigh of age for Orders. Mr. Honyman has been till lately very much indisposed with grief for the loss of his spouse, but is within these few months recovered and married again to one Mrs. Brown, an elderly gentlewoman, mother to Capt. Brown of Newport. With our humble duty to your lady,

I remain, may it please your Lordship, etc.

S. J.

All letters to his English correspondents at this period allude to the action of the General Assembly, and in some of them, he speaks of the fickleness of Mr. Arnold and his removal to Staten Island. In writing to Dr. Astry, April 10, 1740, he said: "I am sorry the Society found themselves under a necessity of removing him to any other mission, though I confess he has not conducted so discreetly of late, especially since he had an intimation of it, as I could wish, and I fear the Church in these parts will much suffer on this occasion. At least his people falling of course again under my care will be a very great addition to my burden."

The memorialists were not disheartened by the refusal to grant their petition, and the clergy renewed it so earnestly that at last, rather than let the Church have its share, a proposition to repeal was adopted, and the proceeds of the sale of the lands by a former act went to the maintenance of popular education. Johnson writing to the Bishop of Cloyne shortly before the repeal took place, referred to the memorial once more, but seemed to be hopeless of any redress: —

June 20, 1740.

My Lord, — I did myself the honor to write to you about a year ago, and ackowledged yours of May 11, 1738, and gave you some account of the condition of things among us in this Colony, and especially the College, which is so much indebted to your Lordship, that I think it is but fit that your Lordship should, at least once a year, have some account of the success of your generous donation to it; and this I hope will apologize for my troubling your Lordship once in a while with some account of our affairs which otherwise would not deserve your notice.

Our College has been in a very unsettled position this last year, which perhaps may be the reason that there has not this May appeared quite so good a proficiency in classical learning as heretofore (though very considerable compared with what used to be), there having been an interregnum of seven or eight months wherein it has had no Rector. Mr. Williams had been much out of health for some months, and last fall was persuaded it was owing to his sedentary life and the sea-side air, and accordingly took up a resolution, from which he would not be dissuaded, to retire up into the country, where he has lived ever since, and where, indeed, he seems to have enjoyed his health better; though some people are so censorious as to judge that, considering the age and declining state of our Governor, his chief aim was to put himself in the way of being chosen into that post. But if this was his view, it is not unlikely that he may be disappointed, for upon a considerable struggle last election for a new Governor, he had but few votes, and Mr. Eliot had a vast many more than all other competitors put together, and will doubtless succeed whenever there is a new choice. However, Mr. Williams was a Representative and Speaker in their Assembly, and was made one of the Judges of the Superior Court, and may possibly get to be one of the Council or Assistants, which is, I believe, the utmost he will attain to.

Upon his leaving the College the Trustees have appointed one Mr. Clap, late minister of Windham, to succeed, who seems to be a well tempered gentleman and of good sense and much of a mathematician, and though he is not so well acquainted with the classics as might be wished, I hope he will improve much in that and all other points of learning, and prove a good governor to the College.

We have again applied to the Assembly about the seven new townships, that I mentioned to your Lordship in my last, and nothing has yet been done. Next October will be the last time of asking, but I do not expect they will finally grant our petition. However, the Church greatly increases, especially in the town. But I grow tedious, and will not add any further save my earnest prayers for your lady and family, to whom my very humble duty. I beg your prayers, and remain, my Lord, your Lordship's, etc. S. J.

The arrival in New England in the autumn of 1740 of the Rev. George Whitefield was followed by an outburst of great religious enthusiasm. He had been ordained by the Bishop of Gloucester, and, before coming to this country, had given specimens of the extraordinary power and erratic zeal for which he was afterwards so celebrated. There had been "very much such a stir among the Dissenters" in some of the Colonies as he had made in England, and the people, therefore, were ripe for his extravagances, and crowded around him when he preached in the open air or in the meeting-houses. He soon put himself beyond the sympathy and sanction of the bishops and clergy of the Church, whose doctrines, worship, and discipline he was ordained to defend; and the more bitter his invectives against them became, the more earnestly did his adherents among the Independent or Congregational ministers encourage his work and promote his irregularities. No doubt many of them regarded him as an angel of light in human form, raised up by Divine Providence to awaken sinners to repentance, to seriousness of life, and the practice of virtue; and there is reason to believe that his preaching in several instances was attended with blessed results. But those who welcomed and caressed him with the idea that his course was calculated to check among their people a growing attachment to the doctrines and worship of the Church, discovered at length that so far from this, it shattered and divided their own churches, and in the end rapidly increased and strengthened the communion which they expected to see dwindle and die.

Whitefield had his imitators as well as his followers —preachers who undertook to adopt his style and imitate his dramatic action, and who travelled about from place to place seeking to make converts, and disregarding all ecclesiastical rights and regulations. Then came a set of lay-exhorters who added to the popular confusions and fomented the flames which had been kindled. Johnson carefully watched the progress of things and was at the head of his clerical brethren in guiding and steadying the Church through such great and manifold perils. He wrote to the Archbishop of Canterbury, and the Bishops of Gloucester, London, and Cloyne to acquaint them with the strange commotions in Connecticut, growing out of

Whitefield's itinerancy. It will be sufficient to quote only his letter to Berkeley, which contains other references, and is dated : —

Oct. 3, 1741.

My Lord, — This comes to your Lordship upon occasion of our recommending to the Society, Mr. Richard Caner (brother to my good neighbor Mr. Henry Caner, Missionary to Fairfield, of whom you may possibly retain some remembrance), who well deserves the Society's notice on this occasion. I have the pleasure to inform your Lordship that upon the occasion of our new Rector, Mr. Clap, and his application to the business of the College, we have the satisfaction to see classical as well as mathematical learning improve among us ; there having been a better appearance the last May than what I gave your Lordship an account of before ; for this gentleman proves a solid, rational, good man, and much freer from bigotry than his predecessor.

But this new enthusiasm, in consequence of Whitefield's preaching through the country and his disciples', has got great footing in the College as well as throughout the country. Many of the scholars have been possessed of it, and two of this year's candidates were denied their degrees for their disorderly and restless endeavors to propagate it. Indeed Whitefield's disciples have in this country much improved upon the foundation which he laid ; so that we have now prevailing among us the most odd and unaccountable enthusiasm that perhaps ever obtained in any age or nation. For not only the minds of many people are at once struck with prodigious distresses upon their hearing the hideous outcry of our itinerant preachers, but even their bodies are frequently in a moment affected with the strangest convulsions and involuntary agitations and cramps, which also have sometimes happened to those who came as mere spectators, and are no friends to their new methods, and even without their minds being at all affected. The Church, indeed, has not, as yet, much suffered, but rather gained by these commotions, which no men of sense of either denomination have at all given in to, but it has required great care and pains in our clergy to prevent the mischief. How far God may permit this madness of the people to proceed, He only knows. But I hope that neither religion nor learning will in the whole event of things much suffer by it.

I humbly beg an interest in your Lordship's prayers and blessing, and remain, etc.,

S. J.

In a similar strain he wrote to his friend, Dr. Astry, two days before, and spoke of the necessity, if possible, of an increase in the number of missionaries, at the same time that he entreated him to be present at the meeting of the Society when the application of Mr. Caner was presented. The reply of Dr. Astry deserves a place in this connection: —

Rev. Sir, — I had the favor of your letter by Mr. Caner, and have out of regard to your recommendation of him attended the Board whilst his business was depending. I hope and believe that you will find him satisfied with what has been done there in compliance with his request; and that he will do me the justice with you to bear testimony that he found me disposed to help him what I could. It would have been agreeable to my inclinations to have had more of his company. But the hurry of his affairs and haste to return to you, have been a bar to that satisfaction. As to his going to Oxford, he mentioned it not to me, and indeed I declined entering into it with him, for that I have very little acquaintance left in the University, and accordingly had little prospect of being instrumental in getting him a degree there, had he attempted it.

I lament the vexations you have had by means of that strange fellow Whitefield, and his successors. But as I find by you that the Church has not in the main suffered so much as might have been apprehended, and was designed by those who maliciously set them to work, one has reason to be content and to thank God that things are no worse. And I have the pleasure to think that among my friends in your parts, there are men capable of dealing with them so as to stop their progress, if not to bring good out of evil. I heartily pray that your endeavors may have that effect, the rather because the Society is very little in a condition to send you more fellow-helpers at present, however your occasions may require more. That they have added one in Mr. Caner [1] I am very glad, as I see in him all good dispositions to answer the ends of his mission. My wife returns her compliments to you and yours, and I am with gratitude, Sir,

Your affectionate friend and servant,

FR. ASTRY.

ST. JAMES'S PLACE, *Feb.* 8, 1741–2.

A bitter and uncharitable spirit grew out of the religious enthusiasm consequent upon the intinerancy of Whitefield. Divines of the standing order were divided — part sympathizing with the new light, and part stoutly maintaining a continuance in the old ways and opposing innovations. The *odium theologicum* was never more fierce, and any attempt to restrain it proved unavailing. Large numbers of sober and thoughtful persons in Connecticut, disgusted with the extravagances of the time and finding in Congregationalism no rest from strife and dissension, broke away from their former associations, and fled for comfort and quietness to the bosom of the Church of England. This excited in an unhappy degree the displeasure of her opponents, and harsh judgments and irritating reflections fell upon the missionaries and upon the doctrines of the communion which they were appointed to teach and maintain.

[1] He was appointed a missionary to Norwalk, Ct., and transferred to the charge of St. Andrew's Ch. Staten Island, 1745, upon the dismission of Mr. Arnold, but died of small-pox in New York, Dec. 14, 1745.

Johnson was brought into sharp conflict with Mr. Gold, the dissenting minister in Stratford, and a correspondence was carried on between them which involved very important principles as well as dangerous precedents. It had been said of him that he was not converted, nor any of the Church of England people in Stratford; that he was a thief, and robber of churches, and had no business in the place; that his church doors stood open to all mischief and wickedness, and other words of like import, which could only be uttered in the heats of angry passion or religious excitement. He was not willing to rest under these charges without calling the author to account, and so he addressed him a letter, which speaks for itself, dated, —

July 6, 1741.

Sir, — . . . . I thought it my duty to write a few lines to you, in the spirit of Christian meekness, on this subject. And I assure you I am nothing exasperated at these hard censures, much less will I return them upon you. No Sir! God forbid I should censure you as you censure me! I have not so learned Christ! I will rather use the words of my dear Saviour concerning those that censure so, and say, "Father, forgive them, for they know not what they do."

As to my having no business here, I will only say that to me it appears most evident that I have as much business here at least as you have, — being appointed by a Society in England incorporated by Royal Charter to provide ministers for the Church people in America; nor does his Majesty allow of any establishment here, exclusive of the Church, much less of anything that should preclude the Society he has incorporated from providing and sending ministers to the Church people in these countries. And as to my being a robber of churches, I appeal to God and all his people, of both denominations, whether I have ever uncharitably censured you, or said or done anything to disaffect or disunite your people from you, as on many occasions I might have done; on the other hand, whether I have not on all occasions put people upon making the kindest constructions possible upon your proceedings, and whether there has ever been anything in mine or my people's conduct that could be justly interpreted to savor of spite or malice, though we have met with much of it from some of our neighbors.

If any of your people have left you, I appeal to them whether it has been owing to any insinuations of mine, and whether it has not been many times owing to your own conducting otherwise than in prudence you might have done, that they have been led to inquire, and upon inquiring to conform to this Church. And pray why have not Dissenters here as much liberty to go to church, if they see good reason for it (as they will soon do if they seriously inquire), as Church people to go to meeting if they see fit, as some have done, without my charging you so highly? In short, all I have done which could be the occasion of any people leaving you, has been to vindicate our best of churches from the injurious misrepresentations she has labored under from you and others; and this it was my bounden duty to do. And indeed I shall think myself obliged in conscience to take yet more pains with Dissenters as well as Church people than I have ever yet done, if I see them in danger of being misled by doctrines so contrary to the very truth and spirit of the Gospel as have lately been preached among us up and down in this country.

And as to my Church being open to all wickedness, I appeal to God and all that know me and my proceedings whether I have not as constantly borne witness against all kinds of wickedness as you have, and been as far from patronizing it as you have been, and must think my people are generally as serious and virtuous as yours. And lastly as to your censuring me and my people as being unconverted, etc., I will only beg you to consider whether you act the truly Christian part in thus endeavoring to disaffect my people towards my ministrations, and weaken and render abortive my endeavors for the good of their souls, when I know not that I have given you any occasion to judge me unconverted, — much less to set me out in such a formidable light to them. However, I leave these things, Sir, to your serious consideration, and beg you will either take an opportunity to converse with me where and when you please, or rather return me a few lines, wherein (as you have judged me unconverted, etc.) I entreat you will plainly give me your reasons why you think me so; for as bad as I am, I hope I am open to conviction, and earnestly desirous not to be mistaken in an affair of so great importance, and the rather because I have not only my own, but many other souls to answer for, whom I shall doubtless mislead if I am misled myself. In compassion, therefore, to them and me, pray be so kind as to give us your reasons why you think us in such a deplorable condition.

In hopes of which I remain, Sir, your real well-wisher and humble servant, S. J.

Replies and rejoinders followed in quick succession, and though Mr. Gold denied having used the severe language attributed to him, yet he appears to have retained his uncharitable feelings, and to have been as far as ever from understanding the true teachings and doctrines of the Church of England. His last letter to Johnson should be quoted, if for no other reason, at least to show the spirit which possessed the most ardent and enthusiastic followers of Whitefield: —

Sir, — I don't wonder that a man is not afraid of sinning that believes he has power in himself to repent whenever he pleases, nor is it strange for one who dares to utter falsehoods of others to be ready at any time to confirm them with the solemnity of an oath, — especially since he adheres to a minister whom he believes has power to wash him from all his sins by a full and final absolution upon his saying he is sorry for them, etc.; and as for the pleas which you make for Col. Lewis, and others that have broke away disorderly from our Church, I think there's neither weight nor truth in them; nor do I believe such poor shifts will stand them nor you in any stead in the awful day of account; and as for your saying that as bad as you are yet you lie open to conviction, — for my part I find no reason to think you do, seeing you are so free and full in denying plain matters of fact; and as for your notion about charity from that 1 Cor. xiii., my opinion is that a man may abound with love to God and man, and yet bear testimony against disorderly walkers, without being in the least guilty of the want of charity towards you. What! must a man be judged uncharitable because he don't think well nor uphold the willful miscarriages and evil doings of others? This is surely a perverse interpretation of the Apostle's meaning. I don't think it worth my while to say anything further in the affair, and as you began the controversy against rule or justice, so I hope modesty will induce you to desist; and do assure you that if you see cause to make any more replies, my purpose is, without reading of them, to put them under the pot among my other thorns and there let one flame quench the matter. These, Sir, from your sincere friend and servant in all things lawful and laudable, HEZ. GOLD.

STRATFORD, *July* 21, 1741.

Johnson waited ten days, and then concluded to "venture the sacrifice of one letter more," in vindication of himself and his people. He would not bear the imputation of having opened a controversy thus closed upon him, but he was chiefly anxious, for the sake of the truth, to disabuse the mind of his neighbor of the idea that the Church of England holds and teaches that a man has power in himself to repent when he pleases, and that the minister has power to wash him from all his sins by a full and final absolution upon his only saying he is sorry for them. These two propositions he regarded as so false and mischievous to the souls of men, that if the Church taught or practiced according to them he owned he would "abhor and fly from her as from the face of a serpent." "As our absolution," he added, "is nothing else but the declaration of God's pardon to all true penitents, so we hold no absolution in any other sense than you do yourself. Pray, Sir, where did you learn these dreadful notions of the Church? Have you lived nigh twenty years so near the Church and all this while understood us no better?"

He wrote to Dr. Bearcroft, the Secretary of the Society, in March, 1742, that the raging enthusiam in this country was "like a kind of epidemical frenzy," and in order to prevent mischief and take advantage of the popular excitement, the clergy were obliged to be continually riding and preaching. He himself had scarcely failed all the previous winter to officiate three times, and frequently six times in a week, going to different parts of the Colony and directing the minds of people to the true plan of salvation and the Scriptural doctrines of the Church. While he was thus fulfilling his ministerial duty with a diligence and prudence equaled only by his learning and firmness, a complaint was brought against him which is best explained in the following note from the Rev. Roger Price, the Commissary for all New England, holding his office under the appointment of the Bishop of London: —

REV. SIR, — Mr. Morris[1] made a complaint to me and

[1] The Rev. Theophilus Morris — an Englishman by birth — who succeeded Mr Arnold at West Haven as an itinerant missionary.

the clergy convened at Boston relating to your going to the dissenting meeting, and suffering your son to do the same, which gave some uneasiness to your brethren. I hope your prudence will always direct you to avoid anything that may show such a favorable disposition towards the separation as will obstruct the growth of the Episcopal Church.

I am your affectionate brother and humble servant,

ROG. PRICE.

BOSTON, *June* 18, 1742.

Johnson lost no time in replying to the reproof thus administered, and the answer reveals the religious habits of his elder son, who was then a student in Yale College: —

July 5, 1742.

REV. SIR, — I received yours of the 18th of June, and do take in good part and with humble submission the tender chastisement which you and my brethren have thought fit to send me relating to my going myself and permitting my son to go to meeting.

As to myself, I cannot think the charge is at all just, for I never have been to meeting since the last convention at Rhode Island that could with any propriety bear that name. All the foundation of Mr. Morris' complaint is only this, that on Commencement night, when Davenport was raving among the people there, Mr. Wetmore and I went in the dark, no mortal knowing us but our own company; and stood at the edge of the crowd and heard him rave about five minutes, and then went about our business; this I humbly conceive could not be called going to meeting any more than a visit to Bedlam, — for we heard no prayers nor anything that could be called preaching, any more than the ravings of a man distracted.

As to my son, I am and so is he, as far as you can be from approving his going to meeting, and would by no means permit it, if it were possible to avoid it consistently with his having a public education. But this is what I must entirely deny him, or not forbid him once in a while to go to meeting, and of two evils I think it my duty to choose the least. He comes home once in a fortnight or three weeks, and when Mr. Morris goes to West-side, he hears him, so that he goes to meeting as little as possible. And in this case I do not think it the unpardonable sin, though I have as little opinion of the meeting as anybody can reasonably have.

I look upon the worst part of going to meeting to be, being present and joining with extempore prayers, and yet this is what Dr. Cutler and Mr. Usher permitted their sons to do every day in the College Hall [Harvard], without being ever found fault with. Upon the whole I can truly say, and thank God for it, my prudence has always directed me and always shall, to avoid anything that could show the least favorable disposition towards the separation as such, or to obstruct the growth of the Episcopal Church. So far from this, that I believe I may say without vanity that I have labored as faithfully, and with as good success, as any of my brethren in promoting that cause. I came alone into this colony a few years ago, when there were but 70 or 80 adult Church people in the whole Government, and now there are above 2000; there are ten churches actually built and three more building, and seven settled in the ministry. I have nigh 150 communicants, of whom there wanted but four of fourscore together and received the Communion last Sunday, and my people are as regular and rubrical in our worship as any congregation that I know of. Can it then be supposed that I have obstructed our growth? In short, I have labored, and studied, and wrote, and rid, and preached, and pleaded, and lived all that was in my power to promote the growth of the best of churches. I have neither farming nor merchandise, nor do I suffer any other pursuit of either pleasure or profit to embarrass or hinder me in promoting the growth of the Church, which is the single point that I have in view. If it would not savor of something like vanity, which I hope may be excused on this occasion, I might almost venture to say I have labored more abundantly than they all, and yet

I must, it seems, be, as it were, singled out by my brethren to be censured as one from whom there is danger apprehended of obstructing the growth of the Episcopal Church. No, Sir; I trust the danger is not from any conduct of mine, but from that spirit of indolence and negligence, of bigotry and bitterness, which has called my conduct in question, and let him that is without fault, or has less fault than I, cast the first stone. For God's sake, Sir, is there nothing but not forbidding a son to go to meeting when he can't help it that can obstruct the Church? Could you find nothing worse than this to except against in the conduct of any of our brethren? I fear you might; if not, God be praised. And particularly, my brother Morris, whom I have ever used in the best and kindest manner, I must think had, of all men, the least reason to complain, and I fear he has much more deserved the censure of his brethren for his violent passion, rashness, and inconsistency in his conversation, and his neglecting his people again and again by such long and needless journeys, especially at this important juncture. And I believe he had better have gone twenty times to meeting, than once have shown such a spirit of ingratitude and malevolence as he has done. But I heartily pity and forgive him, and pray that he, as well as I and all the rest of us, may live to better purpose than to bring our order into contempt, and to disgrace the best Church and religion in the world.

I am, Rev. Sir,
Your most obedient humble servant,
S. JOHNSON.

This apology or explanation, which Johnson wished the Commissary to communicate to as many of the brethren as he had opportunity, was the end of the matter, except that he gently remonstrated with Mr. Morris, and asked what he meant by raising such a "clamor against him both at New York and Boston." He challenged further scrutiny of his conduct, and was willing the complaint should be carried before the Bp. of London and the Venerable Society; but Mr. Morris had misapprehended his intentions, and finding himself unable, from the peculiarities of his temperament, to secure a better living in the Colony, he soon withdrew and returned to England.

The clergy of Connecticut felt the want of an overseer in these critical times more than ever, and as they had been repeatedly refused a Bishop, they asked for a Commissary to reside among them, and for this purpose sent a formal petition to the Bishop of London. Their distance from Boston was such as to render it inconvenient, if not impracticable, to attend the Conventions there, and the growth of the Church in the Colony had been so great that they anticipated many advantages to come from the appointment. They all signed or supported the petition except Mr. Morris. Of their own free will, and without any influence on his part, they presumed to mention for the office the Rev. Mr. Johnson of Stratford, as a person in whose ability, virtue, and integrity they had full confidence. But the Bishop of London was unwilling to revoke or change any part of the commission which he had granted to Mr. Price without his consent, or until his death or resignation, and so no Commissary for Connecticut was appointed. The petition was renewed six years later to Sherlock, then Bishop of London, and the successor of Gibson; but he was so persuaded of his inability to do justice to the Church in the American Colonies, and so bent on the establishment of one or two Bishops to reside in proper parts of them, and to "have the conduct and direction of the whole," that he declined to take a patent from the crown for the exercise of ecclesiastical jurisdiction, and only consented to ordain candidates and supervise the clergy till a better provision could be made. "I should be tempted," said he "to throw off all this care quite, were it not for the sake of preserving even the appearance of an Episcopal Church in the plantations." But Johnson without the appointment of Commissary continued to be the prudent guide and adviser of his brethren, and the calm watcher of all movements that related to the peace and prosperity of the Church, not only in New England but throughout the country.

It was a great gratification to him to receive from the University of Oxford the degree of Doctor of Divinity, which was conferred upon him by diploma February, 1743. Twenty years before, when he visited that ancient seat of learning, his merits had been recognized, and the hope expressed that by his ministry the English Church might be revived on this Continent: *aliam et eandem olim nascituram Ecclesiam Anglicanam.* The hope had been partly fulfilled, and the second and higher distinction, due to his learning and his labors, was spoken of by the Vice-Chancellor, Dr. Hodges, when he resigned his office, as one of the most agreeable things that had been done during his administration. It was stated in the Diploma, *ut, incredibili Ecclesiæ incremento, summam sui expectationem sustinuerit plane et superaverit.* Johnson thanked his friends, particularly Dr. Astry, and Dr. Secker Bishop of Oxford, for their agency in the matter, and wrote to his son at Yale College, April 23, 1744, that he might share in the joy of his success: "I have the pleasure to let you know that my good friend Dr. Astry hath accomplished for me what he so kindly undertook. Dr. Gardiner, lately returned from England, writes to me that he has brought my Diploma. I hope you, as well as I, shall consider this great honor, which the University of Oxford has done me, as a fresh motive to the use of diligence in well-doing, that we may deserve the notice you see they are so ready to take of those that faithfully endeavor to have true merit."

CHAPTER VI.

INCREASE OF HIS PARISH AND NEW CHURCH AT STRATFORD; MORE CONTROVERSY; SYSTEM OF MORALITY; STUDY OF HEBREW, AND HUTCHINSON'S PRINCIPLES; PHILOSOPHICAL CORRESPONDENCE; EDUCATION OF SONS, AND LETTERS TO THE ELDER; PROJECT OF A COLLEGE AT PHILADELPHIA, AND JOHNSON INVITED TO ITS CHARGE.

A. D. 1743–1750.

It was no longer doubtful that the movement towards the Church, in consequence of the extravagancies of Whitefield and his followers, was an earnest and important one. Many things conspired to give it strength, and the growth of the parishes in Connecticut necessitated the erection of larger houses of worship to accommodate the congregations. This was the case at Stratford, where there had been an accession of several of the most influential families of the place; and Johnson was much occupied in 1743 with preparations to build a new edifice suited to the wants of the people. Money was scarce in those days, and contributions of labor, time, timber, and other material were accepted in its place. The subscription of the Rector was for a bell, and he had the satisfaction of seeing the new church opened, though not completed on the 8th of July 1744, when he preached a sermon from Psalms xxvi. 8, on "the great duty of loving and delighting in the public worship of God." The discourse was afterwards printed, with an appendix containing prayers for use in the family and closet. In the same year a church was begun at Ripton (now Huntington), then a part of the town of Stratford and under his pastoral care, and it was this "growing disposition among the people in many places to forsake the tenets of enthusiasm and confusion," that added to the labors of Johnson, and required his unceasing ministrations. Probably no period of his life was filled with greater anxiety than that which immediately followed the itinerancy of Whitefield, and witnessed the results of his disorderly proceedings.

When the spirit that was rampant in the land placed all in predestination and mere sovereignty, and denied that there are any promises to our prayers and endeavors, another controversy arose which engaged his own practiced pen and that of Jonathan Dickinson.[1] He published towards the end of 1744 a pamphlet of thirty-two pages, entitled "A Letter from Aristocles to Authades concerning the sovereignty and the promises of God," and said in his advertisement that what prevailed on him to consent to its publication "was a sincere and firm persuasion, that it is really the cause of God and his Christ that I here plead, and that the eternal interest of the souls of men is very nearly concerned in it. For it is manifest to me, that some notions have of late been propagated and inculcated

[1] So early as 1725, one of his parishioners was sharply attacked by this same gentleman, a Presbyterian divine of Elizabethtown, N. J., upon the subject of Episcopacy, and not being able to cope with his antagonist, Johnson sketched, at his request, the chief arguments in its favor which the parishioner sent in his own name to Mr. Dickinson and soon had an answer. To this a reply was furnished him, and some time after, Mr. Dickinson enlarged and printed his own papers in the dispute, which involved the necessity of publishing what had been written on the other side with the name of the real author. "On this occasion, Mr. Foxcroft, of Boston, took up their cause" against the Church, "and wrote more largely, to whom Mr. Johnson replied but was not answered."

in this country, that are equally destructive to the right belief both of God and the Gospel. I have, indeed, that charity for those that have done it that I do not believe they are sensible of these fatal consequences of what they teach, though I very much wonder they are not aware of them."

Johnson would not be understood to aim at undermining any of the soul-humbling doctrines of the Gospel, for he insisted that his way of explaining the Divine Sovereignty and promises was not a distortion of the Scriptures; but entirely agreeable to them, and such as unprejudiced men of plain common sense might accept and be saved with an everlasting salvation. It was a controversy, as one of the pamphlets of the day characterized it, between a Calvinist and a believer of mere primitive Christianity; and Mr. Dickinson published a first and second "Vindication of God's Sovereign free grace," — the last appearing just before his death; but Dr. Johnson had already issued another letter in defense of "Aristocles to Authades,"[1] and closed it thus: "I will add no more but my earnest wishes that we may, on all sides, be above all things careful, for the sake of the love of God, which is my greatest motive in writing, that we do by no means advance or inculcate any notions or doctrines that may reflect dishonor upon the best of Beings, and upon the Gospel of his grace, or be any ways detrimental to any of the souls which He hath made."

In a letter to a friend, he spoke with the warmest feelings against those who represented the Deity as

[1] Mr. Dickinson, in his first *Vindication*, interpreted these names to represent Johnson, and the Rev. Mr. Cooke of Stratfield, who had printed a sermon in favor of his own side.

consigning some persons to everlasting happiness and others to everlasting misery, by an unconditional decree. "In truth, if it were possible, I would rather believe there is no God than to imagine Him to be such a Being as these teachers not only represent Him, but insist He is; and you must believe so too upon the pain of damnation." [1]

"These controversies" says Johnson in his autobiography, "ended in 1744," but he mistook his own dates; for the pamphlets, which were all printed at Boston, show that they were rather begun at this time, and carried on for the next two years by the principals, and then Mr. Beach of Newtown and "Mr. Jedediah Mills, pastor of a church at Ripton," engaged in the contest and lengthened it out nearly a lustrum.

Mills was an enthusiastic follower of Whitefield, and had broken a lance with Johnson, on original sin, several years before, by writing him letters and calling in question his belief and doctrinal teachings. In one of his replies, dated November, 1741, Johnson said: "You talked about Dr. Clarke, but I never undertook to justify his doctrine of original sin, which I even allowed to be expressed too loosely and unguardedly: only I was willing to put a more favorable construction on it than you did; nor do I remember I ever advised Darby people to read his sermons in public, but I am sure I advised them not to do it, and lent them another book to read that they might not read his."

With a view of counteracting the evil effects of the spirit of the times, Johnson prepared and published in

[2] *Letter to C. Colden*, April 22, 1746.

1746 a "System of Morality," in two parts; one treating of Ethics in a speculative aspect, and the other of the practical duties that result from established truths.[1] It was a useful and seasonable work, and received the approbation of sober and thoughtful men. The following letter was written by one who, though he had no sympathy with him in ecclesiastical matters, yet respected his learning, and was himself, in his day, a guiding mind among the theologians of New England: —

REV. SIR, —I have read your new "System of Morality" with a pleasure which I cannot easily express. You have honored our country by this production of the most perfect piece of *Ethics*, and in the best form, that I have seen in any language, and I like it most in our own. I hope the tutors in our academies may even with the greater advantage read it to their pupils, show them the connection and strength of every part of it, and the force with which it should enter their souls and abide there. For I think it is strongly adapted to inform the mind and affect the heart; and under the blessing of the Holy Spirit to form both into all the emotions of virtue and piety, in its connection with and submission to the Sacred Scriptures, and the revelation of Jesus Christ, who is the end of the law for righteousness to us sinners.

[1] In 1743, a small 18mo volume was published, entitled *An Introduction to the Study of Philosophy*, exhibiting a general view of all the arts and sciences, with a "Catalogue of the most valuable books in the Library of Yale College, disposed under proper heads." It was written by Johnson "for young men at the College," and was the second edition enlarged, the first having been published at London in the *Republic of Letters* for May, 1731. At the end of what must have been the original draught, dated October 5, 1730, he made a note: "This system did not please me well and I drew another." The Catalogue was prepared by Rector Clap, and in his advertisement, addressed to the students, he said: "*The Introduction to Philosophy* will give you a general idea or scheme of all the arts and sciences, and the several things which are to be known and learnt; and the Catalogue will direct you to many of the best books to be read, in order to obtain the knowledge of them. And I would advise you, my pupils, to pursue a regular course of Academical studies in some measure according to the order of this Catalogue."

Yet, sir, I also freely own to you that your words, page 64, "of God's sending a glorious person under the character of his own Son, who had an inexpressible glory with Him before the world was;" although enforced by the following Scripture expressions, "the express image of his person, and the fulness of the Godhead dwelling in Him bodily in his incarnate state;" seem not enough to me in honor of revealed religion, the *Holy Scriptures;* by which it is, Sir, that our reason is illuminated and raised to such a gracious height; as that you, my honored brother, after the diligent study of them for many years, have by their help and the assistance of the blessed Inspirer of them (I am willing to add), been enabled to write this correct and exalted book of *Ethics.*

Your own modesty will not permit you to blame me, if I freely say, that none of the learned Heathen ever wrote to this height, with like perspicuity, method, and enforcement on conscience. It is the Christian Divine, after a diligent search into the religion of Jesus, together with what the masters of morality had wrote before his manifestation in the flesh, or since that blessed day, who exhibits himself in your treatise. And though I am too much a stranger now to Mr. Wollaston's delineation of the Religion of Nature to give my opinion of it, yet I persuade myself also that his performance, praised as it has been by those that I highly esteem, may stand also much indebted to his improvements by Christianity.

Upon all Sir, to lay my whole intention before you in this latter part of my letter, I request you to consider whether those words: "a glorious person under the character of his own Son in our nature, who had an imperishable glory with Him before the world was," with what follows of Scripture expressions in that pious paragraph, is sufficient to answer unto the doctrine of the eternal Godhead of Christ, as it is explained to us in the Athanasian Creed, daily read in your worshipping congregations?

This is the defect that occurs to me in the close of your excellent treatise; which yet I have not observed to any one but yourself. And I hope, Sir, that this freedom, after the high brotherly regards I have been expressing, will be candidly taken by you.

I ask your prayers for me in my age; and wishing you always the presence of God with you in your holy studies and ministrations,

I am, Rev. Sir,
Your affec. brother and servant,
BENJ. COLMAN.

BOSTON, *June* 2, 1746.

The answer was worthy of the subject and of the man: —

June 12.

REV. SIR, — You needed not to make any apology or beseech my candor for so very kind and obliging a letter as you did me the favor to write of the 2d instant. The favorable opinion you express of that small piece of morals I wrote, I wish it would pretend to deserve, and I am highly obliged to you for the candor wherewith you read it, and the brotherly kindness you express towards me.

But what I am particularly obliged to you for is that you was so good as to point out to me the passage you mention as what you apprehended liable to exception. This I take as a singular act of friendship, and what the rather deserves my thankful acknowledgment as it comes from a gentleman of your venerable age and character, and one to whom I had never had the honor of being known. I apprehend, therefore, that as I had the presumption to appear in public, your kind aim was that nothing that I offer should be either liable to misconstruction, or of any mischievous tendency to the disadvantage of our common faith.

In answer, therefore, to your kind suggestion, I beg leave to say, that, as I am sincerely tenacious of the Athanasian Faith, so I beg those expressions may not be understood to be inconsistent with it, but rather expressive of it as they appear to me to be, and that you will do me the favor to assure any gentlemen of this who may be apt to suspect me.

The only reason of my expressing myself as I did was, because I was not willing to meddle with anything controversial, and therefore chose to confine myself to the language of the Sacred Scriptures. However, if it were not too late, I could wish one word were inserted which would put the matter out of all ambiguity. I would express it thus: "Who was truly God of God, and had inexpressible glory with Him from all Eternity, before the world was," and I should be highly obliged to you, if you will desire the printer (provided it be not too late) to insert those words, *Was truly God of God from all Eternity*, in their proper place.

I readily agree with you that even such an imperfect sketch of morals as this could never have been beat out without the help of Revelation, to which no doubt but Mr. Wollaston was also very much beholden; and indeed I am of opinion that those noble pieces of Epictetus, Antoninus, and Hierocles, though they were not professed Christians, were notwithstanding the better for the light which Christianity had brought into the world, though they had it at second hand; which indeed might be the case with Seneca and Tully before, and even Plato and Pythagoras, who in their travels might pick up many notions which originally came from the inspired prophets.

I again repeat my humblest thanks for your kind letter, and especially for your prayer for me with which it concludes, and beg the continuance of it; and I earnestly pray to God for you that He will be your shield and the staff of your age while you continue here, and your exceeding great reward in a better world hereafter.

I am, Rev. Sir, your most obliged, etc.

S. J.

Colman died the next year, and too soon to know the success of the little work, whose author he had so gracefully complimented. Reference will be made to a second edition of it in a future chapter.

Hebrew had been a favorite study with Johnson,

but about this time, his philosophical and theological readings led him to take a new interest in it and to refresh and improve his critical knowledge. Lord President Forbes' "Thoughts on Religion and Letter to a Bishop" fell in his way, and opened to him a scene of study and inquiry both novel and interesting. He found in this author an abridgment or summary of the works of John Hutchinson, then attracting the attention of the learned world. These he procured and read, and considered again and again with the utmost care and with the best helps which he could command; and "though in many things," to use his own words, "he seemed to overdo and go into extremes, and his language was obscure, yet no man in these last ages, ever appeared to have so laboriously studied, and so thoroughly understood the Hebrew language and antiquities, as Mr. Hutchinson." Some of his translations were forced and unnatural, and his criticisms were not all just. It grieved Johnson that he should hurt his own cause by censuring bitterly the great name of Sir Isaac Newton, and representing him and others as no better than atheists who renounced Christianity; and he could not be pleased with his harsh treatment of the Jewish Rabbis, whatever defects in their character might be proved. But still Hutchinson appeared to him to be a "prodigious genius," little inferior, if not superior to Sir Isaac himself, and to have established several very important philosophical and theological principles. He wrote to his friend John Berriman in London to know more about him and the estimation in which he was held, and the answer which he received was not very flattering to his cultured mind: "Mr. Hutchinson, I never saw in my life but once; he had rather the appearance of a plowman than a philosopher. He was not bred to learning; but by the leisure he enjoyed, while he was steward to the Duke of Richmond, he found means to attain a good measure of knowledge in the Hebrew tongue; upon which he became so conceited that he thought nobody knew anything of the matter but himself; and those few that learned of him to be so sharpsighted as to see in the Old Testament the only true principles of philosophy, quite contrary to the Newtonian, and clearer accounts of the Trinity than are to be found in the New."[1]

Johnson may have had the feeling to which Jones of Nayland gave expression in the preface to the second edition of his life of Bishop Horne, when, speaking of the Hutchinsonian principles, he said: "These things came down to us under the name of John Hutchinson, a character *sui generis*, such as the common forms of education could never have produced; and it seems to me not to have been well explained, how and by what means he fell upon things, seemingly so new and uncommon; but we do not inquire whose they are, but what they are, and what they are good for. If the tide had brought them to shore in a trunk, marked with the initials J. H., while I was walking by the sea-side, I would have taken them up, and kept them for use; without being solicitous to know what ship they came out of, or how far, and how long they had been floating at the mercy of the wind and the waves. If they should get from my hands into better hands, I should rejoice; being persuaded they would revive in others the dying flame

[1] MS. Letter, June 19, 1747.

of Christian faith, as they did in Bishop Horne and myself."

A correspondence, chiefly upon philosophical subjects, was carried on for some time between Johnson and Cadwallader Colden, afterwards Lieutenant-governor of the Province of New York. Colden was the son of a Scotch divine, and finished a course of studies at the University of Edinburgh, and devoted himself to medicine and mathematics. While yet a young man, he emigrated to America and finally settled in New York, where he was appointed the first surveyor-general of the lands of the Colony, and at the same time master in chancery. His botanical and medical essays were numerous; but the work upon which he bestowed the most labor was first published under the title of the "Cause of Gravitation," and then enlarged and printed with the title of the "Principles of Action in Matter," to which was added a "Treatise on Fluxions." Among his correspondents were such distinguished characters of the time as Linnæus, Gronovius, and Franklin. His letters to Johnson are full of the principles involved in his chief work, and in one of them he said: "I am now printing something on the subject of material agents, which I hope may be of use to enlarge our knowledge in moral philosophy. I print only so many copies as may submit it to the examination of the learned. As soon as it shall be printed, it will kiss your hands for that purpose."

Johnson directed his attention to the philosophy of Berkeley, and sent him some of his productions, as the following letter will show: —

Coldengham, *March* 26, 1744.

Sir, — I now take this opportunity, by Mr. Watkins, to

return you my hearty thanks with the books you were pleased to send me. As to the Bishop's "New Theory of Vision," I think he has explained some things better than had been done before, but as to the main design he labors at, I cannot say that I comprehend it. I allow that the object which reflects light is not in a proper sense the object of vision, no more than a bell or any other sounding body is the object of the sense of hearing, and yet I think we may without much impropriety say that we see or hear a bell as well as that we feel it, though it be certain that the bell is not the immediate object of the senses of seeing and hearing, as it is of the sense of feeling, and that it is only from reasoning and experience that we form the conception of the same objects affecting all the senses. If his sentiments do not differ from this conception of the matter, then I must look on a great part of his books to contain a most subtle disputation about the use of words. If his sentiments be different, I can form no conception of them. His mistake in the "Analyst," in my opinion, may be made very apparent, that he does not understand the doctrine of Infinites or Fluxions, as received by mathematicians, and this I think I can demonstrate. I formerly had illustrated the principles of that doctrine in writing, in order to assist my own imagination in forming a regular and true conception of it.

Since I received that book from you I have carefully re-examined what I had formerly wrote, and am so far from finding any defect in what was formerly clear to me, that I think I clearly see his error, that he has no conception of the principles of that doctrine. If you have a curiosity to be satisfied in this, I will send you a copy of my paper. It is contained in about two sheets of paper.

I assume the liberty always to be allowed in philosophizing to differ from any man without disrespect or disregard to his character, as I now do with respect to Bishop Berkeley, whose merit is very conspicuous, and whom I highly esteem. I am sir, your humble servant,

CADWALLADER COLDEN.

In replying, Johnson as usual defended his friend and favorite author, and said: "I am much obliged to you for the observations you have made upon Bishop Berkeley's pieces that I sent you. I take it that the great design of that gentleman in what he wrote was to banish scholasticism, and all talk without any meaning, out of philosophy, which, you very well know, has been the bane of science in all other parts of learning, as well as in religion and morality." He did not claim to be competent to understand all his reasonings: "As to his mathematical pieces," said he, "I confess I am not versed enough in the sublime mathematics to be a judge of them, and so cannot pronounce on this subject. I am very loth to give you the trouble of transcribing, otherwise I should have a great curiosity to see what you have wrote upon it, in order that I might make a better judgment; but this is too great a favor for me to ask."

In another letter of later date he showed his independent thinking, and confessed: "Your notions of prescience and liberty are entirely agreeable to the apprehensions I have of those matters; nor could anything have been expressed better, nor can the greatest authority in the world induce me to think otherwise. You knew good Dr. Turner's works. He takes for his motto: *Nullius in verba.* It is a very good one; and for the same reason, though I have a profound veneration for Mr. Locke and Sir Isaac Newton, yet I will not be determined by their authority, nor by their reasons, any further than I can see for myself. I am not attached to Hutchinson. Sir Isaac was doubtless very exact; but no wonder if even he, in matters very abstruse, should sometimes be mistaken; nor is it less to be wondered at, if this should be the case now with Bishop Berkeley, though I cannot but think him one of the first men of the age. I have lately read his "Siris," and have desired Mr. Nicholls to send it you, if he can consistent with his engagements with Mr. Franklin, of whom he was so obliging as to borrow it for me. Be it so that there may be some things in it that may be thought fictitious, yet I cannot but wish I had your opinion upon the philosophical part of it."

Colden paid his respects to Bishop Berkeley's "Treatise on Tar Water," and published his reflections by themselves, "which" said he, "turned out to the benefit of the printer." But in his correspondence with Johnson his pen ran chiefly upon mental and moral philosophy; and the several letters which passed between them serve to illustrate as much the character of the one as the other: —

COLDENGHAM, *June* 2, 1746.

REVEREND SIR, — I now desire Mr. Nicholls to send you a copy of the "Treatise" which I mentioned to you in my last. In it you will find my thoughts on some things which were the subject of your last to me by the Rev. Mr. Watkins. One thing I am desirous to be more fully informed of from you, how consciousness and intelligence become essential to all agents that act from a power in themselves. As to my own part, I do not perceive the necessary connection between power or force and intelligence or consciousness. We may certainly in a thousand objects of our senses discover power and force without perceiving any intelligence in them. And though this power or force should be only apparent and the consequence or effect of some other primary cause, yet I am certainly to be excused in my thinking it real till it appear otherwise to me, as I believe every man is to be excused who does not understand astronomy, and thinks that the sun moves, and this opinion cannot in any proper sense be called an absurdity in him.

In the next place I must beg you will give me a definition of matter, or of any other being merely passive, without any power or force or action. Such a being I cannot conceive, and therefore as to me does not exist.

You will oblige me exceedingly by giving your opinion of the printed "Treatise" or of any part of it without reserve. For my design only is to discover and be assured of the truth. You will find by some parts of that piece that though I have the greatest esteem of Sir Isaac Newton's knowledge and performances, I take the liberty to differ from him in some points. That man never existed who never erred. As I have a great esteem of your judgment, I am very desirous to have your opinion of what I send as soon as may be with your conveniency, and thereby you will very much oblige,

Sir, your most humble servant,

CADWALLADER COLDEN.

June 19.

SIR, — I now return you my hearty thanks for yours of the 2d instant, and especially for your kind present that accompanied it. It is my sincere opinion of it that it is a very ingenious piece, and the result of much and deep thought. There is one thing in it that I am much pleased with, which is, that you make the resistance of what you call matter to be an action deriving from a self-exerting principle. This I take to be a point of very great importance and use, both in physics and metaphysics as well as in religion. All the odds between you and me is, that you imagine matter to be a self-exerting principle, whereas I suppose matter to be a mere passive thing, and if it is spirit pervading and agitating all things, that is one principle of action according to Virgil's philosophy: *mens agitat molem*, etc., which though it be the most ancient notion, I believe is nevertheless true; and that elasticity and gravitation or attraction and repulsion as well as resistance, or what Sir Isaac calls *vis inertiæ*, and perhaps several others, are so many various exertions of the one self-exerting active principle Who pervades all things, and in Whom we live, move, and have our being.

Your attempt to assign the cause of gravitation appears to me a curious dissertation, but I have hardly furniture and force of mind enough to comprehend it, having for many years discontinued these kind of studies, and indeed never turned my thoughts that way so closely as I find you have done. Your system seems to me pretty near of kin to Mr. Hutchinson's, as far as I have had opportunity to be acquainted with his from my Lord Forbes, but I believe you have much outdone him in the exactness of your method and methodical reasoning.

And now in answer to your candid inquiries, you ask me how consciousness and intelligence become essential to all agents that act from a power within themselves? where, by a power within themselves I take you to mean a principle of activity belonging to their essence, and not either arbitrarily annexed to them, or exerting itself in and by them. To which I answer, a power of action without a principle of self-exertion and activity, I can form no notion of, and a blind power or principle of activity — were it possible — would be so far from being of any use that it could be only mischievous in nature. In fact we find that all these motions and consequently actions in nature are conformable to the wisest laws and rules, ever aiming at some useful end or design, and must therefore be under the management of a most wise and designing principle, so that it seems to me repugnant to place intelligence and activity in or derive them from different principles; for if you suppose a blind principle of action in matter, you must still suppose it under the ever ruling force of an intelligent and designing principle; and as it is not the part of a philosopher to multiply beings and causes without necessity, it seems plain to me that we ought not to imagine any other principle of action than the principle of intelligence, which we know from our own soul in fact has, and in nature must have, a power of self-exertion and activity. We must come at it eventually in our inquiries, and I see not how one can avoid admitting it immediately. I can find nothing of activity in the idea of matter; nothing but what is merely passive, and therefore can only conceive it as a mere passive instrument acted on by the one principle of intelligence and activity. Thus I say things appear to me, nor can I with the utmost force of mind that my little capacity will admit of, conceive of them any otherwise, but I submit what I am about to advance on this subject to your better judgment, and remain Sir,

Your most obliged friend and humble servant,

S. J.

A letter from Colden, dated November 19, 1746, continued his speculative inquiries, and met very emphatically the apprehension, reported to him by Johnson, of one of the Fellows of Yale College, that there was a "tendency in his system towards atheism." This was a misfortune in his view which had happened to all new discoveries in philosophy, and after rejecting the thought that he was an enemy to true religion, he proceeded to say: —

I shall add something on this occasion, in defense of my system, that from it a certain proof may be given of the evidence of spirits, or immaterial beings. For as in the idea of all immaterial beings, quantity or shape or form is included, and their actions are all divisible into degrees or quantities of action; the being from whence thinking proceeds cannot be material, because no kind of quantity enters our conception thereof, neither can any kind of measure or division be applied to it, so much as in imagination.

All allow that when God created matter, He gave it some essential property; otherwise there can be no essential difference between matter and spirit, and why may not I say, in my way of speaking, that God gave at the creation to different kinds of matter, different and distinct kinds of action. As to my part, I can discover no kind of ill consequence in the one more than in the other.

In answer to your demand of my opinion of Dr. Berkeley's book "De Motu," I shall give it with the freedom requisite to Philosophy. I think that the doctor has made the greatest collection in this and his other performances, of indistinct and indigested conceptions from the writings of both the ancients, and the moderns that I ever met with in any man's performances; that he has the art of puzzling and confounding his readers in an elegant style not common to such kind of writers; and that he is as great an abuser of the use of words as any one of those he blames most for that fault. I hope you will pardon me for writing so freely of your friend, and of so great a man. I do it with the less concern in hopes thereby to provoke you to use the same freedom with me. Compliments without sincerity spoil all philosophy.

I am so often interrupted at this time with business, and which I wish I could avoid, that you must excuse the incoherence of this scrawl, and likewise that I say nothing on the subject of your treatise. I will do it when I can apply my thoughts to it in the manner you desire. I must still stay some days on business in this place, which deprives me of that pleasure which I had hoped to obtain in old age; that is, free thoughts and conversation with my friends on philosophy.

The next letter contained the notice of the treatise which Johnson had desired him to examine, and is dated: —

COLDENGHAM, *January*, 27, 1746–7.

REV. SIR, — In my last I told you how much I had been involved in the public affairs, that I had not been able to consider your new System of Morality with the attention which I designed to give to the reading of it, and which it truly deserves. Nothing has been a greater injury to true religion than the pretenses that some people have set up that religion is not the object of the understanding, but is merely founded on authority, for in such case it could not with any propriety be designed for the use of an intelligent being, and there are no means left to distinguish between true and false Religion when we are not allowed to use our understanding in forming our judgment, and the false may set up as strong pretenses to authority as the true, and in fact always does.

You have by your performance clearly evinced the contrary of this, that true religion is founded on the reason or nature of things, and you have shown this in a manner adapted to common capacities and the commonly received conceptions, which makes it more generally useful and the more valuable.

I have considered the same in my own Principles of Natural Philosophy, and I have done this for two reasons: viz. thereby to remove some metaphysical objections which you made to my principles, and which I hope by this method to remove more easily than by a direct answer; the other reason is in hopes to give you some hints which may perhaps be of use to you in reconsidering your subject, as you tell me that you intend to publish a second edition of that work. I hope you will give me your sentiments with the same freedom that you see I write to you, and thereby I shall judge that the freedom I take is not disagreeable to you. I have no other view but truth, and for that reason I shall myself be more obliged by having my mistakes shown to me than by any applause. I am, Sir,

Your most humble servant,

CADWALLADER COLDEN.

Johnson waited nearly three months, and then returned the following answer: —

April 15.

SIR, — I have been so much taken up of late in several journeys and various other affairs, that this must be my apology for not sooner answering your kind letter of Jan. 27. Your beautiful little draught of the first principles of morality is what I have been very much pleased with; I have read it with attention three times, and every time with a fresh increase of pleasure, and I now at length return my hearty thanks for it, and for the candor you express towards the piece I had the presumption to publish. You have in this little piece of yours made such an easy, gradual, and natural progress from physics to metaphysics, and from thence to morality, as is very pleasing to the mind; and I think, if I rightly apprehend, you have now so explained yourself that we do not much differ, and what difference yet remains I believe is but merely verbal. My chief objection was against your using the term *action* as expressing anything in matter, which I take to be a mere passive thing, and that action cannot in strict propriety of speaking be attributed to it; for which reason that expression still grated upon my mind till I came to your 7th section, in which, when you come to explain the difference between spirit and body, you say "the actions of the latter are altered by efficient causes *always* external to themselves."

This seems evidently to conclude what I would be at, and that at the bottom we think alike, viz. that when we speak of matter and the *action* of it we use that word for want of a better, in a sense rather figurative than literal, and understand it in a vulgar sense rather than a sense that is strictly philosophical, [as we] do the rising and setting of the sun. So we may call writing the action of the pen, when it is only in reality merely acted [on], and consequently that by the *action* of matter you do not mean any exertion of its own, much less a designed conscious self-exertion which always enters into my notion of efficient causes; and that therefore when you say it is *determined* by the (exertion I would say of) *efficient causes always* external *to itself*, those efficient causes must always be self-exerting and intelligent beings *i. e.*, spirits, which therefore only are properly agents, and consequently that all the actions in all nature that affect our senses and excite ideas in our minds are really the actions of that Great Supreme Almighty Being or Spirit whom you call (25) *the soul of the universe.*

I do not, with Sir Isaac in § 9, quite like that expression. It may however be admitted, if it means that He animates and governs the world as the soul does the body, which is merely passive to it: it is so far right, — He being in this sense the natural Governor of the natural world; but this seems not sufficient unless you also conceive Him as the moral Governor of the intelligent or moral world, rewarding or punishing men according as they behave, — which is what I would apprehend you to mean by the real words.

You say very truly, § 9, *We have no idea of matter;* by which it is plain that by matter you mean something that is not the object either of our senses or minds. Of what use then is it in philosophy? Why may we not wholly drop it, and do as well without it, perhaps much better, and suppose what you call the action of it to be the action of that Almighty Spirit in whom we live, move, and have our being, and consider all nature as being the glorious system of his incessant exertions and operations, with which by his own action governed by fixed rules of his most wise establishment called the laws of nature, He perpetually and with endless variety of objects affects our senses and minds This will sufficiently account for everything, whereas matter whereof we have no idea, can account for nothing.

You use the expression, §§ 20 and 21, *During the time of our existence*, which sounds as though it was to have a period with this vain life. This I cannot suppose your meaning (and therefore might perhaps be better left out), because I apprehend you must think it evident from the wisdom, justice, and goodness of God, compared with that excellent nature He has given us, that we must be designed for nobler ends than can be answered by our existence only in this short, uncertain, and troublesome life. Thus, Sir, I have used the freedom you desire, and which I doubt not you will take in the same good part, and with the same pleasure as I do yours, and always shall. I am glad to find by your "Gazette" that you are at last resolved to have a College in your Government. This is what I doubt not you have much at heart, and I heartily wish success to it, and shall be glad to correspond with you in anything in my little power that may tend to promote it, and wish it may take effect speedily that you may not suffer the Jersey College (which will be a fountain of nonsense) to get ahead of it.

I am, Sir, etc. S. J.

The business of his official position crowded upon him, and Colden found little leisure to pursue his favorite speculations, but he wrote again to Johnson in answer to the foregoing letter, and then there appears to have been for a short time a suspension of their correspondence : —

NEW YORK, *May* 18*th*, 1747.

REV. SIR, — Yours of the 15th of last month, in which you express some satisfaction in the little rude sketch I sent you on the first principles of morality, gave me a good deal of pleasure, though I cannot be fully clear that either of us has received clear conceptions of the other's thoughts. But in the first place I must thank you for your taking notice of some expressions in my paper liable to exceptions. I own they are justly so, but as what I wrote was only for your private amusement, and to obtain your opinion on my thoughts, I did not much attend to the accuracy of expression.

I did not think of the old opinion of the soul of the world when I wrote that paragraph. My design was only to avoid all expressions which could raise any idea of matter or corporeity, as the word spirit in its natural signification is apt to do, and for that reason only I made use of the words soul or mind. Please then to put in their place *infinitely Intelligent Being*. It was by the same inadvertency the words, — *During the time of our existence*, were made use of, and I am obliged to you for the correction which you have made of them.

But now to come to the matter itself, I cannot have any idea of anything merely passive or without any kind of action. I can have no idea of a mere negative, and since, as I observed, all our ideas of everything external to us must arise from the actions of those things on our minds, everything of which we have any idea must be active. This is my fundamental argument, to which I suspect you have not given sufficient attention; and from whence I conclude that all matter is active. You seem likewise not to have alluded to the distinction which I make between the substance and the action of that substance. We have no idea of the substance of intelligent Beings, as little as of material. We have only ideas of their actions. Or the ideas are the effects of their actions on our minds. But, Sir, if you attribute all action immediately to that *Almighty Spirit in whom we live, move, and have our Being, all nature* (as you say) *being a system of his incessant exertions, etc.*, I do not see how anything or action can be morally evil in a proper sense, and the foundation of morality seems merely to be sapped. It seems to be a kind of Spinozism in other words. But as this is inconsistent with the whole tenor and end of your treatise I can only conclude that I have not been able to form any conception of the first principles of your and Dr. Berkeley's system of Philosophy. I am afraid you will find me of a much duller apprehension than you at first imagined, and that if you are willing to make me understand your system, it will give you more trouble than perhaps anything, that can be expected from me on the subject, can deserve.

The public affairs have employed my time so much that I cannot write more fully at this time on this or any other subject, and I must desire that the same excuse may serve for my not answering your letter sooner. But if you be at more leisure, a line or two from you will be exceedingly agreeable to me, that I may know whether I have been so lucky as to explain anything to your satisfaction, or to free me from my mistakes. I hope soon to be freed from these clogs to the pleasantest amusement in old age, and to have time to show how much I am, Sir,

Your most obliged humble servant,

CADWALLADER COLDEN.

June 7.

SIR, — Could you be sensible of the manner of life I am obliged to live, I should have little occasion to make any apology for my being so long before I answer your obliging letters, and especially your last of May 18, for which I now return you my sincerest thanks; or for my incorrectness of expression when I do write, which doubtless is the chief occasion of my not being clearly understood, as well as of my not sufficiently attending to what you write. For my case is not altogether dissimilar to that of the great Apostle, particularly in being in journeyings often and in perils among false brethren.

I am entirely satisfied and well pleased with the amendments you allow me to make in the ingenious draught you were so good as to send me of your notion of the first principles of morality; with which it now runs clearly to my mind and is equally pleasing to my friends here, to whom I have communicated it. As for the incidental turn I made upon an expression of yours in favor of Bp. Berkeley's system, I was little more than jocular on that occasion, being not dogmatically tenacious of his peculiar sentiments, much less zealous of making you a proselyte to them. I would however observe that you have made a considerable approach towards them, at least as far as I am concerned to wish you to do, particularly in your allowing that all our ideas of sensible things are the effects of the actions of something external to our minds, and that even resistance is an action. Your supposing an active medium which you call matter intervening between the action of the Deity and our minds perceiving, to which they are immediately passive, though I am not clear in it, does not affect me so long as you allow all action throughout all sensible nature to derive originally from Him.

I doubt I expressed myself sometimes uncouthly, at least very incorrectly, otherwise you would not have inferred from what I wrote that I attributed "*all action* immediately to the Almighty Spirit." I meant only all the actions in sensible nature only, or which produce in our minds the ideas of sense and imagination; but I was far from meaning that there are no other actions besides those of the Deity. For this would be in effect to deny or doubt whether there be any other Beings besides Him and our ideas. This would sap the foundation of morality sure enough, and would be at least as bad as Spinozism. Bp. Berkeley any more than I, never doubted of the existence or actions of other inferior created spirits, free agents and subject to moral government. All he contends for is that there are no other than two sorts of beings, the one active the other passive, — that spirit, the Deity, and created intelligence alone are the active beings, and the objects of sense alone are merely passive; and that there is no active medium intervening between the actions of the Deity and our minds whom He has made to be perceptive and self-active Beings. These I take to be the first principles of his system. But however at a loss you may be about his peculiar system, there is a very pretty book published in England in 1745, called "Dialogues Concerning Education," being a plan for training up the youth of both sexes in learning and virtue, which I have lately seen, and long to have you read; and in which I don't doubt we should perfectly agree. I have recommended it to Mr. Shatford of New York to procure several copies, and do not think we could put a better thing into the hands of our children. It is the prettiest thing in its kind, and the best system both in physical, metaphysical, and moral philosophy I have ever seen.

Dr. Johnson had two sons; the birth of the elder has been already given, and that of the other — William — took place March 9, 1731. He saw as their intellects opened, that if they had such an education as he desired for them, it would be necessary for him to give his personal attention to it, and carry them through the preliminary course, and "that it might be the more agreeable to them to have companions, he took several gentlemen's sons of New York and Albany." When the youngest was born he wrote in his private diary: "O God, I give this child as well as the other to Thee. Bless them both," and "let me live to see them well educated and engaged in Thy service." At the age of about thirteen they were each admitted to the lowest class in Yale College, but "it was a great damage to them," said the father "that they entered so young, and that when they were there, they had so little to do, their classmates being so far behind them." He regretted that he had not taught them Hebrew before they entered; a study which they could not pursue in College, as there was no competent teacher. William Samuel, the eldest, received the degree of B. A. in 1744, and was the single "scholar of the house," for that year, to whom was adjudged the premium under the bounty of Dean Berkeley. He chose the law for his profession, and in the last week of May, 1747, he took a journey to Boston, that he might attend a few Lectures, be present at the Commencement, and admitted a Master of Arts in Harvard University.

Some external preparation for the occasion appears to have been necessary, since he wrote to his father from Cambridge that he had spoken for a wig and could not have one under £10; everything being "monstrously dear." The cost of his degree exceeded his expectations: "Commencement is now over" said he, "and I have taken a Degree which cost me £8; four of which I was unwilling to pay, but the Corporation appointed the charge when they granted my request, and it was then too late to hesitate about it."

The letters which passed between the father and the son at this time are full of affection, and because it was the turning point in the son's life, the most important of them deserve a place in this connection. He had reported his pleasant journey and safe arrival, and given some account of the old friends of his father, — Dr. Cutler and Mr. Caner,[1] — as well as his inclinations about a profession and his desire to be governed by the paternal counsels, before he penned the following letter: —

HONORED SIR, — When I wrote last it was in great haste, and only that you might just know that I was well. Since which I have met with nothing very remarkable. The small-pox, which, when I wrote first, I informed you was in town, is now only in the pest-house, and there only one negro has it, so that there is now no danger. The gentleman also, I then mentioned, is since taken up and buried; he was found with his money and watch about him, and therefore 'tis thought was not murdered as was suspected. It proved to be the gentleman from London. He was son to a Deacon of Dr. Guise's Church, of a fine fortune, and came recommended to Dr. Colman, who never saw him but once. He preached a sermon about it last Sunday, and told them that the last was the most afflicting week that he ever endured.

About £40 of the money I brought with me was of the Rhode Island last emission, and consequently of no use here, for it is £50 fine to tender it to any one. What I mention it for is because I got Captain Prince to change it, and he expects that you will indemnify him, if the law prohibiting the bills of the neighboring colonies (which we hear our Assembly is

[1] Rev. Henry Caner, long his neighbor over the Church at Fairfield, Conn., had recently been made Rector of King's Chapel Boston.

about to enact) should take place before he gets home. If it should, I believe you must repay him and send it down to me if you have an opportunity, that I may exchange it at Newport on my return home.

The precepts you gave me in your letter are excellent, and the method you prescribe is no doubt the best; for I find by experience that vice is not to be reasoned with, but the temptation to it to be avoided, and none is there greater than that of bad company. It is almost impossible to associate with ill men and not sometimes do as they do, and even though we do not, yet their converse leaves a stain upon the mind which it is very difficult to get rid of. For this reason it shall be, as you advise, my greatest concern to avoid them, and chief care not to consent with them in their wickedness.

It is the greatest desire of my soul to be useful to mankind, but the difficulty is to determine in what way; for as we must necessarily be confined to some one kind of business or profession for a subsistence, so I think every man ought to choose that which is most agreeable to his dispositions and abilities, for in that he is most likely to succeed; and here it seems that what is really the best profession, in itself considered, is out of the question, but the point is what is best for this or that particular man. For as it is impossible that all men can live by any one profession, though it be really the best, so the Wisdom of Heaven has almost infinitely diversified the dispositions and powers of men, that they may not only follow but also delight in the different pursuits of life; and he I take it as much answers the end of his being who adorns a lower as he who fills a higher station of life, provided he is apparently calculated for it, and, therefore, it seems I must consider not in what profession the greatest good may be done to mankind, but in what station I, with these dispositions, these abilities and acquirements which I possess, am most likely to serve them; for where there is one that succeeds in an employment for which he is not calculated there are thousands that fail.

You may perhaps think from that warmth and eagerness of

temper which is natural to me, that I am for rushing into life and business hand over head without due deliberation and forecast. But in this you are really mistaken, for I am fully sensible that all my future happiness in life depends upon my taking a right course; so I have employed my most serious and intense thought upon it for this long time past, and have endeavored so far as I am able to consider everything relating to it, and to view my case, in every possible light I could place it. But I am resolved to do nothing rashly, yet I think it is high time for me to have some particular business in view, and to be qualifying myself for it. And as I chiefly and above all (under the conduct of Heaven) depend upon your advice, direction, and approbation in this most important case, so I hope you will be prepared when I come home to give me your last and best advice in the affair, that I may earnestly apply myself more immediately to fit myself for business. And pray, Sir, consider the distinction I mentioned above, and consider not what profession is best in itself (for if I am not fit for it, that must be the very worst of all for me), but what is best for me such as I am. We cannot unmake ourselves. We may correct but can never eradicate the first principles of our constitution either in body or mind. I know and am fully persuaded you would do what to you appears best for me in every case, and you know my temper, dispositions, abilities, etc. as well, perhaps better than I do myself; therefore, Sir, consider these and direct me to a course of life that is suitable for me; for by this means, and by the practice of virtue in such a course, I apprehend it is most likely I may become an instance of the *generis humani debitio*, and an instrument of doing all the good I am capable of among this degenerate race, and may best secure both my temporal and eternal interest. . . . . .

I am, honored Sir,

Your most dutiful son and humble servant,

WM. SAM^{L} JOHNSON.

CAMBRIDGE, *June* 13, 1747.

STRATFORD, *June* 23, 1747.

DEAREST SON, — I thank you for yours of the 13th, and am glad to find the small-pox is not likely to spread. That is a very melancholy story you tell of the young gentleman, and must come with a most shocking force to his poor father's ears, whom every human breast must tenderly compassionate, though perhaps the less, if what I heard be true, that that idle passion called *love* was the occasion of it, on account of which, it being unequal, he forced him away. I conclude the affair of the Rhode Island money need give us no concern, since though Prince told me of his changing it, he said nothing further about it.

I am extremely well pleased with the remarks you make on the advice I gave you about the infectiousness of vice and the great danger of bad company, and the resolution you express to be upon the strictest guard, which I pray God you may steadfastly abide by; and remember that that loose, weak, inconstant humor, abusively called *Free Thinking*, is equally infectious with vice, of which it is always either a cause or an effect, or most commonly both. I hope, therefore, you will be no less upon your guard against that, and any conversations leading to it, especially those of the ludicrous kind, which can be no more reasoned with than vice itself, or the most violent temptation to it. And as I doubt not but the infidelity of this wicked age is chiefly occasioned by an unbounded self-conceit and the unconstrained indulgence of lust, I would particularly recommend it to you above all things to be *clothed with humility* and to *flee youthful lust.*

I am also equally well pleased with the reflections you make upon the subject of making a wise choice of a course of life wherein to be useful to mankind. They are very just. If a man is not pleased with the business he follows, it cannot be expected he will succeed in it. For which reason I have always resolved as far as possible to indulge your inclinations, though at the expense of my own, for I am so much concerned, if possible, that you may be happy, that I should gladly undergo a great deal of uneasiness rather than stand in the way of it: nay, I have said, though I could never enjoy myself if you should follow war, yet I would rather submit to that, than that you should not be able to enjoy yourself well in some other calling.

But with regard to the question before us, I agree with you, that in choosing a course of life much allowance must be made to one's natural genius and inclination. Genuine nature must always be consulted. Notwithstanding which, I cannot quite agree with you in saying that what is really the best profession in itself considered is out of the question. Methinks it ought by all means to be taken into consideration with other things, in order to make a just judgment how to steer. If indeed it is plainly *humoris impar*, or one has an unconquerable aversion to it as a business of life, as I have for husbandry (though a great opinion of it), it must be doubtless a duty to choose rather some other course. But if I am equally qualified for that with another, perhaps better, and have only some little reluctances and misgivings, I ought in that case, for the sake of the superior intrinsic excellency and usefulness, to set my reason to work to conquer those reluctances if possible. And I know by experience, agreeable to what you allow, that the nature cannot be eradicated yet it may be corrected; that what one has no genius for, and even a reluctance to, may by dint of resolution and application be rendered not only tolerable but even delightful, as was my case with regard to Mathematics.

You are, my son, and I bless God for it, by genius and ability equally qualified to shine either in the pulpit, at the bar, or at arms. As to the last, I hope that is now at least in a great measure out of the question. And as to the two former, I shall for my part be entirely easy whichsoever you choose, though I prefer the first, for which you are already so well qualified that you can well afford to spend a year or two in making a trial of the study of Law, which would by no means be lost time, if you should afterwards quit it for Divinity. On the other hand, if you like it you may abide by it.

You say well (as being so young you well may), that you are not for rushing suddenly into life. And as you can spare yet three or four years to consider and qualify yourself, I doubt not but by that time you may begin in either of those professions with good advantage. Meantime assure yourself it is my daily and earnest prayer both for you and your brother not only that you may be duly qualified, but also directed to such a choice of business for life as may enable you to do God the greatest honor and mankind the greatest good you are capable of, and at the same time, in the best manner to enjoy yourselves here, and be qualified for the most ample reward hereafter. And to my prayers I shall willingly add my best advice and endeavors, and I am glad you have opened the way to a particular and free correspondence and conversation upon these subjects, and would wish you always to converse with me in the freest and most unreserved manner upon any subject that may be of importance to you, nay even upon the choice of a companion as well as a business for life, as occasion may offer. For there is nothing pleases me better than a decent, open, and unreserved freedom. You will make allowance for the extreme haste of my writing. It is now half an hour past 12, and high time to break up, so I conclude. With our hearty love to you,

Dear son,

Your most tender and affectionate father,

S. JOHNSON.

The answer to this letter caused the father to write another with more advice about plans for the future; and he addressed it to his son at Guilford, where he would stop on his return to visit relations. It closed the correspondence, and nothing more was needed to fix him in the choice of a profession: —

STRATFORD, *July* 7, 1747.

DEAR SON, — I do not now write to you as at Boston, having been informed you was to leave it this week. However as writing rather than speaking may be most agreeable to you on some of the subjects of your letter, I send this to meet you on the road.

Methinks you are rather too severe upon that instance of human frailty which is called *Love.* I believe there are few of us without some tincture of distraction, and I take that to be a species of it, which, in some degrees, of which there have been many instances, deserves as great a compassion and tenderness as any other kind of distraction, it being sometimes equally impossible even for a good genius to be master of himself in that case, as in any other case of distraction, which makes it a matter of great importance with regard to that, as well as other dangers, to think much of the Apostle's aphorism, *Let him that thinketh he standeth take heed lest he fall.*

I am pleased with the declaration you make of your sense and resolution about *Free Thinking.* Indeed I have thought (nor am I yet secure) that you are in too much danger of it, I mean in the bad sense; instances of which, you complain you have met with. But it is rather too cold an expression you use, that the more you know of this humor the less you esteem it. This seems to imply as if you had had too much of a favor for it, and upon the experience and observations you have had opportunity to make of it, I should hope you might have said, the more you know of it the more you abhor it.

You suspect my tenderness may carry me too far. It may have been so in some instances. It is a pardonable esteem, for which I hope you know how to make allowances. But give me leave to say, that there is at least as great a danger in youth of being too secure and self-sufficient; and, in consequence of that, of thinking too hardly of the caution and anxiety of age, and being not sufficiently sensible of the great advantage which age has of youth, in having gone through a long course of experience, and having had larger opportunities of trial, both of the treachery of a tempting world, and of the instability and deceitfulness of the heart of man, — our own as well as that of others; and consequently of the great dangers to which youth is particularly exposed, and of which it is not sufficiently aware.

I did not allege the case of Mathematics, as being at all concerned with choosing a course of life (as you seem to understand me), but only as a case, wherein a choice being made of any pursuit, even though somewhat against the grain, a resolute practice and application might, as I experienced, render it not only tolerable but even delightful.

Perhaps it is only the knowledge of yourself as you now are, in the heat of youth, that makes you apprehensive that you are not well calculated for Divinity (of which you give so just an encomium). I doubt not but with a careful management of yourself, you will in a few years grow more sedate, and your taste may much alter. However, as you profess that you have no notion of hurrying into life, you will do well to study law industriously two or three years. I would only observe, that so far as temper and disposition and conduct in life are concerned, such a management of them as is necessary to make a good Christian will be equally consistent with being a divine; and if you should not follow divinity as your profession, I beg to depend that your conduct be such as would be an ornament to it, and that you so order your manner of life, as vastly more to serve than disserve that cause; much less would I fear as you seem to do, that if you were a divine you should do more hurt than good to it.

You abhor the thought of making a woman unhappy, *i. e.*, in matrimony, or a family miserable. You are very right in this, and I hope I may take this as a good omen that you are resolute (and then you will succeed in it) so to act your part in life, as will not fail by God's blessing to make all those happy in a good measure to whom you may ever be related. And I would hope the same tenderness for that tender and unwary sex will always make you equally careful while you are in a state of celibacy to guard against anything that may have the least tendency to make any of them miserable, which often proves the effect of a frequent intercourse with them when no thoughts of anything further than mere conversation are intended. This is an affair of great tenderness, and has occasioned in time past a great deal of grief to me, and were I to go over life again I would never frequently or much converse with a person I had not even remote thoughts of making a partner in life, or when I was in no condition for it.

You say you are not worth a farthing, etc. It is true you are not in possession, but whenever you are disposed to settle yourself, I can spare you 2,000 pounds worth of lands to dispose of for that purpose, and hope in God's time I may leave you at least as much more. Meantime, I am,

Your most affectionate father,

S. JOHNSON.

In the year 1749 a project was set on foot to establish a college at Philadelphia, and several gentlemen of the first rank in the province gave it their support. One of this number was the celebrated Benjamin Franklin, who drew up and published the original proposals for erecting the English, Latin, and Mathematical schools of the institution under the name of an Academy, "which was considered as a very proper foundation on which to raise something further at a future period if these should be successful." He consulted Dr. Johnson, for whose opinion on such matters he had the highest respect, about the plan of education; and was very urgent to get him to assume the Presidency, and for this purpose, in company with another gentleman, visited him at Stratford. A similar movement was begun about the same time in New York, and Johnson, in writing to his fast friend, Bishop Berkeley, desired his good offices and "advice upon the undertaking." The following letter in reply was inclosed to Dr. Franklin, that he might have the benefit of the suggestions and thoughts which it contained:—

CLOYNE *August* 23, 1749.

REV. SIR, — I am obliged for the account you have sent me of the prosperous estate of learning in your College of New Haven. I approve of the regulations made there, and am particularly pleased to find your sons have made such a progress as appears from their elegant address to me in the Latin tongue. It must indeed give me a very sensible satisfaction to hear that my weak endeavors have been of some use and service to that part of the world. I have two letters of yours at once on my hands to answer, for which business of various kinds must be my apology. As to the first, wherein you inclosed a small pamphlet relating to tar-water, I can only say in behalf of those points in which the ingenious author seems to dissent from me, that I advance nothing which is not grounded on experience, as may be seen at large in Mr. Prior's narrative of the effects of tar-water, printed three or four years ago, and which may be supposed to have reached America.

For the rest, I am glad to find a spirit towards learning prevail in those parts, particularly New York, where you say a college is projected, which has my best wishes. At the same time I am sorry that the condition of Ireland, containing such numbers of poor uneducated people, for whose sake Charity Schools are erecting throughout the kingdom, obligeth us to draw charities from England; so far are we from being able to extend our bounty to New York, a country in proportion much richer than our own. But as you are pleased to desire my advice upon this undertaking, I send the following hints to be enlarged and improved by your own judgment.

I would not advise the applying to England for charters or statutes (which might cause great trouble, expense, and delay), but to do the business quietly within themselves.

I believe it may suffice to begin with a President and two Fellows. If they can procure but three fit persons, I doubt not the college from the smallest beginnings would soon grow considerable: I should conceive good hopes were you at the head of it.

Let them by all means supply themselves out of the seminaries in New England. For I am very apprehensive none can be got in Old England (who are willing to go) worth sending.

Let the Greek and Latin classics be well taught. Be this the first care as to learning. But the principal care must be good life and morals to which (as well as to study) early hours and temperate meals will much conduce.

If the terms for degrees are the same as in Oxford and Cambridge, this would give credit to the College, and pave the way for admitting their graduates *ad eundem* in the English universities.

Small premiums in books, or distinctions in habit, may prove useful encouragements to the students.

I would advise that the building be regular, plain, and cheap, and that each student have a small room (about ten feet square) to himself.

I recommended this nascent seminary to an English bishop, to try what might be done there. But by his answer it seems the colony is judged rich enough to educate its own youth.

Colleges from small beginnings grow great by subsequent bequests and benefactions. A small matter will suffice to set one a going. And when this is once well done, there is no doubt it will go on and thrive. The chief concern must be to set out in a good method, and introduce, from the very first, a good taste into the society. For this end the principal expense should be in making a handsome provision for the President and Fellows.

I have thrown together these few crude thoughts for you to ruminate upon and digest in your own judgment, and propose from yourself, as you see convenient.

My correspondence with patients who drink tar water, obliges me to be less punctual in corresponding with my friends. But I shall be always glad to hear from you. My sincere good wishes and prayers attend you in all your laudable undertakings.

I am your faithful, humble servant, G. CLOYNE.

The Philadelphia gentlemen matured their plans, and the subscriptions obtained for carrying them out were a strong proof of the public spirit and generosity of their fellow-citizens. The hints of Berkeley[1] appear to have been carefully studied, and Johnson was importuned to become the head of an institution which he showed himself so well qualified to direct, and which promised to be such a nursery of classic and Christian learning.

[1] The memory of this distinguished prelate as interested in Christian Education is perpetuated in Connecticut. His name designates one of its most useful and prosperous Institutions, — the "Berkeley Divinity School" at Middletown, incorporated in 1854, and conducted, since its foundation, under the immediate charge of the Bishop of the Diocese.

CHAPTER VII.

CORRESPONDENCE WITH FRANKLIN; DECLINES PHILADELPHIA; "ELEMENTA PHILOSOPHICA"; DEATH OF BERKELEY AND LETTER FROM HIS SON; ENGLISH EDITION OF "ELEMENTS OF PHILOSOPHY"; SPECULATIVE INQUIRIES, AND NOTIONS ABOUT EDUCATION.

A. D. 1750–1754.

THE fondness of Johnson for learning and colleges induced him to take into serious consideration the overtures from Philadelphia. They were urged upon him in a way which made them somewhat attractive, but his reluctance to leave the region of his nativity and separate himself from the cherished associations of his brethren formed a great obstacle to their acceptance. He spoke freely of his age as against the change, and did not think it was warranted by the prospect of increased usefulness and better pecuniary support. Dr. Franklin's letters to him present the subject very fully, and show the points on which Johnson dwelt in his replies. The first that has been preserved is dated: —

PHILADELPHIA, *Aug.* 9, 1750.

REV. SIR, — At my return home I found your favor of June the 28th, with the Bishop of Cloyne's letter inclosed, which I will take care of, and beg leave to keep a little longer.

Mr. Francis, our Attorney General, who was with me at your house, from the conversation then had with you, and reading some of your pieces, has conceived an esteem for you equal to mine. The character we have given of you to the other trustees, and the sight of your letters relating to the academy, has made them very desirous of engaging you in that design, as a person whose experience and judgment would be of great use in forming rules and establishing good methods in the beginning, and whose name for learning would give it a reputation. We only lament, that in the infant state of our funds, we cannot make you an offer equal to your merit. But as the view of being useful has most weight with generous and benevolent minds, and in this affair you may do great service not only to the present but to future generations, I flatter myself sometimes that if you were here, and saw things as they are, and conversed a little with our people, you might be prevailed with to remove. I would therefore earnestly press you to make us a visit as soon as you conveniently can; and in the mean time let me represent to you some of the circumstances as they appear to me.

1. The Trustees of the Academy are applying for a charter, which will give an opportunity of improving and modeling our constitution in such a manner as, when we have your advice, shall appear best. I suppose we shall have power to form a regular college.

2. If you would undertake the management of the English Education, I am satisfied the trustees would, on your account, make the salary £100 sterling, (they have already voted £150 currency which is not far from it), and pay the charge of your removal. Your son might also be employed as tutor at £60 or perhaps £70 per annum.

3. It has been long observed, that our church is not sufficient to accommodate near the number of people who would willingly have seats there. The buildings increase very fast towards the south end of the town, and many of the principal merchants now live there; which being at a considerable distance from the present church, people begin to talk much of building another, and ground has been offered as a gift for that purpose. The Trustees of the Academy are three

fourths of them members of the Church of England, and the rest men of moderate principles. They have reserved in the building a large hall for occasional preaching, public lectures, orations, etc.; it is 70 feet by 60, furnished with a handsome pulpit, seats, etc. In this Mr. Tennent collected his congregation, who are now building him a meeting-house. In the same place, by giving now and then a lecture, you might, with equal ease, collect a congregation that would in a short time build you a church, if it should be agreeable to you.

In the mean time, I imagine you will receive something considerable yearly, arising from marriages and christenings in the best families, etc., not to mention presents that are not unfrequent from a wealthy people to a minister they like; and though the whole may not amount to more than a due support, yet I think it will be a comfortable one. And when you are well settled in a church of your own, your son may be qualified by years and experience to succeed you in the Academy; or if you rather choose to continue in the Academy, your son might probably be fixed in the Church.

These are my private sentiments which I have communicated only to Mr. Francis, who entirely agrees with me. I acquainted the trustees that I would write to you, but could give them no dependence that you would be prevailed on to remove. They will, however, treat with no other till I have your answer.

You will see by our newspaper, which I inclose, that the Corporation of this city have voted £200 down and £100 a year out of their revenues to the Trustees of the Academy. As they are a perpetual body, choosing their own successors, and so not subject to be changed by the caprice of a governor or of the people, and as 18 of the members (some the most leading) are of the trustees, we look on this donation to be as good as so much real estate; being confident it will be continued as long as it is well applied, and even increased, if there should be occasion. We have now near £5,000 subscribed, and expect some considerable sums besides may be procured from the merchants of London trading hither. And as we are in the centre of the Colonies, a healthy place, with plenty of provisions, we suppose a good academy here may draw numbers of youth for education from the neighboring Colonies, and even from the West Indies.

I will shortly print proposals for publishing your pieces by subscription, and disperse them among my friends along the continent. My compliments to Mrs. Johnson and your son; and Mr. and Mrs. Walker your good neighbors.

I am, with great esteem and respect, Sir,

Your most humble servant,

B. Franklin.

P. S. There are some other things best treated of when we have the pleasure of seeing you. It begins now to be pleasant travelling. I wish you would conclude to visit us in the next month at farthest. Whether the journey produce the effect we desire or not, it shall be no expense to you.

The Rev. Richard Peters, though he had no personal acquaintance with him, wrote him on the same day, and invited him to his house. Mr. Peters was an Englishman of culture and good manners, who came to this country in Holy Orders, with his young wife, and served for a time as an assistant in Christ Church, Philadelphia. He afterwards accepted the appointment of Provincial Secretary, and acquired a considerable fortune, but did not relinquish his ministerial character, and continued occasionally to perform clerical duty. The letter below has allusion to his official position in the government which he still held: —

Philadelphia, *Aug.* 9, 1750.

Reverend Sir, — I am obliged to you for the honor you did me in your compliments by Mr. Franklin and Mr. Francis. They said so many good things of your abilities and inclinations to promote useful knowledge, and the Trustees of the Academy are so much in want of your advice and assistance, that, though personally unknown to you, I must take the freedom, from a hint that such a journey would not be disagreeable to you, to give you an invitation to my house. Let me, good Sir, have the pleasure of conversing with a gentleman whose character I have a long time esteemed, and provided your journey be not between the 20th October and 1st November, when I am obliged to attend the Governor and Assembly at New Castle, I will meet you at Trenton or Brunswick, or any other place you shall appoint. I will tell you beforehand, that can my friends or I find any expedient to engage your residence among us, I will leave nothing unattempted in the power of, Reverend Sir,

Your affectionate brother and humble servant,

RICHARD PETERS.

Johnson replied: —

Aug. 16.

SIR, — I am extremely obliged to you for the honor you have done me in writing so kind and polite a letter to me, who am a perfect stranger to you, and a person whose real character I doubt you will find much below what the candor of the openly friendly gentlemen have represented. You will see by my letter to Mr. Franklin what difficulties lie in my way with regard to my residence among you, which otherwise would, doubtless, be vastly agreeable to me. However, as I do think in earnest, if practicable, to make a tour to Philadelphia in acknowledgment of the great kindness you express towards me, I shall most gratefully accept of your kind invitation, and let you know beforehand when to expect me. If I can come at all it will be before the time you mention, but I would first see my brethren here together at our Commencement on the 2d week in Sept., by conversing with whom I shall be the better able to make a judgment whether a remove would be practicable. Meantime,

I remain, Sir, etc.,

S. J.

The next letter of Franklin, so characteristic of the man, goes more deeply into the objections which

Johnson had raised, and intimates to him that his "talents for the education of youth were the gift of God," and it was his duty to employ them for the public service.[1] It shows too the writer's practical wisdom in regard to the extension of the Church: —

PHILADELPHIA, *Aug.* 23, 1750.

DEAR SIR, — We received your favor of the 16th inst. Mr. Peters will hardly have time to write to you per this post, and I must be short. Mr. Francis spent the last evening with me, and we were all glad to hear that you seriously meditate a visit after the middle of next month, and that you will inform us by a line when to expect you. We drank your health and Mrs. Johnson's, remembering your kind entertainment of us at Stratford.

I think, with you, that nothing is of more importance for the public weal, than to form and train up youth in wisdom and virtue. Wise and good men are, in my opinion, the strength of a state far more so than riches or arms, which, under the management of ignorance and wickedness, often draw on destruction, instead of promoting the safety of a people. And though the culture bestowed on youth be successful only with a few, yet the influence of those few, for the service in their power, may be very great. Even a single woman, that was wise, by her wisdom saved a city.

I think, also, that general virtue is more probably to be expected and obtained from the education of youth than from the exhortation of adult persons; bad habits and vices of the mind being, like diseases of the body, more easily prevented than cured.

I think, moreover, that talents for the education of youth are the gift of God; and that he on whom they are bestowed, whenever a way is opened for the use of them, is as strongly called as if he heard a voice from heaven. Nothing more surely pointing out duty, in a public service, than ability and opportunity of performing it.

[1] This letter was first printed in the *Port Folio*, 1809, and it also appears in Sparks' *Works of Franklin*, vol. vii. pp. 47–50.

I have not yet discoursed with Dr. Jenney concerning your removal hither. You have reason, I own, to doubt whether your coming on the foot I proposed would not be disagreeable to him, though I think it ought not. For should his particular interest be somewhat affected by it, that ought not to stand in competition with the general good; especially as it cannot be *much* affected, he being old, and rich, and without children. I will however learn his sentiments before the next post. But whatever influence they might have on your determinations about removing, they need have none on your intention of visiting. And if you favor us with the visit, it is not necessary that you should previously write to him to learn his dispositions about your removal, since you will see him, and when we are all together those things may be better settled in conversation than by letters at a distance. Your tenderness of the Church's peace is truly laudable; but, methinks, to build a new church in a growing place is not properly dividing but multiplying; and will really be a means of increasing the number of those who worship God in that way. Many who cannot now be accommodated in the church go to other places or stay at home; and if we had another church, many, who go to other places or stay at home, would go to church. I suppose the interest of the Church has been far from suffering in Boston by the building of two new churches there in my memory. I had for several years nailed against the wall of my house, a pigeon-box that would hold six pair; and though they bred as fast as my neighbor's pigeons, I never had more than six pair; the old and strong driving out the young and weak, and obliging them to seek new habitations. At length I put up an additional box, with apartments for entertaining twelve pair more, and it was soon filled with inhabitants, by the overflowings of my first box and of others in the neighborhood. This I take to be a parallel case with the building a new church here.

Your years, I think, are not so many as to be an objection of any weight, especially considering the vigor of your constitution. For the small-pox, if it should spread here, you might inoculate with great probability of safety; and I think that distemper generally more favorable here than further northward. Your objection about the politeness of Philadelphia, and your imagined rusticity, is mere compliment; and your diffidence of yourself absolutely groundless.

My humble respects, if you please, to your brethren at the Commencement. I hope they will advise you to what is most for the good of the whole, and then I think they will advise you to move hither.

Please to tender my best respects and service to Mrs. Johnson and your son.

I am, dear Sir,

Your obliged and affectionate, humble serv[t],

B. FRANKLIN.

Illness prevented Johnson from making his contemplated visit. Franklin wrote him again and gave up all expectation of seeing him immediately, as the small-pox was spreading in the city, and it would not be prudent to expose himself to its dangers: —

DEAR SIR, — I am sorry to hear of your illness. If you have not been used to the fever-and-ague let me give you one caution. Don't imagine yourself thoroughly cured, and so omit the use of the bark too soon. Remember to take the preventing doses faithfully. If you were to continue taking a dose or two every day for two or three weeks after the fits have left you, 'twould not be amiss. If you take the powder mixed quick in a tea-cup of milk, 'tis no way disagreeable, but looks and even tastes like chocolate. 'Tis an old saying: That an ounce of prevention is worth a pound of cure, — and certainly a true one, with regard to the bark; a little of which will do more in preventing the fits than a great deal in removing them.

But if your health would permit I should not expect the pleasure of seeing you soon. The small-pox spreads apace, and is now in all quarters; yet as we have only children to have it, and our Doctors inoculate apace, I believe they will soon drive it through the town; so that you may possibly visit us with safety in the spring. In the mean time we should be glad to know the result you came to after consulting your brethren at the Commencement. Messrs. Peters and Francis have directed me on all occasions to present their compliments to you. Please to acquaint me if you propose to make any considerable additions to the "Ethics," that I may be able in the proposals to compute the bigness of the book.

I am, with sincere esteem and respect, dear Sir,

Your most obliged humble servant,

B. FRANKLIN.

PHILADELPHIA, *September* 13, 1750.

Inclosed I return the good Bishop's letter with thanks.

Before this correspondence was begun, Dr. Johnson received a second invitation to the Rectorship of Trinity Church, Newport, made vacant by the death of his friend, the Rev. James Honyman. But he felt that his removal would prejudice the interests of the Church in Connecticut, and he finally declined it, and suggested to the Vestry whether it would not be advisable to think of Dr. Cutler's son for the place. He had been a long time officiating in England, and was "doubtless," he said, "very well experienced and accomplished." The same motive which led him to decline Newport helped him to come to a determination about Philadelphia. He had been quite ready to give his friends there the benefit of his counsels in regard to their Institution; but the following letters were the last that related to the acceptance of their proposals.

PHILADELPHIA, *December* 24, 1751.

DEAR SIR, — I received your favor of the 11th inst. and thank you for the hint you give of the omission in the "Idea." The "Sacred Classics" are read in the English school, though I forgot to mention them. And I shall propose at the meeting of the Schools, after the Holidays, that the English master begin and continue to read select portions of them daily with the prayers as you advise.

But if you can be thus useful to us at this distance, how much more might you be so if you were present with us, and had the immediate inspection and government of the schools. I wrote to you in my last that Mr. Martin our Rector died suddenly of a quinsy. His body was carried to the Church, respectfully attended by the trustees, all the masters and scholars in their order, and a great number of the citizens. Mr. Peters preached his funeral sermon, and gave him the just and honorable character he deserved. The schools are now broke up for Christmas, and will not meet again till the 7th of January. Mr. Peters took care of the Latin and Greek School after Mr. Martin's death till the breaking up. And Mr. Allison, a dissenting minister, has promised to continue that care for a month after their next meeting. Is it impossible for you to make us a visit in that time? I hope by the next post to know something of your sentiments, that I may be able to speak more positively to the Trustees concerning the probability of your being prevailed with to remove hither.

The English master is Mr. Dove, a gentleman about your age, who formerly taught grammar sixteen years at Chichester in England. He is an excellent master, and his scholars have made a surprising progress.

I shall send some of the "Œconomies" to Mr. Havens per next post. If you have a spare one of your "Essays on the Method of Study," the English edition, please to send it me.

My wife joins in the compliments of the season to you and Mrs. Johnson, with, dear Sir,

Your affectionate humble servant,

B. FRANKLIN

Answer: —

Dear Sir, — I now write my most thankful acknowledgments for your two kind letters of December 24 and January 8, and have received your most obliging letters of the summer before last, to which you refer me. There was one of August 23, to which I did not make a particular reply by reason of my illness at that time. In that you reasoned, I own, in a very forcible manner upon the head of duty. You argued that ability, with opportunity, manifestly pointed out duty, as though it were a voice from Heaven. This, Sir, I agree to, and therefore have always endeavored to use what little ability I have that way in the best manner I could, having never been without pupils of one sort or other half a year at a time, and seldom that, for thirty-eight years. And, thank God, I have the great satisfaction to see some of them in the first pulpits, not only in Connecticut, but also in Boston and New York, and others in some of the first places in the land. But I am now plainly in the decline of life, both as to activity of body and vigor of mind, and must, therefore, consider myself as being an *Emeritus*, and unfit for any new situation in the world or to enter on any new business, especially at such a distance from my hitherto sphere of action and my present situation, where I have as much duty on my hands as I am capable of and where my removal would make too great a breach to be countervailed by any good I am capable of doing elsewhere, for which I have but a small chance left for much opportunity. So that I must beg my good friends at Philadelphia to excuse me, and I pray God they may be directed to a better choice. And as Providence has so unexpectedly provided so worthy a person as Mr. Dove for your other purpose, I hope the same good Providence will provide for this. I am not personally acquainted with Mr. Winthrop, the Professor at Cambridge, but by what I have heard of him, perhaps he might do. But I rather think it would be your best way to try if you cannot get some friend and faithful gentleman at home, of good judgment and care, to inquire and try if some worthy Fellow of one or other of the Universities could not be obtained. Perhaps Mr. Peters or Mr. Dove may know of some acquaintance of theirs, that might do likely: *dulcius ex ipsis fortibus.* Your son intimated that you had thought of a voyage home yourself; if you should you might undoubtedly look out a fit person to be had, and you had better do as you can for some time than not be well provided. I could, however, wish to make you a visit in the Spring, if the way were safe, but it seems the small-pox is propagating at New York, and perhaps you will be scarcely free of it. Meantime you have, indeed, my heart with you as though I were ever so much with you in presence, and if there were any good office in my power you might freely command it.

I thank you for sending the two sheets of my "Noetica" which are done with much care. I find no defects worth mentioning but what were probably my own. At page 62, l. 19, there should have been a (;) after "universal," and l. 21 a (;) after "affirmative." On reviewing the former sheets I observe a neglect, p. 30, l. 24, "on account of which," and p. 36, l. 3, there should be a (,) after "is."[1]

I am very much obliged to you for Short and the Almanac and my wife for hers. I have had five parcels of the "Œconomies" and Fisher. I think you told me they were a dollar each parcel, besides that of Havens, who desires you to send him another parcel, and begs you to send one or more of your pieces on "Electricity," published in England. By your son's account I am much charmed with this, and beg if you have a spare copy to send it me. And as you desire a copy of my "Introduction," since I had many sent me from home, I send half a dozen, of which with my humble service to Messrs. Peters and Francis and your son, pray them to accept each a copy. My wife and son, with me, desire our service may be acceptable to them and Mrs. Franklin and your son.

I am, Sir, etc.

S. J.

[1] In the copy before me there are pen corrections of these and other errors by Johnson himself.

The work referred to in the foregoing letter was the "Elementa Philosophica: containing chiefly Noetica, or Things relating to the Mind or Understanding; and Ethica, or Things relating to the Moral Behaviour." This was the summary title, and three great philosophers were grouped together in the issue of the work. It was written by Johnson, dedicated, "from the deepest sense of gratitude," to the Bishop of Cloyne, and printed by Benjamin Franklin. The first part, *Noetica,* was mainly new, prepared for young beginners to show them the principles of knowledge and the progress of the human mind towards its highest perfection; and in the advertisement, Johnson said: "Though I would not be too much attached to any one author or system, exclusive of any others; yet whoever is versed in the writings of Bishop Berkeley will be sensible that I am in a particular manner beholden to that excellent philosopher for several thoughts that occur in the following Tract." The remaining part was a second edition of his "System of Morality," described in the previous chapter.

The graceful dedication to Berkeley was too late to be seen by that eminent man. The correspondence between them had been kept up, and every opportunity improved to communicate with each other, as the following letters will show.

CLOYNE, *July* 17, 1750.

REV. SIR, — A few months ago I had an opportunity of writing to you and Mr. Honyman by an inhabitant of the Rhode Island Government. I would not, nevertheless, omit the present occasion of saluting you, and letting you know that it gave me great pleasure to hear from Mr. Bourk, a passenger from those parts, that a late sermon of yours at New Haven hath had a very good effect in reconciling several to the Church. I find also by a letter from Mr. Clap, that learning continues to make notable advances in Yale College. This gives me great satisfaction, and that God may bless your worthy endeavors and crown them with success, is the sincere prayer of, Rev. Sir,

Your faithful brother and obedient servt,

G. CLOYNE.

P. S. I hope your ingenious sons are still an ornament to Yale College, and tread in their father's footsteps.

Answer: —

December 17.

MY LORD, — I yesterday received your Lordship's most kind letter of July 17, from New Haven, and as there is a vessel soon going from New York, I take the opportunity of making my most humble acknowledgments to your Lordship, though I lately wrote by the way of New York, my humble thanks for your kind letter before received which came not to hand till last summer. In that letter I informed you of the death of good Mr. Honyman, and of the controversy between the Governor of New York and their Assembly, which hath hindered their College from going forward, — since which, things have been so far accommodated that they have nominated the Trustees, and I hope they will proceed. They are very thankful for the notice you so kindly took of what I had mentioned to you in their behalf, and will form their College upon the model you suggested to me. I intended to have written by Mr. Bourk, but he was just going when I saw him, and I had not time, nor had I then received your Lordship's last kind letter.

We should soon have a flourishing Church at New Haven, if we could get a minister, — but the Secretary of the Society writes very discouragingly about expecting any more ministers for these parts. Here is one of your Lordship's scholars, one Colton,[1] that is a worthy candidate, and another equally deserving, one Camp,[2] but we cannot yet have leave for their

[1] Jonathan Colton was afterwards admitted to Holy Orders in England, and died on his returning voyage to this country in 1752.

[2] Ichabod Camp, his companion, a graduate of Yale College, 1743, was ordained at the same time.

going home for Orders. No endeavors of mine shall be wanting, my Lord, while I live, to promote sound learning and religion in these parts, and particularly your Lordship's excellent system, in order to which I am preparing a short draught for the use of pupils, but it will much want your Lordship's correction.

I thank God my sons yet give me good hopes, and there is scarce anything I want to hear of more than of Mr. Harry's welfare and of your Lordship's family, for whom I most ardently pray. I heartily thank your Lordship for your prayers and good wishes for me and mine, and beg the continuance of them, and remain, my Lord, your Lordship's, etc.

S. J.

Berkeley wrote one more letter to Johnson, partly in answer to the foregoing, and it is believed to have been his last to the great American friend who never ceased to love him for his virtues, and to honor him for his learning and philosophy. It was dated : —

CLOYNE, *July* 25, 1751.

REV. SIR, — I would not let Mr. Hall depart without a line from me in acknowledgment of your letter which he put into my hands. As for Mr. Hutchinson's writings, I am not acquainted with them. I live in a remote corner where many modern things escape me. Only this I can say, that I have observed that author to be mentioned as an enthusiast, which gave me no prepossession in his favor.

I am glad to find by Mr. Clap's letter, and the specimens of literature inclosed in his packet, that learning continues to make a progress in Yale College, and hope that virtue and Christian charity may keep pace with it.

The letters which you and Mr. Clap say you had written, in answer to my last, never came into my hands. I am glad to hear, by Mr. Hall, of the good health and condition of yourself and family. I pray God to bless you and yours, and prosper your good endeavors. I am Rev. Sir,

Your faithful friend and humble serv^{t},

G. CLOYNE.

As soon as his "Elementa Philosophica" was published, Johnson wrote to Berkeley and sent him a copy, not knowing that he had broken up at Cloyne, and exchanged its gloomy retirement and the life of a recluse philosopher for the classic shades and ideal beauty of Oxford. His son George had been entered a student at Christ Church, and parental tenderness, joined to other considerations,[1] led him to follow him with his family and make his future residence at the seat of the venerable University in the "fair vale of the Cherwell and the Isis." The issue of "Elementa Philosophica" must have been about the time when he was settling his affairs, preparatory to the final departure from Cloyne. The following letter shows this as well as the use to which the work was put and the estimation in which it was held. It gives, moreover, a sketch of the progress of the Institution of which Johnson had declined the oversight.

PHILADELPHIA, *July* 2, — 52.

REV. SIR, — I have sent you, via New York, twenty-four of your books bound as those I sent per post. The remainder of the fifty are binding in a plainer manner, and shall be sent as soon as done and left at Mr. Stuyvesant's as you order.

Our Academy, which you so kindly inquire after, goes on well. Since Mr. Martin's death the Latin and Greek school has been under the care of Mr. Allison, a Dissenting minister, well skilled in those languages and long practiced in teaching. But he refused the Rectorship, or to have anything to do with the government of the other schools. So that remains vacant, and obliges the Trustees to more frequent visits. We have now several young gentlemen desirous of entering on the study of Philosophy, and Lectures are to be opened this week. Mr. Allison undertakes Logic

[1] See Fraser's *Life of Berkeley*, ch. ix.

and Ethics, making your work his text to comment and lecture upon. Mr. Peters and some other gentlemen undertake the other branches, till we shall be provided with a Rector capable of the whole, who may attend wholly to the instructions of youth in the higher parts of learning as they come out fitted from the lower schools. Our proprietors have lately wrote that they are extremely well pleased with the design, will take our Seminary under their patronage, give us a charter, and, as an earnest of their benevolence, Five Hundred Pounds sterling. And by our opening a charity school, in which near one hundred poor children are taught Reading, Writing, and Arithmetic, with the rudiments of religion, we have gained the general good will of all sorts of people, from whence donations and bequests may be reasonably expected to accrue from time to time. This is our present situation, and we think it a promising one; especially as the reputation of our schools increases, the masters being all very capable and diligent and giving great satisfaction to all concerned.

I have heard of no exceptions yet made to your work, nor do I expect any, unless to those parts that savor of what is called *Berkeleyanism*, which is not well understood here. When any occur I shall communicate them.

With great esteem and respect, I am, dear Sir,

Your obliged humble serv[t],

B. FRANKLIN.

Berkeley had not long enjoyed the academic repose of Oxford before his family and friends were thrown into the deepest affliction by his sudden death. He had received neither the book nor the letter from Johnson when it occurred, on the evening of Sunday, the 14th of January, 1753, but the author had sent another copy of his work to Dr. Thos. Secker, then Bishop of Oxford and almost the only survivor of the distinguished men in England with whom

Berkeley corresponded in his later years. The funeral solemnities were scarcely over when he wrote to his son and apprized him of its reception and offered it to his acceptance, and he in acknowledging the Bishop's kindness said — "Dr. Johnson's book I have not seen, but shall be greatly obliged to you for a copy of it, as I suppose it is not reprinted in England, and as my dear father had a great esteem for the author." The best and most authentic account of Berkeley's death is contained in the following letter to Dr. Johnson, written by this son, and dated: —

CHRIST CHURCH, *October* 16, 1753.

REV. SIR, — With inexpressible sorrow I repeat the dismal account (for I suppose you have heard it before) of my dearest and ever honored father's removal to the enjoyment of eternal rewards, which happened suddenly and without the least previous notice or pain on Sunday evening, Jan. 14th, as he was sitting with my mother, sister, and myself, and although all possible means were instantly used, no symptom of life ever appeared after, nor could the physicians assign any cause for his death, as they were certain it was not an apoplexy. He had made his will at Cloyne a few days before he left it (which he did in the middle of August), and has very wisely left us all entirely under the care, and in the power of the best of mothers. He arrived at Oxford on the 25th of August and had received great benefit from the change of air, and by God's blessing on Tar Water, insomuch that for some years he had not been in better health than he was the instant before he left us. He had been indeed much out of order the whole summer at Cloyne, which prevented his coming over with me in May, 1752. His remains are interred in the Cathedral of Christ Church, and next week a monument to his memory will be erected with an inscription by Dr. Markham, a student of this College.[1] A few

[1] Berkeley provided in his will that his body should be buried in the Churchyard of the parish where he died.

days after this greatest of human misfortunes befell us I received from Cloyne your letter to my dearest father, but his agent there has not yet got an opportunity of sending me the Book mentioned in it, but the Bishop of Oxford has been so good as to send it to me, and you must give me leave to say that (except those wrote by him to whom this was dedicated) I never read any with equal pleasure, and the more so as it shows that a person so very capable and willing to spread his Philosophy, understands it so thoroughly. This little book contains and teaches the wisdom of ages and numberless volumes, and I entreat you would accept my hearty thanks for the honor you have done my dearest parent by choosing him for its patron, and also for the improvement I have met with in it.

It is now high time that I should apologize for the liberty I have taken, and which nothing should have encouraged me to but the great friendship that subsisted between you and him whose image is ever fresh before me, and whose memory shall ever be most dear to me. I have inherited his high esteem for you, Sir, and this will, I hope, plead my excuse for giving you this trouble. My mother, who remembers you with the truest regard, desires me to assure you of her most sincere services. Your countryman, my brother,[1] has been near two years abroad in the south of France for his health, which has been very bad ever since a violent fever which he had some years ago. He is now, I thank God, much better, and is lately returned to Dublin, from whence we expect him here next summer. Not knowing any other way of

In the summer of 1870, in company with two friends, I spent a day at Cloyne, and walked through its narrow streets, and under the ancient elms that overshadow the dwellings of this thriftless village. I thought of Berkeley at every turn and was disappointed when we entered the Cathedral to find no memorial of the great name associated with it for nearly a score of years. The mysterious Round Tower, the Cave, the See House and the Palace garden, were there as they were a century ago, and the myrtle and the ivy grew in wonderful luxuriance, but there was nothing to perpetuate the memory of the good Bishop, or to show that there had ever been a people here who knew his intellectual greatness.

[1] Henry, the eldest son, born at Newport. In Fraser's admirable *Life of Berkeley*, p. 336, it is conjectured that he "had been left behind in Ireland," when the removal to Oxford took place.

conveyance, I have taken the liberty of inclosing this to Dr. Bearcroft, the Secretary of your Society (of which I have the honor to be a member), to forward it. If ever you can think of anything in which I can render you the least service, I assure you that nothing will more highly oblige me than receiving any commands from one whom I so honor and esteem, and to whom I am a most dutiful and faithful humble servant.

GEO. BERKELEY.

A third edition of Dr. Johnson's "Elements of Philosophy," corrected and enlarged, was published in London in the spring of 1754, under the editorship of Rev. William Smith, afterwards Provost of the College of Philadelphia. He sent by him letters to several of his friends, and among the rest to Mr. Berriman, who answered, —

February 7, 1754.

DEAR SIR, — I had the pleasure of yours by Mr. Smith, but have as yet had but little of that gentleman's company; I once called at his lodgings, and found him at home; but having no time to stay then, he promised to favor me with a visit, which promise he has not yet fulfilled: however, I hope he will do it hereafter, as I understood by him he intended to continue some time in England before he returned to your parts.

Dr. Bearcroft is made Master of the Charter House, but still holds his place of Secretary to the Society. There has been some talk of Capt. Thomlinson for Treasurer. Perhaps I may let you know more about it before I seal up this letter.

Mr. Pollen is appointed Missionary to Rhode Island. He is a worthy clergyman and esteemed a good scholar; he was contemporary at C. C. C. Oxon. with your friend Dr. Burton, who is now Vice Provost of Eton College. I would beg leave to recommend him to your favorable notice, and that you would advise and assist him in any case that may need your helping hand. He is a traveller, and has seen the world; and has been lately employed in an Episcopal chapel at Glasgow, but never was in your parts, and being quite a stranger to such a kind of settlement, may often have occasion to consult you, who are so much known, and so well esteemed by all around you. We have had such bad accounts of poor Mr. Checkley that we fear the next news will bring an account of his death.

I thank God I am rather the better for the change of my situation, and at this time in tolerable good health; but I must never expect to get free from my old companions, the cough and shortness of breath, but God be praised, they are not by many degrees so bad with me as with many others: and I ought to be very thankful for the long intervals I have, and the health and strength afforded me to attend my duty in the Church. I quitted my Lecture at Aldermary at Lady-Day last and have done scarce any duty in the Church but supplying my own pulpit or desk on Sunday mornings, since midsummer. I find my strength somewhat decayed, and my eyes begin to wax dim (though I can make no use of spectacles), and I have this day completed my grand climacteric.

Feb. 15. — The choice of a Treasurer came on at the anniversary meeting of the Society in the Vestry at Bow Church. Mr. Pearson (recommended by the Bishops) was elected, and nobody named in opposition to him.

I am affectionately yours,

J. Berriman.

To the London edition of the "Elements of Philosophy" was annexed "A Letter containing some Impartial Thoughts concerning the Settlement of Bishops in America, by Dr. Johnson and some of his Brethren." In this connection the following letter is important, written by the Bishop of Oxford from the —

Deanery of St. Paul's, *March* 19, 1754.

Good Dr. Johnson, — I should have returned you my hearty thanks before now, if extraordinary business had not put it partly out of my power, and partly out of my thoughts, for your favors by Mr. Smith. He is indeed a very ingenious and able, and seems a very well disposed young man. And if he had pursued his intention of residing a while at Oxford, I should have hoped for more of his company and acquaintance. Nor would he, I think, have failed to see more fully, what I flatter myself he is convinced of without it, that our Universities do not deserve the sentence which is passed on them by the author whom he cites, and whose words he adopts in page 84 of his "General Idea of the College of Mirania."[1] He assures me they are effaced in almost all the copies. I wish they had not been printed, or that the leaf had been cancelled. But the many valuable things which there are in that performance and in the papers which he published at New York, will atone for this blemish with all candid persons. And there seems a fair prospect of his doing great service in the place where he is going to settle.

I am particularly obliged to you for sending me your Book; of which I made a very acceptable present to the late excellent Bishop of Cloyne's son, — a most serious, and sensible, and prudent young man, whom his father placed at Christ Church, and who, with his mother and sister, spent the last summer with me in Oxfordshire. I have now lately received from Mr. Smith another copy of it, printed here, and have read several parts of it, and all with much pleasure. You have taken very proper care to keep those who do not enter into all the philosophy of the good and great man from being shocked at it, and you have explained and recommended just reasoning, virtue, and religion, so as to make them not only well understood, but ardently loved.

Would God there were any present hopes of executing what the concluding piece unanswerably proves to be harm-

[1] This was an imaginary scheme drawn up and published at the desire of some gentlemen of New York, who were appointed to receive proposals relative to the establishment of a college in that province, and it contained a pretty exact representation of what the author endeavored to realize in the Institution over which he afterwards presided at Philadelphia.

less, useful, and requisite. But we have done all we can here in vain; and must wait for more favorable times; which I think it will contribute not a little to bring on, if the ministry of our Church in America, by friendly converse with the principal Dissenters, can satisfy them that nothing more is intended or desired than that our Church may enjoy the full benefit of its own institutions, as all others do. For so long as they are uneasy and remonstrate, regard will be paid to them and their friends here by our ministers of state. And yet it will be a hard matter for you to prevent their being uneasy, while they find you gaining ground upon them. That so much of the money of the Society was employed in supporting Episcopal congregations amongst them, was industriously made an argument against the late collection. And though, God be thanked, the collection hath notwithstanding proved a very good one, yet unless we be cautious on that head, we shall have farther clamor; and one knows not what the effect of it may be. Our friends in America will furnish us, I hope, from time to time, with all such facts, books, observations, and reasonings, as may enable us the better to defend our common cause.

I am with great regard and esteem, Sir,

Your loving brother and humble servant,

THO. OXFORD.

Johnson felt some disappointment that his work was not more generally appreciated, and appeared to regret that he had ventured on its publication. The cost of printing it was likely to exceed the amount of sales, — as it was not so well calculated for popular reading as for use in educational institutions. Franklin relieved him from any anxiety on this subject, and wrote him a kind and encouraging letter, offering to assume the loss, should there be any: —

PHILADELPHIA, *April* 15, 1754.

DEAR SIR, — When I returned from Maryland in February last, I found your favor of Jan'y 1, but having mislaid it soon after, I deferred answering till I should find it again, which I have now done. I think you ought not to be, as you say you are, vexed at yourself that you offered your "Noetica" to be printed; for though the demand for it in this part of the world has not yet been equal to the merit of the work, yet you will see by the inclosed newspaper they are reprinting it in England, where good judges being more plenty than with us, it will, I doubt not, acquire a reputation that may not only make it extensively useful there, but bring it more into notice in its native America.

As to the use of it in our Academy, you are to consider that though our plan is large, we have as yet been able to carry little more into execution than the grammatical and mathematical parts: the rest must follow gradually, as the youth come forward and we can provide suitable masters. Some of the eldest scholars, who have now left us, did read it; but those at present in the Academy are chiefly engaged in lower studies. For my own part, I know too well the badness of our general taste, to expect any great profit in printing it; though I did think it might sell better than I find it does, having struck off five hundred, and not disposed of more than fifty in these parts. There were parcels sent to New York, Rhode Island, and Boston, and advertised there, though it seems you have not heard of it. How they sold I have not learnt, and did not remember to inquire when I was there last year. I am far from thinking it right that the loss should fall on you, who took so much pains in the composition. You gave me no other expectation than what I might gather from your saying in your letter of May 10, 1750, you believed you could dispose of one hundred copies in Connecticut, and perhaps another hundred might be disposed of at Boston. All I would request of you is, that if you think fit, you would take the trouble of writing to such of the Ministers of your Church in New England and New

York as you are acquainted with, and desire them to recommend the book to their friends; and if, with those you have had, all that shall be disposed of in those Colonies amount to two hundred, I will cheerfully take my chance with the remainder. And if you cannot procure the sale of so many, make yourself easy nevertheless; I shall be perfectly satisfied with your endeavor. With my best respects to good Mrs. Johnson and your valuable sons,

I am, dear Sir, very affectionately,

Your most humble servant,

B. FRANKLIN.

Among the friends and correspondents of Dr. Johnson, Lieutenant-governor Colden was not forgotten in the distribution of the spare copies of his "Noetica." It has been seen how these two men discussed philosophical subjects and exchanged publications, and the following letters, after glancing at the points of their disagreement, advert to matters of domestic interest, and show the concurrence of their ideas upon the subject of education: —

December 20, 1752.

SIR, — I sometime since received your book which Mr. Nicholls told me you was pleased to send me. Since that time my thoughts happened by several incidents to be so much engaged that I could not write to you in the manner I inclined to do, and they continued so when I sent you the "Principles of Action in Matter," about ten days or a fortnight since. I had at that time just received three copies of it from England, and had only time to run it cursorily over to correct the most obvious errors in the press, which happen to be numerous. I know we (you and I) differ in the fundamentals of that Essay, and for that reason I expect from you the strongest arguments that can be brought against it, and therefore, if I am under an error, you are the most capable to set me right, and I assure you that I have that esteem of your judgment that I unwillingly differ from you. Pray then, Sir, let me have your objections to those principles with that freedom that ought always to subsist in philosophical inquiries.

In the sixth page of your "Noetica," you say our perceptions cannot be produced in our minds *without a cause* (so far we agree); or, which is the same thing, by any *imagined, unintelligent, inert, or unactive cause.* I likewise agree that an unactive cause and no cause are synonymous; but I am not convinced that intelligence is an essential concomitant to all action, for then I could not conceive the action of a mill without supposing it endowed with intelligence. You seem likewise to think that the words *inert* and *unactive* are synonymous. Sir Isaac Newton was certainly of a different opinion, as appears by the third definition in the beginning of his "Principia," viz.: Materiæ vis inerta est Potentia resistendi, etc. We certainly can have no conception of Force or Power devoid of all kind of action. Now, Sir, these are fundamental differences. One of us must be under a very great mistake, and if you incline to write with the same freedom that I incline to think on these subjects, I hope we shall not continue long of a different opinion. Inert in common discourse is often synonymous with unactive, but I take it in the sense that philosophers of late use the word Inertia when they say *vis inertiæ*, which certainly cannot mean mere inaction. I shall say nothing more on these matters of speculation, that I may pass to a subject of more immediate concern.

It gave me a great deal of pleasure when Mr. De Lancey resolved to send his children to you for their education in learning, as I am confident they will thereby imbibe principles which will be of the greatest use to themselves and to their neighbors in whatever course of life they shall afterwards take to. I am under little concern as to their learning languages, or as to their skill in what may be called the learned sciences, but I am earnestly desirous that they have the true principles of good manners early implanted in their minds; to have their affections always moved by universal benevolence, and to have a true sense of honor wherein it really consists. It is from you that I hope they will receive these great advantages, of which they will find the benefits in every station of life and in all emergencies or turns of fortune. These I beg you will again and again explain to them and never cease to inculcate upon their minds. As it is not determined what course of life any of them shall pursue, it may be best to instruct them in such parts of learning as will be of use in every station. I think knowledge in geography as useful as any other part for these purposes, especially the modern geography with an account of the present state of the kingdoms and republics in Europe and of the great monarchies in other parts of the world. Peter, in a letter he wrote to me from West Chester, tells me that he inclines to study Divinity and to fit himself for that study with you. I shall be far from diverting these thoughts, because he may be as useful in that way as in any, and the more so that few of any distinguished families in America apply themselves to the Church. His applying to it may (if others follow his example) prevent a contempt of the character which otherwise may in time be produced. For this reason I do not doubt but the bishops in England will think it for the interest of the Church to encourage any young gentlemen in America who shall turn their thoughts that way from worthy principles.

I had thoughts of writing to my grandchildren,[1] but I have said all to you that I had in my thoughts to write to them, and therefore if you think proper you may communicate it to them and remember me affectionately to them and tell them that we are all in health. I hope to hear often from you. Mr. Nicholls will take care of your letters.

I am affectionately, Sir,

Your most humble servant,

CADWALLADER COLDEN.

[1] Elizabeth Colden, daughter of the Lieutenant-governor, married Peter De Lancey, and was the mother of eleven children, six sons and five daughters. Peter, one of

January 29, 1753.

The river being full of ice has deprived me of any opportunity of sending this letter till now. We continue in health. Remember us again to the children. Their grand-mamma, uncles and aunts all join with me.

Yours, C. C.

Answer: —

February 19.

SIR, — I sent you that Book without any imagination of its being worthy your perusal. I only meant it as a testimony of my humble respect and gratitude, though not without my wishes that so far as you should condescend [to] cast your eye upon it, if you see anything that might much tend to mislead youth in the entrance of their studies, for whose use it was written, you would be so good as to intimate it to me. I now return you my humble thanks for your very ingenious performance and this kind letter upon it. I have perused it with some care, though I have not yet had it long enough to spend so much thought upon it as I intend. I am glad to see the whole of it published, and doubt not but it will be an acceptable present to the public, and must own that now I see the whole of it together, it appears to me in a much more advantageous light than that piece of it did before, and do not think we differ so much in the principles you set out with as you seem to imagine. I do not differ with you at all, considered as a natural philosopher, which is the light in which you are principally to be considered in that Treatise. For it is evident there are those three distinct principles of action in nature you go upon, — media or endings of action I should call them as a metaphysician, referring the same origin of them to the one great principle of natural discovery and action; but which you as a natural philosopher, — as such going no higher, — do very well to

the sons, did not fulfill the promise of his boyhood in regard to the Church, — having been killed in a duel at a comparatively early age; but a grand-nephew of his father, Wm. Heathcote De Lancey, was consecrated the first Bishop of Western New York, May 9, 1839, and died April 5, 1865. — *MS. Letter D. Colden Murray*, Dec. 10, 1872.

consider as distinct principles. The principle of resistance of motion and of elasticity — and the contemporative (if I may so speak) of those principles in their various exertions and operations you seem to have happily demonstrated — will well account for the phenomena, and as to what is metaphysical in your Treatise, I think you have explained yourself to my satisfaction in your chapter of the Intelligent Being, § 10 — where you allow the Intelligent Being to be the real author of all material (I should call them sensible) beings, and to govern or direct their actions in such a manner as is most conducive to the advantage of the whole, which you rightly deduce from the power of our minds over the ether in the nerves which we observe to quiesce till put in action by our hands. The reasons indeed we know not, but it is the fact.

So that I believe what we seem to differ in, if at all, will amount to little more than words. I agree with you in saying "we can certainly have no conception of Force or Power devoid of all kind of action," and when I do so, it seems to me that you must with me allow that Sir Isaac's *vis inertiæ* is a contradiction in terms, and that that great man, in that definition and the explication of it, has some expressions that have no meaning; for I must think it is plain that by Inertia (as in Ovid, *pondus iners*) the old Romans meant an utter destitution of any principle of activity *in se*, or power of self-exertion or action, terminating on anything without, and I don't see what right he had to use or define it in a quite contrary sense; at best his expressions are figurative.

As to that question whether the same Being that is the principle of action must as such be also a principle of Intelligence, I have nothing to say for it more than I said in a former letter, that it seems to follow from that principle "Non est philosophia extera multiplicare sine necessitate," and that a blind principle or power of action without Intelligence seems repugnant and useless. However it seems a question of little real consequence, or indeed of scarce any meaning after what you allow in the chapter of the Intelligent Being; the action of what you call matter being according to you derived originally from and directed by the Intelligent Being. And so matter is no more than merely His instrument, so that what you call the action of a mill or watch is really only a successive series of passions till you come to the principle of Intelligence, which will ultimately prove to be also the principle of the action.

That expression of yours, page 164, "That perfect Intelligence will not act in contradiction to the action of matter," I should have chosen to express thus: Will not in the settled course of things act in contradiction to the Laws He hath established according to which He wills matter to act. For I cannot conceive you to imagine the action of matter to be independent of the Divine will. I rather imagine from other passages that you do with me conceive it to be entirely dependent, as well as matter itself, on the constant free exertion of the Divine will and power.

I don't deny, Sir, but that I am yet a little in the dark about the operations of that elastic fluid by which you account for gravitation. I should scarce ever say that there should be a perpetual return of the ethereal fluid to the sun as well as a perpetual flow from it, agreeable to Mr. Hutchinson's notion, who imagines a perpetual circulation of it from the sun, and after a kind of condensation of it at the utmost bounds of the system, a reverberation and return of it to the sun again; so that according to that great man the effects of gravitation, circular motion, and rotation, will be the result of the struggle between those contrary tendencies. This being supposed, you and he seem well to coincide. I wish you had opportunity, if you have not had, to read his system with some attention and exactness, if not in his works, which are something tedious, at least in that beautiful short sketch of them set forth by your excellently great and good countryman, Lord President Forbes, in his "Letter to a Bishop and Thoughts on Religion." But what you call the different principles of Light and Ether, he supposes to be the one ethereal fluid or fire of the sun in the different conditions of Light and Spirit as it flies from or returns to its fountain. Perhaps your notion and his may come nearly to the same thing. The Abbe Pluche of France, as well as he and Bp. Berkeley, agree that this ethereal fire is the light and life of the whole sensible world, and grand agent in all nature, or the immediate engine from whence all the phenomena mechanically derive: and that this was the original philosophy of Moses and in all the Hebrew Scriptures, and taught mankind from the beginning. And I am pleased in thinking that your demonstrations and Mr. Franklin's experiments illustrate and confirm it to be the only true and genuine philosophy. Pardon, Sir, my incoherent and rambling way of writing. I hope you may pick out my meaning. I would transcribe, but my care of your grandchildren and other duties will not admit of time for it.

As to your grandchildren, I have the same notion of education with you (my plan you may see in my 6th chapter), and do not fail, as you desire, to inculcate those principles you mention as far as I am able. And besides the moral and classical part (in which they have almost finished "Cornelius Nepos" and two thirds of "Justin"), I have gone over and explained a short History of England and a short Geography you gave them, and am now going over a short system of Universal History and Chronology, and point out to them in maps the Ancient Geography of the Classics as well as the modern. But they have (the eldest especially) such a violent impetuosity to their play that I find it exceeding difficult to gain so strong an attention as I could wish to their books and studies. They seem well cut out for business, as farming and merchandise, but Peter has an excellent turn for learning, and it is a pity but he should go through an entire course of education. As to what he wrote to you, I am exceeding glad his dispositions are such and that you approve of them, and agree with you and thank you for your remark of the vast importance to religion and the public weal that any of distinguished families should apply themselves to Divinity. Mrs. De Lancey first mentioned it to me, and I ventured to encourage it, and shall henceforward encourage myself to hope that your daughter has borne, and that I am educating one who, in God's time, may become a bishop in America. I communicated your letter to them and inculcated it. They send their humblest thanks and duty to you and their grandmamma and uncles and aunts. They have had an uninterrupted course of perfect health.

I cannot take leave without giving you my humble thanks for the favor you have done me in the good character you gave of me in your account of Pokeweed, etc., which was published in the "Gentleman's Magazine," and wish I may deserve it. I have since heard of several others of the eating cancers cured by it, but a man in this town has a strange sore on his legs they call a heaving or gnawing cancer, on which it was tried without success; and both cutting, burning, and several caustics have since been tried, which have only made it grow the faster, and it is now larger than the hand can cover, and is like to cost the poor man his life.

I am, Sir, your most obliged humble servant,

S. J.

CHAPTER VIII.

PROPOSED COLLEGE AT NEW YORK; JOHNSON INVITED TO THE PRESIDENCY; OBSTACLES TO A CHARTER, AND FINALLY GRANTED; LETTERS TO PRESIDENT CLAP; REMOVAL TO NEW YORK AND LECTURER IN TRINITY CHURCH; HIS YOUNGER SON CHOSEN TUTOR IN KING'S COLLEGE; GOES TO ENGLAND FOR ORDINATION AND DIES THERE OF THE SMALL-POX.

A. D. 1754–1756.

THE proposition to establish a College in New York was pursued with more vigor after the settlement of the Institution at Philadelphia. A few gentlemen, chiefly members of the Church of England, were leading spirits in the movement, and guided it so as to secure the erection of the College on the broad grounds of Christian liberality. It appears to have been the intention in the original endowment of Trinity Church, in the city of New York, to connect the promotion of learning with the interests of religion, and a lot of land in a favorable locality belonging to the Vestry was given for the use of the proposed College, upon condition, that the President thereof for the time being should be in communion with the Church of England, and that the morning and evening service in the College should be the Liturgy of the Church, or such a collection of prayers out of the Liturgy as should be "agreed upon by the President or Trustees or Governors of the said College." This gift was accepted by the Commissioners empowered to receive proposals for the Trustees.

The Trustees, who had been appointed by an act of the Colonial Legislature, consisted of "the eldest Councilor of the Province, the Speaker of the Assembly, the Judges of the Supreme Court, the Mayor of the city of New York," *ex officio* (Churchmen), and one more Churchman, together with the Treasurer of the Colony, and a "member of the Dutch Church, and one of the Presbyterian congregation." [1] The same act which fixed the appointment of Trustees, vested in them the sum of "three thousand four hundred and forty-three pounds, eighteen shillings, *raised by way of Lottery for erecting a College within the Colony;*" and by a supplementary act passed on the 4th of July, 1753, the Treasurer of the Colony for the time being was enabled and directed to pay unto the Trustees out of "the moneys arising from the duty of excise, the annual sum of five hundred pounds, for and during the term of seven years, to commence from and after the first day of January next ensuing;" this annuity to be distributed by them in salaries to the officers of instruction.

In pursuance of other powers granted by this act, the Trustees invited Dr. Johnson, who from its inception had been consulted about perfecting the scheme and carrying it into execution, to become the President, and to remove to New York and enter upon his duties without delay. The position was congenial to his tastes, for he loved learning and colleges; but there were two great obstacles in the way of his acceptance. One was he had not had the small-pox, and in New York he would be much more exposed

[1] See a *Brief Vindication of the Proceedings of the Trustees, etc., by an Impartial Hand*, p. 4.

to it than in Stratford; and the other, which was perhaps the greater, was the consideration of his advanced years. He was almost three-score, and on this account was less inclined to sunder the happy pastoral relations which had subsisted between him and his people for the best part of his life. And then the social refinement, the bustle and stir, and demands upon his time in a city did not contrast pleasantly in his mind with the studious retirement and quiet repose of a rural parsonage. But his friends in New York and the principal managers of the enterprise assured him they would abandon it, and it would come to nothing if he declined the invitation. He finally consented to make a trial, but would not absolutely accept the office till the charter should be obtained, and he could see what sort of an institution he was to preside over. With this view he left Stratford on the 15th of April, 1754, but neither removed his family nor resigned his parish. The Vestry of Trinity Church unanimously chose him an Assistant Minister and voted him the sum of one hundred and fifty pounds per annum; but he replied, "My advanced years, verging towards the decline of life, are great matters of discouragement to me, and render me extremely fearful whether I shall be able to answer your expectations." [1]

The design of the College underwent a violent struggle before Dr. Johnson arrived in New York. It was intended to be a common blessing to all denominations, with no other preference for the Church than that one of her communicants should be at the head; "but Mr. W. Livingston, a virulent Presby-

[1] Berrian's *Hist. Trinity Church*, p. 106.

terian, joined with other leading Presbyterians and Free-thinkers, violently opposed it, and raised a hideous clamor against it, and printed a paper of Twenty Reasons to disaffect the Assembly against granting the money raised by lotteries."[1] This paper was styled a Protest, and much was written and published in reply. Johnson himself dipped into the controversy, and even asked his elder son, who was then rising into eminence in the legal profession, to try his hand in an argument to demolish the Twenty Reasons and vindicate the proceedings of the Trustees. The opinion which he returned to his father should not be omitted from these pages: —

I must add a word to what you say of an answer to the Protest. You know I am generally averse to disputes of this kind, as tending more to irritate the passions than to convince the understandings of the people. What is wrote in this way, is most generally read only by those persons who are before prepossessed on one side or other of the question. But especially averse am I towards engaging myself in any controversial writings, as knowing myself to want both ability and leisure to perform anything as it should be. I never yet wrote anything but I was both sick and ashamed of it before it was half done. In regard to the present case, Mr. Wetmore on conference agrees with me that it is not, as we can see, worth while to write or publish any answer, most of what is here said having been already thrown out in the "Reflector," or consisting of such far fetched reasons and strained constructions of the act of Assembly and purport of the petition and charter, that they demonstrate the gentleman to be determined to oppose and find fault with everything that does not coincide exactly with his favorite scheme of absolute independency both in religion and government. And when men are resolved to wrangle and find

[1] *MS. Autobiography.*

fault, what end is there in answering them? But especially I imagine that of all persons, you nor I nor any of the family should be in the least concerned in any disputes with respect to the College. For those in the opposition to have it in their power once to suggest that you are at the head of a party, or promoting any particular scheme, must be highly prejudicial, and will give them great strength in their endeavors to bias the Assembly. A very small matter in this way may be magnified and improved to the most pernicious purposes. Let us by all means at present stand perfectly neuter. If they, whose business it is, form a college whose model you approve, you can in this case accept the Presidentship with cheerfulness. If they do not, you can retreat with honor. Should I write anything, it would certainly be discovered by them, and must in these circumstances do vastly more hurt than in any case it would possibly do good. This I humbly suggest as my opinion in the matter. However, if an answer be finally thought necessary, Mr. Wetmore will doubtless be ready to write, and I have suggested to him, what has occurred to me in reading of it. The Protest I think goes upon a wrong supposition, namely, that the charter petitioned for is to establish a college without the approbation and almost independent of the Assembly or Legislature, to the support of which nevertheless the moneys granted by the two acts of Assembly are to be applied, contrary to the intentions and design of the Assembly in making the grant, which I take it is by no means aimed at by anybody, nor indeed I conceive can possibly be. The question I think truly is whether it be advisable for the Trustees to recommend or the Legislature to accept the generous offer of Trinity Church on the condition they give, or not. In this light nothing I think in the Protest can have any great weight. It would be plainly unreasonable for the Church to make the offer without the condition annexed. And TWENTY reasons, I think, might be given why it would be advisable for the Legislature to accept it on those terms. What is said about the establishment of the Church of England, and several other things which are hinted at, are manifestly designed to raise a clamor and excite jealousies, as they have not even the remote resemblance of a reason *pro* or *con.* on any just or reasonable state of the question. However, let us by all means let them entirely alone. Let those whose proper business it is exert themselves. 'Tis enough for us to say, ... God speed ye. I know you will excuse my freedom, and am, honored Sir,

Your obedient son and servt,

WM. SAML. JOHNSON.

June 13th, 1754.

In writing to him, June 17, 1754, the father said: "I very much commend your prudence; but even caution, one of the best things in the world, may be carried too far as well as humility itself. We must have resolution to do good in spite of opposition, as well as discretion to direct it to the best purposes. As to the Protest, I hope there will be no occasion for you or me to answer it." He may have known at this time what was already contemplated, if not begun; for "A Brief Vindication of the Proceedings of the Trustees relating to the College, containing a sufficient Answer to the late famous Protest, with its Twenty unanswerable Reasons," was written "by an Impartial Hand,"— this hand representing Mr. Benjamin Nicoll, a son of Dr. Johnson's wife by her first husband. He was a lawyer of distinction in New York, one of the governors of the College, and "the life and soul of the whole affair." While the contest was going on, Dr. Johnson published his plan of education, and appointed a day for examining and admitting candidates. He commenced with a class of ten students, including two from other colleges, who met him for the first time on the 17th of July in the vestry-room of the school-house belonging to the Corporation of Trinity Church. He continued his instructions without intermission till September 1st, when he was summoned to the sick-bed of his elder son, whom he had little expectation of finding alive, but who, after remaining a long time in a critical state, finally recovered. During his absence, which continued till November 10, the Royal Charter passed the seals, incorporating the Governors of King's College in New York; and thus what had been the subject of such violent opposition became a fixed provision of law. The time had now come for him to make a decision whether he would remain in Stratford or go to New York. The services of his Church had been conducted in his absence by his younger son, who was preparing for Holy Orders, and with the aid of the neighboring clergy he had managed to keep the people from much uneasiness during the protracted struggle for settling the question about a charter for the College. The following letter from the Rector of Trinity Church sums up the final contest, and puts before him the responsibility of resigning his pastoral charge, and entering upon the full duties of the Presidency: —

DEAR SIR, — Mr. Nicoll being obliged to go out of town, communicated your letter to me in order that I might answer it. On Thursday last the Charter passed the Governor and Council, and was ordered to be forthwith engrossed. On Friday, the Trustees appointed by act of Assembly, according to order of the House, delivered in a report of their proceedings conformable to the act, which report was signed by all but William Livingston, who objected to the report as not being complete, because no notice was taken of the proceedings with regard to the Charter, which the Governor and the rest of the gentlemen thought unnecessary. Whereupon Livingston delivered in a separate report in full, containing his famous Protest, etc. This occasioned a great ferment in the House, and issued for that day in a resolve that Livingston's Report should be printed at large, and the affair postponed to farther consideration on Wednesday next. They had a majority of fourteen to eight, but three of our friends were absent, and it was with much difficulty that they were prevented from censuring the conduct of the Trustees and returning thanks to Livingston. We were all afraid that this would have retarded the Sealing of the Charter, and some well-wishers to the thing would have consented to the retarding of it, had not the Governor appeared resolute and come to town on Saturday and fixed the Seal to it; and to do him justice, he has given us a good majority of Churchmen, no less than eleven of the Vestry being of the number. There are but eight of the Dutch Church, most of them good men and true, and two Dissenters. We are, however, puzzled what to advise you as to resigning your mission. I have been with Mr. Chambers this morning, and though it be the opinion of most of the gentlemen that you ought to resign and trust to Providence for the issue of things and come away immediately, yet we would rather choose if possible, that you should put off the resignation for a fortnight or three weeks, and come down immediately, because some are not so clear with regard to the £500 support, though others think we cannot be deprived of it. But since this conversation with Mr. Chambers we have had some glimmering light. I went from Mr. Chambers' to Mr. Watts' (who is unhappily confined with the rheumatism), and met two Dutch members coming out of his house, who, as he told me, came to make proposals for an accommodation, and all they desired was a Dutch Professor of Divinity, which, if granted, they would all join us, and give the money. This I doubt not will be done unless the Governor should oppose it, who is much incensed at the Dutch for petitioning the

Assembly on that head, but I make no doubt but he may be pacified.

Upon the whole, it is the opinion of all that you must come down as soon as possible, and the advice of Mr. Chambers and myself, in which I believe Benny concurs, that you defer the resignation of your mission a little longer, as it will be a means of getting a good subscription for your support in case this accommodation with the Assembly should fail, which, however, I am inclined to think will not fail. In a word, it seems you have put your hand to the plow, and I know not how you can now look back. Providence, I trust, is still on our side, and everybody is solicitous for your return.

I am, dear Sir, in the greatest hurry,
Yours, etc.
HEN. BARCLAY.

I have not time to give you a list of the Governors, nor indeed can I recollect them all. The whole number is forty-one: seventeen *ex-officio* and twenty-four private gentlemen, in which number there are at present but eight of the Dutch Church, the French, Lutheran, Presbyterian Ministers, and Will. Livingston, — so that we have a majority of twenty-nine to twelve, and in these twelve are included Mr. Richards, John Cruger, Leonard Lispenard, and the Treasurer, all our good friends.

MONDAY, 10 *o'clock, Nov.* 4, 1754.

Dr. Johnson returned to New York to find the controversy about the College not yet closed. The opposition set their pens running to prevent the Assembly from granting any more favors; but he did not heed them, and sent for some of his furniture and books, and wrote to his son Wm. Samuel, December 2, to say: "It is not doubted but the next session will give us the money to build. Meantime it is resolved to have a subscription to begin with, and doubtless money enough will be got twice told to build a President's house, which will begin early in the spring. And as to my security, the Trustees resolve to meet this week and confirm what they did before, nothing doubting but the £500 per annum is in their power, and unalterably at their disposal for my support." By the advice of his friends, he was to lodge during the winter with his son, Mr. Benjamin Nicoll, with whom he appears to have previously made his home; and the Vestry of Trinity Church voted to pay him the salary as usual, and "in consideration of his advanced years and the duties of the College," to require of him "only to read prayers on Sunday, and to preach one Sunday in a month at church and chapel," or as might be agreed upon by the Rector and occasion might demand.

His endeavors met with much embarrassment, and "nothing," he wrote again to his son after the Holidays, "I assure you could have induced me to endure it, but the hopes of rendering the little remainder of my life more useful to mankind, and especially in laying a foundation for sound learning and true religion in the rising and future generations." He worked vigorously on to bring things into shape and order, drew from the Liturgy a form for the daily prayers, composed the Collect for the College, and had them printed with the Psalter. It added to his anxiety that his flock in Stratford was without a shepherd. Both his sons acted as lay-readers, — the elder taking his place after the younger had joined the father in New York to pursue his theological studies. Mr. Beach of Newtown had been thought of for his successor, and all would have welcomed him to the post, but he could not conscientiously leave his own church vacant. In a letter to his son Wm. Samuel, January 20, 1755, Johnson said: "The melancholy condition of my poor destitute people is very affecting to me. I talked with Ogilvie and Chandler to no purpose; nor do I think there is the least probability that Mr. Brown, or Mr. Seabury, Jun., would entertain the least thoughts of a removal, and since there is no hope of Stiles,[1] I am sorry he should have had it in his power to make a merit of his refusal. I am very sorry Mr. Beach cannot be prevailed upon to remove; and what course you can now take, I cannot conceive. Methinks I should be for trying Mr. Leaming, with the utmost endeavor to get him for Stratford or Newtown. I confess from his talk to me, there seems little hope, yet it seems to me worth while to try. Who knows what may be done? Can there be no thoughts of Sam. Brown for Newtown? or is there no young man that would go for so valuable a parish? It is certainly much preferable to anything the Dissenters can give. There was some talk once of one Street, of Wallingford. What has come of him?"

The establishment of a separate religious society and church in Yale College, at first unacceptable to many of the Congregationalists, and the adoption about this time of regulations which infringed upon the rights of Episcopal students, gave importance to the position of Dr. Johnson as the head of King's College. It was the fault of the times to take a narrow view of Christian liberty; but after a parish had been formed, a church built, and a Missionary of the

[1] Ezra Stiles, afterwards President of Yale College.

Society for the Propagation of the Gospel stationed in New Haven, it was expected and claimed that Episcopal students should be allowed to prefer their own mode of worship on the Lord's day, and not subjected to a penalty for declining to attend those services in the College Chapel, designed to guard and perpetuate the Puritan faith. The two sons of the Missionary (Punderson) were not exempted from the rigor of the offensive statute. The separation and withdrawal of all students from the First Ecclesiastical Society, where with the officers of the College they had been hitherto accustomed and required to worship, and limiting them to the chapel, involved questions of internal orthodoxy; and the long and fierce contention which sprung up and affected to some extent the whole colony, was entirely outside the rights of Episcopalians, and only concerned them so far that it made them more desirous to keep their sons as much as possible under the teaching of the Church.

President Clap defended the law in its full operation, and undertook to show that it was "inconsistent with the original design of the founders," to grant special favors to Episcopal students. Johnson, who for many years had been on the most friendly terms with him, replied warmly to his statements, and insisted that the chief benefactors of the College and the proportionate share of Churchmen in its yearly support contemplated a common benefit, and forbid the supposition that the children of Episcopal parents should ever be required to "go out of their own houses to meeting, when there was a church at their doors." The following letter is an earnest vindication of his views: —

STRATFORD, *February* 5, 1754.

REV. AND DEAR SIR, — Tho' I am but in a poor condition for writing, I can't forbear a few lines in answer to yours of January 30th.

I thank you for your kind congratulation on my being chosen President of their intended College at New York, and I shall desire by all means, if I undertake it, to hold a good correspondence not only as Colleges but as Christians, supposing you and the Fellows of your College act on the same equitable, catholic, and Christian principles as we unanimously propose to act upon, *i. e.*, to admit that the children of the Church may go to church whenever they have opportunity, as we think of nothing but to admit that the children of dissenting parents have leave to go to their meetings; nor can I see anything like an argument in all you have said to justify the forbidding it. And I am prodigiously mistaken if you did not tell me it was an allowed and settled rule with you heretofore.

The only point in question, as I humbly conceive, is, *whether there ought of right to be any such law in your College as, either in words or by necessary consequence, forbids the liberty we contend for!* What we must beg leave to insist on is, *That there ought not; and that it is highly injurious to forbid it;* unless you can make it appear *That you ever had a right to exclude the people of the Church belonging to this Colony, from having the benefit of Public education in your College, without their submitting to the hard condition of not being allowed to do what they believe in their conscience it is their indispensable duty to do, i. e., to require their children to go to church whenever they have opportunity, and at the same time a right to accept and hold such vast benefactions from gentlemen of the Church of England, wherewith to support you in maintaining such a law in exclusion of such a liberty.* Can you think those gentlemen would ever have given such benefactions to such a purpose! And ought it not to be considered at the same time, that the parents of these children contribute also their proportion every year to the support of the College?

Your argument in a former letter was, That it is inconsistent with the original design of the founders, which was only to provide ministers for your churches. But pray, Sir, why may not our Church also be provided for with ministers from one common College as well as your churches? And ought not the catholic design of the principal benefactors also in strict justice to be regarded, who, in the sense of the English law, are to be reckoned among the founders? See *Viner*, on the Title FOUNDERS. What *Mr. Yale's* views[1] were, I had not opportunity of knowing, though, doubtless, they were the same that we suppose. But I was knowing to Bp. Berkeley's, which were, that his great Donation should be equally for a common benefit, without respect to parties. For I was myself the principal, I may say in effect the only person in procuring that Donation, and with those generous, catholic, and charitable views; though you (not willing, it seems, that Posterity should ever know this) did not think fit to do me the justice in the History of the College (though humbly suggested), as to give me the credit of any, the least influence on him in that affair; when the truth is, had it not been for my influence it would never have been done, to which I was prompted by the sincere desire that it should be for a common benefit, when I could have easily procured it appropriated to the Church. But at that time *Mr. Williams* also pretended a mighty catholic charitable conviction that there never was any meaning in

[1] Jeremiah Dummer, agent of the Colony of Connecticut, writing to Gov. Saltonstall, from "Middle Temple [London], 14th April, 1719," says: "I heartily congratulate you upon the happy union of the Colony, in fixing the Colledge at New Haven, after some differences which might have been attended with ill consequences. Mr. Yale is very much rejoyc'd at this good news, and more than a little pleas'd with his being the Patron of such a seat of the Muses. Saving that he express't at first some kind of concern, whether it was well in him, being a Churchman, to promote an Academy of Dissenters. But when we had discours't that point freely, he appear'd convinc't that the business of good men is to spread religion and learning among mankind without being too fondly attach't to particular Tenets, about which the world never was, nor never will be, agreed. Besides, if the Discipline of the Church of England be most agreeable to Scripture and primitive practice, there's no better way to make men sensible of it than by giving them good learning." — State Library, Hartford. *Extract from Document* 110 *of vol. ii.* "*Foreign Correspondence with Colonial Agents*, 1661–1732."

it; it being at the very same juncture that he, with the Hampshire ministers, his father at the head of them, were, in their great charity, contriving a letter to the *Bishop of London* by means of which they hoped to deprive all the Church people in these parts of their ministers, and them of their support; the same charitable aim that *Mr. Hobart*[1] and his friends are pursuing at this day! And now you, Gentlemen, are so severe as to establish a law to deprive us of the benefit of a public education for our children too, unless we will let them, nay require them, to go out of our own houses to meeting, when there is a church at our doors.

Indeed, Sir, I must say this appears to me so very injurious, that I must think it my duty, in obedience to a rule of the Society, to join with my Brethren in complaining of it to our superiors at home, if it be insisted upon, — which is what I abhor and dread to be brought to; and, therefore, by the love of our dear country (in which we desire to live, only upon a par with you, in all Christian charity), I do beseech you, Gentlemen, not to insist upon it. Tell it not in *Gath!* much less in the ears of our dear mother-country, that any of her daughters should deny any of her children leave to attend on her worship whenever they have opportunity for it. Surely you cannot pretend that you are conscience-bound to make such a law, or that it would be an *infraction of liberty of conscience* for it to be repealed from home, as you intimate. This would be carrying matters far indeed. But for God's sake do not be so severe to think in this manner, or to carry things to this pass! If so, let Dissenters never more complain of their heretofore persecutions or hardships in England, unless they have us tempted to think it their principle, that *they* only ought to be tolerated, in order at length to be established, that they may have the sole privilege of persecuting others. But I beg pardon and forbear; only I desire it may be considered, how ill such a principle would sound at this time of day, when the univer-

[1] Noah Hobart, a Congregational minister at Fairfield, who published two *Addresses to Members of the Episcopal Separation in New England.* He died 1773.

sal Church of England as much abhors the persecution of Dissenters as they can themselves. It may also deserve to be considered that the Government at home would probably be so far from going into the formality of *repealing* this law that they would declare it a nullity in itself; and not only so, but even the corporation that hath enacted it; inasmuch as it seems a principle in law *that a corporation cannot make a corporation*, nor can one be made without his Majesty's act. See *Viner*, under the titles, CORPORATION and BY-LAWS.

You mistake me, Sir. I did not say that Professors of Divinity do not preach. I knew they and the Heads, etc., do preach in their turns at the common church, to which all resort to sermon. But what I say is, that they do not preach as Professors, nor do they ever preach in private Colleges, there being no such thing as preaching in the College chapels, but only at *St. Mary's* and *Christ Church*, which are in effect cathedrals, where the scholars resort, but not exclusive of the town's people, tho' they generally go to their parish churches.

I wonder how you came to apprehend I had any scruples about the divinity of Christ. I am with you, glad we agree so far; and I would desire you to understand, that my zeal for that sacred *Depositum*, the Christian faith, founded on those principles, — a coessential, coeternal Trinity, and the Divinity, incarnation, and satisfaction of Christ,— is the very and sole reason of my zeal for the Church of England, and that she may be promoted, supported, and well treated in these countries; as I have been long persuaded that she is, and will eventually be found, the only stable bulwark against all heresy and infidelity which are coming in like a flood upon us, and this, as I apprehend, by reason of the rigid Calvinism, Antinomianism, enthusiasm, divisions, and separations, which, through the weakness and great imperfection of your constitution (if it may so be called), are so rife and rampant among us. My apprehension of this was the first occasion of my conforming to the Church (which has been to my great comfort and satisfaction), and hath been more and more confirmed by what has occurred ever since. And I am still apt to think that no well-meaning *Dove* that has proper means and opportunity of exact consideration, will ever find rest to the sole of his foot amid such a deluge, till he comes into the Church as the alone *ark* of safety, — all whose Articles, Liturgy, and Homilies taken together and explained by one another, and by the writings of our first Reformers, according to their original sense, shall ever be sacred with me; which sense, as I appehend it, is neither Calvinistical nor Arminian, but the golden mean, and according to the genuine meaning of the Holy Scriptures in the original, critically considered and understood. I beg pardon for this length, which I did not design at first, and desire you will also excuse my haste, inaccuracy, and this writing *currente calamo*, and conclude with earnestly begging that neither your insisting on this law nor anything else, may occur to destroy or interrupt our harmony and friendship, with which, on my part I desire ever to remain, dear Sir,

Your real friend and humble servant,

S. JOHNSON.

P. S. — I wish you to communicate it to the Fellows.

Another letter from President Clap received his attention when he was on the eve of departing for New York. The issue was made in the case of the sons of the Missionary, and here the first relaxation of the law began. For Dr. Johnson's son William wrote him from Stratford a few months later: "I don't hear any talk of printing against the President; am told he has given up the point with Mr. Punderson's sons." He could not well do otherwise after the following letter, dated: —

STRATFORD, *February* 19, 1754.

DEAR SIR, — My unsettled condition in view of my removing to New York, must be my apology for not being more particular in answer to yours of the 10th.

If there was not good reason offered to support my *warmth* you might justly fault it, but I must think it was supported with abundant reasons which you have nothing like answered. I am sure the Dissenters in England had never half so much reason to excuse their many pathetic declamations. You would have us, it seems, be deprived of our birthright as Englishmen, and at the same time be perfectly calm and easy under it. Truly, Sir, I must think it sufficient to raise our passions to be denied a public education for our children, unless we will in direct violation of our consciences enjoin them to go to dissenting meeting when we have a church at our doors.

I have always been very tender of the charter privileges of this Government, and ever advised our Church people to be easy, and do all they could to promote the public peace and weal as things stand; but by your proceedings you seem resolved to provoke us to be enemies to the Government, when we are content to be only upon a par with our neighbors, and to live in entire love and peace with them in a cheerful submission to the Government. I am surprised at your *Politics* in this way of proceeding with us, supposing the *injustice and uncharitableness* of it were out of the question. However, since you are resolved (being, as you say, *in possession*) to go on in your own way, you must even proceed; but I am very much mistaken if you do not eventually prove your own greatest enemies.

It is strange to me that merely opening a church at New Haven should be considered by any of you, gentlemen, as a justifiable provocation to interrupt the harmony that had subsisted between us, when we do not aim at disturbing you, but only at judging and acting for ourselves. Indeed I own I have never been very zealous and active in the affair, but rather hung back, as I apprehended danger of some gentlemen's making disturbance on such an occasion; but I do not remember that I told you I was with you — of the mind it would not be for the public good to have a church there, as you state it. However, when I saw what loose principles were obtaining among you and the confused state you were in, I thought it might be much conducive to the public good to have a church there, especially after such a virulent and abusive spirit as Mr. Hobart thought fit to raise against the Church, to whose pious labors I suppose it was chiefly owing that the Society fixed a mission and Mr. Punderson there.

If there had been such a general law before, as you say, yet this I very well remember, that you told me you had made certain Rules under the name of *Customs*, which I understood to be written and agreed to by the Fellows; one of which was that the children of the Church, their parents so desiring, should have free liberty to go to church whenever they had opportunity, or to this effect.

I may be, perhaps, mistaken in saying there is *never* preaching in any of the College chapels. There may be those two or three exceptions you mention; my copy of the Oxford Laws was and is at New York; so that I could not turn to those paragraphs you cited; but surely you cannot think them anything to your purpose of holding constant meeting only in your Hall,[1] and requiring the Church children to attend them when they have a church to go to, and their parents order their attendance there!

If, indeed, you are an independent Society or Government, or the Charter had given you such unlimited and uncontrollable powers, I own there would have been something plausible in your reasoning; but then it would equally conclude against any toleration of the Dissenters in England, and consequently must *now* be interpreted to be contrary to law, and as far as in you lies to aim at a subversion of the present English Constitution.

I much wonder you cannot understand my stating of the case. I cannot conceive of any words that could make it more intelligible. If, indeed, with *Hobbes*, etc., you thought *power* to do anything would give a *right* to it, then your argument from *possession* is just; but I trust that is not your

[1] Public worship was established in the College Hall preparatory to the erection of a chapel.

tenet. The question then is, 1st. Whether it be right in itself for any Society, however voluntary or independent, to *require as a condition of enjoying the privileges of it (and especially so great a privilege as that of a public education), that any person that is free of that Society, or born in it, should be obliged to act contrary to his conscience, or to what he is really persuaded is his duty in matters of religion, supposing that his religious principles be not in their nature subversive of the State?* And then, 2dly. Supposing this could be resolved in the affirmative, *Whether your Charter has given this government such a right, or a right to erect any Corporation with such a right or power as to insist on such a condition; or indeed could do it consistent with the English Constitution?* I trow not. And it is plain to me, that unless you prove the affirmative of both these questions, which you don't attempt, you really do nothing to the purpose. But I humbly conceive it is most proper to have these questions canvassed before our Assembly here, before we trouble our Superior at home.

But in truth the College is ours in proportion as really as yours, and you can no more be bound to pursue the intention of the founders in your sense, exclusive of the Church, than Oxford was to continue their Colleges appropriated to the Roman Catholics, if so much; I mean in point of equity. There may be some small inconveniences in granting such a liberty, but they are not to be compared with the inconveniences which will attend denying it.

If what was mentioned was no *designed omission* in the first draught of your History, yet it seems to have been designedly persisted in after what I humbly suggested to you. Indeed, Sir, your College never had a more hearty friend, without respect to any party, than I was and desire still to continue, if we can only stand upon an equal foot, but I am really and tenderly hurt by this disputed prohibition. It is hard, very hard indeed, if in an English colony the Church must be treated upon the same foot with every idle sectary. But I am insensibly got much further than I intended.

However, if I can find leisure to answer your state of the case and reasoning upon it more particularly, which I think may be easily done, and with as much calmness as you can desire, you may expect to hear further from me. Meantime, I remain, dear Sir,

Your friend and humble servant,

S. JOHNSON.

His time and thoughts were so much absorbed in the controversy about the College in New York, that he does not appear to have answered President Clap, as he intimated. He and his friends were determined to construct it on a liberal basis; but there was as much opposition among Presbyterians to allowing Episcopalians to dominate therein, as there was among the authorities of Yale College to giving the children of the Church the privilege of worshipping on Sundays in their own sanctuary. His son William wrote him, August 2, 1754, and in the course of his letter said: "We had yesterday a visit from President Clap; I suppose on his return from advising with his brother *Hobart*. He was very inquisitive about your College, and wanted much to see your 'Oxonia Illustrata,' which I handed to him. He pored upon it a considerable time, and at length said: 'Really, I think it seems to agree very well with a pretty long History (I forget the author's name) that I have lately been reading, which I sent for from Cambridge Library.' He said not a word about the controversy, though I believe he does not intend to give it over, by his studying the History of Oxford so much."

Dr. Johnson finally resigned the Mission of Stratford,[1] which he had held thirty-two years, and settled

[1] The Rev. Edward Winslow was appointed his successor, May 2, 1755.

with his family in New York, where he devoted himself to the duties of the College at the same time that he fulfilled the office of a lecturer in Trinity Church. When he came to admit a second class, he needed some assistance, and as Mr. Whittelsey, who had previously been chosen Tutor, was prevented by the failure of his health from accepting the appointment, the Trustees gave the place to the younger son of Dr. Johnson. The internal affairs of the College were now prosperous, and liberal subscriptions and benefactions were obtained to further its interests. But the war without was unended. The Presbyterian faction went on with its clamor, and expected to find in Sir Charles Hardy, the new Governor of the Province, a sympathizing friend, and prepared an inflammatory address, against his arrival, to disaffect him towards the College. But it was received with coldness, while the address of the Governors or Trustees delivered by the President, was listened to "with the utmost complaisance;" and signifying his desire to see the subscription paper, it was taken to him the next day, when the Governor "immediately took his pen and subscribed £500. All this," says Johnson in his autobiography, "was such a mortification to the faction, that from this time forward they shut their mouths, and the College met with no more opposition. And in a little time it was agreed, for peace' sake, with the Assembly, to divide the money equally between the College and the public." This was the money raised by lottery.

His younger son had completed his theological studies, and resigning his tutorship, embarked for England for Holy Orders, Nov. 8, 1755, with a view to assist and succeed the venerable Mr. Standard at West Chester. It was a painful thing for the father to part with him. He wrote his other son shortly before the decision: "Your brother can never go with better advantage than now, so that it is doubtless best he should now go. But I tremble at the thoughts of the difficulties and dangers to which he must be exposed, and pray God I may live to see him safe returned again, and could then cheerfully sing my *nunc dimittis*."

He had already acquainted the Venerable Society with the foundation of the College and his own election to the Presidency; and Sherlock, the Bishop of London, had written him a letter of congratulation in view of the good service which this Institution might do for the Church of England in the Northern Colonies. But the Vestry of Trinity Church took occasion to write to the Rev. Dr. Bearcroft, Secretary of the Society, and appeal directly for sympathy and aid in behalf of the new enterprise. The letter thus written was intrusted to the care of Mr. George Harison, one of their number, and Mr. William Johnson, and after speaking of the opposers, it went on to say of the friends of the College: —

They have begun a subscription amongst themselves, and are daily purchasing materials to lay the foundation of a handsome, convenient edifice, which, God willing, they purpose to begin next spring; and they are induced to hope, that as the dissenting Seminary in New Jersey has had the General Assembly of the Kirk of Scotland engaged in its behalf last year, as well as the dissenting interest in England, and, as we are informed, have collected a very considerable sum of money, so our brethren in England will be ready to contribute to preserve the Church in this part of the world from the contempt its enemies are endeavoring to bring upon it.

The Dissenters have already three seminaries in the Northern Governments. They hold their synods, presbyteries, and associations, and exercise the whole of their ecclesiastical government to the no small advantage of their cause; whilst those churches which are branches of the National Establishment are deprived not only of the benefit of a regular church government, but their children are debarred the privilege of a liberal education, unless they will submit to accept of it on such conditions as Dissenters require; which, in Yale College, is to submit to a fine as often as they attend public worship in the Church of England, communicants only excepted, and that only on Christmas and sacrament days. This we cannot but look upon as hard measure, especially as we can with good conscience declare that we are so far from that bigotry and narrowness of spirit they have of late been pleased to charge us with, that we would not, were it in our power, lay the least restraint on any man's conscience, and should heartily rejoice to continue in brotherly love and charity with all our Protestant brethren." [1]

Four months elapsed and no intelligence had been received by Dr. Johnson of the arrival of his son in England. He reached his destination, however, after an extremely perilous voyage, a week before Christmas, and landing at Deal, proceeded to Canterbury, where of all the clergy who befriended the father and his companions thirty-three years before, Mr. Gosling alone survived to welcome the son and give him hospitality. But on arriving in London, the seat of the Society's operations, he found several of his father's old friends and correspondents, and writing to him January 10th, he expressed some disappointment that

[1] Berrian's *History Trinity Church*, p. 103

his application to be ordained for West Chester was heard with so little favor. He had called on Dr. Bearcroft, Christmas Eve, who received him rather coldly; and again he had waited on him ten days later, when he was more kind, and "talked very freely of Dr. McSparran and his ambitious views; of Fowle and Norwalk, Mr. Gibbs,[1] the state of the Church throughout New England; of the hasty recommendations of young gentlemen for orders from America, and their being sent many times very raw, without first obtaining leave to come, etc.; but always mentioned you with a great deal of kindness and respect. He said the Society did not intend to maintain assistants abroad, and that the sending me as curate to Mr. Standard would be a bad precedent for others to ask the same favors. I urged the infirmities of the old Doctor, and the miserable condition of the Church there as well as in many parts of the County." He was assured that if the Society thought proper to grant the request, much missionary duty would be done outside of the parish.

Mr. Berriman and Dr. Astry received him cordially and promised him all the assistance in their power, but both regretted that he and Mr. Samuel Fayerweather,[2] who arrived in London a week after Mr. Johnson, "were come upon such a slender basis." Further on in this same letter, he says: —

[1] Rev. Wm. Gibbs, of Simsbury, Ct., then in poor health.

[2] He was a native of Boston, and graduated at Harvard College, 1743. He was for several years settled as a Congregational minister in Newport, R. I., but after conforming to the Church of England, and receiving Holy Orders therein, he was appointed a missionary in South Carolina. The climate impaired his health, and petitioning the Society to be removed North, he was transferred in 1760 to St. Paul's Church, Narragansett, vacant by the death of Dr. McSparran, in 1757. Mr. Fayerweather died in 1781.

Last Tuesday, with Fayerweather, waited on his Lordship of London at Fulham. He appeared very kind; he seemed desirous to converse with us, but it was very difficult to understand him: his voice is almost gone, but his understanding yet very good. He spoke at first pretty roughly to Fayerweather, and said his bond from Taunton people was good for nothing; they meant only to impose upon him. He had, he said, known instances of it from other places, and Taunton he knew never intended to pay what they promised him. At our coming away he asked whether I should write soon, and bid me give his services to you and tell you that writing was grown very difficult to him, and his infirmities such that he could scarce hold a pen in his hand to write his name, which was the reason you had no letter from him for some time. He then told us we must wait upon Dr. Nicholls next week, who does all his business for him, and thus we are referred to another tribunal. They all seem to agree (and especially the Secretary) that Taunton must not be made a mission. Poor Fayerweather is frighted out of his wits about it. However, I endeavor to encourage him to hope that all things will turn out right for us both, by and by.

The good Bishop of Oxford I have waited on twice. He truly deserves Pope's character — *Secker is decent.* He converses with me with all the familiarity of an intimate friend, promises to write for me to Oxford, and hopes a degree may be obtained. I heard him preach on Christmas Day at the Cathedral (the congregation was in tears), and received the Sacrament at his hands. There is to be a meeting of the Society next Friday, at which he promises to attend, and I am to be there myself and urge my cause. The Committee meet on Monday to prepare matters ready. Thus you see I am at present lying at the pool, and waiting for the moving of the waters, in hopes some good friend will then take me up and cast me in, so that in my next I hope I shall be able to give you a more agreeable account of a favorable turn to my affairs. Meantime I shall endeavor to possess myself in patience and wait the event.

He seized every opportunity to communicate with his father, and keep him informed of the progress of his affairs. He knew his anxieties about him, and would do what he could to quiet them, and gladden the hearts of all his friends at home. His letters, intended for the family eye, do not fail to mention any change of plan or new proposition, though he was so far away that it must be carried into effect before he could have the parental advice. He left himself in the hands of Providence and his London counselors, and wrote as follows to his father: —

LONDON, *February* 6, 1756.

HONORED SIR, — I am told this morning, with the greatest secrecy, of an opportunity to New York, but who it is that is going, I know not; however, 'tis satisfaction enough for me that I can inform you with what pleasure I received yours by the *Grace* via Bristol. There is no happiness here equal to that of hearing that you all continue well, as blessed be God, I am at present. You mention in this letter that you had wrote a few days before, I suppose by the *Albany*, but she is not yet arrived, and we begin to be anxious for fear the French have got her. I am sorry to hear of Mr. Colgan's death; neither do I know what to say about succeeding there.[1] I have just mentioned it to Dr. Nicholls and Dr. Astry, and they both seemed rather to discourage me from thinking of it, as there must be a lawsuit, and perhaps a good deal of trouble to get things quietly settled; however, if I should hear nothing further from you about it, I shall endeavor to get leave of the Society to succeed there, if they should choose me upon my return, and all things considered, it be thought most advisable.

I wrote you a long letter by the *General Wall* Paquet for New York, which hope you will receive. Since that I have waited on his Grace of Canterbury, who received me in

[1] Jamaica, L. I.

a very familiar manner and inquired much about the College at New York, and the affairs of religion there. I was surprised to find by him that he had never yet seen a charter, or received any proper account of his being a Governor of the College. I suppose it was left with our late Governor, De Lancey, to write and send a charter to him, but you know his indolence, and therefore 'tis not strange it never was done.

As to my own affairs, I can inform you nothing certain. I have waited upon the Committee at the Charter House, and afterwards was introduced to the Venerable Board at Abp. Tenison's Library. His Grace of York sat in the chair. On his right hand, the Bp. of Oxford, and three other Bishops. On his left, a very grand assembly! Your letters were read, and that from the Vestry, publicly before the Board; Mr. Harison was asked by the Bp. of Oxford to be present, and accordingly when we were introduced, we were questioned by his Grace and the Bp. of Oxford publicly about the College and the opposition it had met, and was like to meet with from the Dissenters, etc., to all which we answered in the best manner we could. I was then desired by Dr. Bearcroft to tell his Grace and the Bishops the story of our persecutions at Yale College, and in particular that of our going to hear Mr. Morris preach in the jail at New Haven (which I had told the Committee before); and they all heard it with much attention, and seemed disposed to patronize the College at New York. Mr. Harison, by your letters and Dr. Astry's recommendation, was mentioned at the Board for a member of the Society. I have myself taken a good deal of pains among the members, to have him made one, and Dr. Nicholls assures me it will be done at the next meeting. Mr. Fayerweather and myself are recommended by the Society to the Bp. of London for orders, and have leave afterwards to apply to them for their favor, which I suppose will be near £20 for me, an annual present, but not a settled salary as Dr. Nicholls thinks. Mr. Fayerweather I know not how they will dispose of, perhaps to Norwalk, for the Secretary tells me they must dismiss poor Fowle. I expect Dr. Nicholls will examine us next week, and we shall be ordained (if found worthy) in the Ember Week in March. 'Tis this day the general Fast, and I had engaged myself to wait on some company to Westminster Abbey to hear the sermon before the House of Lords, before I knew of the opportunity for writing.

. . . .

I trust in God for his protection and blessing upon us all, and hope we shall have a happy meeting again. Meantime, I remain, Honored Sir,

Your most dutiful and obedient son,

W. JOHNSON.

The examination referred to in the foregoing letter was held, and he wrote his father on the 19th of March, to inform him that he and Mr. Fayerweather and several other candidates were ordained Deacons the previous Sunday by the Bishop of Bangor, Dr. Pierce, in the Chapel of the Palace at Fulham, — Dr. Sherlock, the Bishop of London, being too infirm to go through the ordination. Dr. Nicholls, Master of the Temple, presented them, and "after the service," he added, "we had a very grand and elegant dinner served up. The Bishop of London's lady, my Lord of Bangor, Dr. Nicholls, etc., sat at the table with us. The particular notice with which I was treated above the rest of my fellow-candidates had almost put me to the blush several times. My Lord of London desired to be affectionately remembered to you. He expresses a very great regard for you, and on your account treats me with the greatest kindness, and intends (as I am told by Dr. Nicholls), as soon as ever he can hear from Boston whether or not Dr. McSparran accepts the Chaplaincy, which Mr. Brockwell held, to give me the refusal of it, as he does not much expect the Dr. will think best to have it. If it should be offered me I shall be at a loss how to act, as I shall be unwilling to refuse, and unworthy to accept it."

He wrote again on the 31st, and said: "I have now the satisfaction to acquaint you that Mr. Fayerweather, myself, and two others were ordained Priests on Lady Day, at the Bishop of London's palace again, by the Bishop of Carlisle, Dr. Osbaldistone." Three days later he had another opportunity to write his father, when he mentioned: "I forgot in my last to tell you that my good friend, Mr. Cutler, had been in London almost a week, and took much notice of me. He came from Bocking, forty miles, almost on purpose to see us, and would have me with him every day, and visit all his friends with him here in London. He is hearty and lusty, a very true picture of his father; only more merry. When he went away he made me and Mr. Fayerweather promise to preach for him at Bocking in our journey to Cambridge. He particularly desired to be affectionately remembered to you, but says he believes he shall never be tempted to see America again."

Young Johnson still tarried in London, and had not left its precincts since his arrival, to visit other parts of the kingdom. He preached with good acceptance in several churches of the metropolis, and then communicated to his brother his final plans in the following letter. His ordination had not fixed his post in America, and the hesitancy or uncertainty about this occasioned him some anxiety: —

Dear Brother, — I have yet received but one letter from you and that above a month ago, to which I gave you an answer by Captain Jacobson, in the *Irene*, by whom also I sent you a box of books, marked W. S. J., No. 2, which I hope will come safe to you. I have still the pleasure of acquainting you of the continuation of my health (blessed be God), as I hope you all have; but am quite weary of the smoke of London, which I propose on Friday next to change for that of Windsor, and Oxford, where I was about ten days since honored with a degree of Master of Arts, and through my intercession with the good Bishop of Oxford, had Mr. Fayerweather joined with me, so that we have been now sounding in the newspapers almost a week, till I am quite weary of the compliments. Messrs. Harison and Fayerweather will accompany me to the University where we propose to spend about eight days, and then go to Cambridge and Bocking to see Mr. Cutler, etc. After which I shall return to London again, and begin to settle my affairs here that I may turn my attention to America again, and the pleasing hopes of seeing you in health and peace once more.

I don't know whether I told you that my Lord of London designs me the Chaplaincy at Boston, if Dr. McSparran refuses it, as 'tis expected he will; his own being better, and the Bishop won't let him hold both as the Dr. intended, and my Lord is now waiting his answer that he may give it to me, so that I am, at present, in a quandary whether Boston, West Chester, or Jamaica, will finally be my place of abode, though I can't but rather wish one of the latter, and that I may be the nearer to Daddy in his decline of life, as well as to you, though Boston be in itself the most eligible otherwise, as well as most honorable.

Be so good as to make my compliments to Mr. Winslow, and tell him his acquaintances here are well, particularly Mr. Bromfield and Jackson. I have had several agreeable little rides with Mr. Jackson into the country about London, as Mr. Winslow can tell you he did before me. He dislikes the grounds and rudiments of law, etc., that you mentioned, but advises me to get you Peere Williams' Reports, a celebrated thing, just published, in 3 vols. folio, price £4 10*s*

But as it is so costly I am a little at a loss what to do. Mr. Jackson offers to do you any little service that shall come in his way, and is obliged to you for the little memorandum you gave me about his land, which I showed to him. His Grace of Canterbury has been very ill, so that his life has been despaired of, but is now better, though 'tis thought he will not live long, as he is imagined to be in a consumption. I am to-morrow to attend at the grand rehearsal for the Sons of the Clergy at St. Paul's, and after sermon to be at the great feast with the stewards, gentry, etc. I have nothing particular to inform you as to public affairs. 'Tis neither peace nor war here; our eyes are fixed upon America, and I hope you will do worthily. I shall add no more, but my most affectionate love to sister, and hearty service to all friends as though named, and that

I am your most affectionate brother and friend,

W. Johnson.

London, *May* 5, 1756.

A letter to his father, twenty days later, describing the reception at Oxford, was the last which he wrote to his friends in America. The journey to see Mr. Cutler at Bocking does not appear to have been made, for the visit to Cambridge was cut short by his illness and speedy return to London. What happened to him after this is best detailed in the following pathetic letter, conveying the tidings of his death: —

London, *June* 24, 1756.

Dear and ever Honored Sir, — The occasion of my writing to you is melancholy and distressing. But O how can I speak it — my heart is pained within me, my spirit is troubled for you. The sovereign God has made a great breach in your family. Your beloved son William is dead — is dead.

It pleased God, after a short illness of about nine days with the small-pox, to take him out of this world. The task in sending such a letter of condolence to one of the best and tenderest of parents is exceeding irksome and disagreeable to me. But the duty I owe to Doctor Johnson, as well as the particular regard I had for his amiable son, will not allow me to refrain. And while I thus drop a tear with you over my departed friend, wouldn't be forgetful of what Christianity forbids, "to mourn as those who are without hope."

And though you, Rev. Sir, may say in the midst of your distress and sorrow, — "O William, my son, that I had died for thee — William, my son, my son," yet you have all the reason imaginable to be greatly comforted in his death, and even to rejoice because he is gone to his heavenly Father. Certain I am that you will be better able to make suitable reflections on such a providence, and improve it to your soul's comfort through the gracious assistance of the Divine Spirit than I can direct to. However, as it may be some satisfaction to you to know the particulars of his death, I will just put down some of the circumstances of it.

Your son and I who were as one, united in the bonds of natural love and affection, and engaged in one and the same cause, were as often together as our circumstances would allow of (which was almost every day). And as we had one interest to serve, and recommended to the same gentlemen, we in all respects fared alike, and had the same honors to be unitedly thankful for. This leads me to observe that your letters (and Doctor Cutler's which I procured in behalf of us both) to the Bishop of Oxford introduced us to his acquaintance, and our conduct recommended us still more to his esteem and notice. That worthy gentleman, who was indefatigable to serve us, went down to Oxford and procured, after making all the interest he could, a degree of Master of Arts, which was conferred on us by Diploma in the fullest convocation ever known before, and the more honorary this was, being done when we were not present ourselves. His Lordship, upon his return to London, advised us in consequence of so high an honor to pay a visit to the University, which we did, and were there received with all the demonstrations of joy and respect possible by the Vice-chancellor and the other governors of it, with whom we staid a fortnight, with the most inexpressible pleasure and delight, — the Vice-chancellor himself presenting to each of us his Diploma in the handsomest form and order.

In about a month after, we agreed to visit the University of Cambridge also, where we were admitted *ad eundem*, and previous to it we passed through all the forms and ceremonies of it. And there we were likewise treated with uncommon civility and kindness by the Vice-chancellor, Professors, Doctors, Proctors, etc. We spent four days at this seat of the Muses, and came back to London, but with this disagreeable circumstance of my brother traveller being sick of that fatal distemper whereof he died. Where he took the infection, or by what particular means, I cannot trace out, but very well remember his first complaints were in Trinity Hall, Cant.; though some say he was out of order by overheating his blood, and worrying himself by excessive walking in bad weather the day before we sat out upon our journey.

As soon as he got back to his lodgings from this unfortunate tour, a surgeon of eminence — Mr. Kinnersly — bled him, which was on Saturday evening about eight o'clock, June the 12th. The next day, which was Sunday, a physician and an apothecary of the first rank and character — Doctor Hyberton and Channing — were sent for, who immediately pronounced his case dangerous, he having the worst of symptoms, and those of the confluent sort. On the Friday following, growing worse, the help of another physician was found necessary, and accordingly, by the advice and desire of good Mr. Berriman, Doctor Nichols, a gentleman of great renown and formerly of your acquaintance, was applied to, and the three consulted together, and did everything for dear Billy that they possibly could do. This I was an eye-witness to, as I took lodgings in the house where he was from his first being put to bed, and constantly staid with him (at his desire), and the rather as Mr. Harison was gone into Wales and

Ireland. He had also a careful nurse and the best of friends about him to keep up his spirits. The Revd. minister above mentioned was exceeding kind in praying with him. I likewise prayed with him at several different times, for which he always expressed his most humble and hearty thanks.

In the whole course of his sickness as he had the exercise of his reason and understanding, so I observed him full of devotion. And when any prayers were offered up in his behalf, his attention was fixed to every sentence and period. On Sunday, the 20th of June, about two hours before he died, [he] begged of me to pray with him before I went out to church (for then I was just going to preach for the Rev. Doctor Bristowe), which I readily complied with, and couldn't help remarking his particular emphasis on the concluding word, *Amen*. This he would speak out distinctly, and audibly, with his innocent hands lifted up to the God of Heaven when he could scarcely be heard to say anything else.

As I sat by his bed-side observing him to breathe hard, I asked him "whether he thought himself dangerous, — whether he thought he should die," to which he answered, "I know not; I cannot tell." I asked, "whether he was anything uneasy about a future state." His answer was "No, no, not in the least." To which he further added, "If it be the will of God that I may live to see my dear father again, I shall be thankful; if not, his will be done. I can, I do entirely resign myself to the blessed will of my Creator to dispose of me as He thinks best."

This, this was his language, and I may say too, the song of his soul. Towards the close of his precious life, he had one or two considerable struggles and conflicts, yet still meek, silent, patient, resigned, —

"And smiling pleased in Death."

Death was no surprise to him in the least; being disarmed of its stings and horrors, he bid it welcome, breathing out his last in the hands of Jesus. May the dear parents be prepared to hear the tidings, and supported under so sore a bereavement.

Ah me! my companion and friend! very pleasant hast thou been unto me in thy life-time, and now at death not divided. O Lord make me to know mine end and the measure of my days what it is, that I may know how frail I am.

Quis talia fando temperet a lachrymis ?

And after all, the greatest comfort, Rev. and Hon. Sir, to you is, that your beloved son only sleepeth; that you shall see him again risen with a more beautified body, like unto his Saviour's, and distinguished with the glory of the Lord, — a crown — a laurel. The young prophet hath ascended; may I in particular catch his mantle, his spirit descending and resting upon me. To conclude, may both Mr. Harison, who was your worthy son's intimate friend, and I, imitate him as he imitated Christ, and follow him who through faith and patience is now inheriting the promises. Then shall we be together with him as one, where there will be no parting any more in the beatific presence, and ever rejoice in shouting forth the praises of God and the Lamb. Even so, come, Lord Jesus.

I most heartily sympathize with you, venerable and much afflicted Sir, and the whole distressed family, and wish you and them the great consolations which are contained in the covenant of grace, and promised to good men under Divine chastisement.

I am, believe me to be, with the utmost sincerity,
Your very affectionate sympathizing friend,
SAMUEL FAYERWEATHER.

He was carried on Thursday the 25th of June into the Church of St. Mildred in the Poultry, and, after the usual funeral rites, was laid in a vault, under the Church, belonging to Mr. Morley, a near relation of Mr. Harison. A handsome marble monument was afterwards erected to his precious memory at the expense of his most loving brother.

CHAPTER IX.

GRIEF FOR THE DEATH OF HIS SON AND CORRESPONDENCE WITH FRIENDS; PROGRESS OF THE COLLEGE AND ERECTION OF A BUILDING; LEAVES THE CITY ON ACCOUNT OF THE SMALL-POX; DEATH OF HIS WIFE; FIRST COMMENCEMENT; AND INCLINATIONS TO RESIGN.

A. D. 1756–1759.

It is impossible to describe the sorrow of the father at the loss of his son. He had written to his friends in Stratford as late as the first week in September, to say that no new intelligence had been received from him, and that he hoped by that time he was "well on his way over." The first tidings of his death came through a London paper, and followed quickly upon the hope thus expressed. He seized his pen and wrote again as follows: —

September 13, 1756.

Dearest Son, — You will find by an article in the news which is out of the London paper, that it hath pleased our Heavenly Father to take to himself your dear brother, and to deprive me of one of the best of sons and you of the best of brothers. May He support and comfort you under these heavy tidings, as I hope I may say with thankfulness He does us. The wound is exceeding deep, but we have nothing to say upon these occasions but *Thy will be done!* and to make the best use we can of it to disengage us from this world, and fit us for a better where he is doubtless gone, and where we may hope in a little time to meet him never to part more. This is all the intelligence we have of it (via Boston), but you see him in the case so exactly described that there is no possible place left to doubt of it. Your sister is at Staten Island. I dread at the shock it must give her. Thank God we are all in health and send our tender sympathies with you on this melancholy occasion. This makes us the more long to see you again, but must wait till your affairs make it practicable. Meantime may God sanctify this sad event to you and to us all, and ever have you under his most gracious protection. I am, dear son,

Your most afflicted and affectionate father,

S. JOHNSON.

Several letters passed between them before the tidings were confirmed by Mr. Fayerweather's communication, — in one of which Dr. Johnson said: "Dear son, you are now my all; pray for my sake as well as your own be very careful of your health. I have always a sort of terror at the sound of Litchfield ever since the sickness you got there. I shall long to hear you are well returned." Another letter, written after all the particulars of William's death had been received, is so full of parental tenderness and solicitude for his surviving child that it must not be omitted in this connection: —

NEW YORK, *October* 18, 1756.

MY DEAR AND ONLY SON, — I had yours of the 12th and thank God for your health and ours. I conclude you had my last by the post with Mr. Fayerweather's, though I have no answer by Hurd.

Your kind intentions towards your brother, had he lived, are very pleasing to me. You may remember I once wished you to assist him, as I was concerned how he would be able to get decently along in life. But God, I am persuaded, has provided infinitely better for him than we both of us could have done, and yet it is so difficult a thing to be disengaged from the hopes and wishes we had of happiness in his continuance with us, that I believe we would both be content to be stripped of all we have, if that could fetch him back. But God's will is done, and to that we must submit.

What you mention of his taking away such young persons, and especially in prospect of great usefulness, always appeared to me one of the most difficult phenomena of Providence to account for. It did so, on his taking away my dear friend, Mr. Brown, who was certainly the best of us three, and much such another as your brother. What you suggest is the only thing that can satisfy us that there are wise and good reasons with that infinitely perfect and best of Beings, though it is infinitely beyond us to see them. It is impossible for us to judge what is wisest and best, unless we knew the whole of things. But He hath kept that future world impenetrably out of our sight, doubtless (wisely and kindly) to teach us to live by faith, not by sight. A heathen would say, *Prudens, futuri temporis exitum, calignosa nocte premit Deus.* It is certain we can make nothing of Providence without taking both worlds into the account; and in this view let us rest.

Mr. Walker was so kind as to write me a large and elaborate letter on this melancholy occasion, to which I inclose an answer open for your perusal, which I desire you to seal and deliver to him. I am very sorry you can't be here at Christmas. After having had two such desirable sons for near thirty years almost always under my eye, now to be totally deprived of one, and so very seldom to see the other, seems very hard. I shall be so out of all patience not to see you till spring that I beg of you, if possible, to let us see you in that first week in December you mention.

My dear son — This is your birthday; [1] you now enter upon your thirtieth year. I bless God for preserving you both so long to me as He has. May He preserve you still, and lengthen out to you a useful life to a good old age, and bestow ten thousand blessings on you and yours. And as I always set my heart upon your being, both, great and public

[1] He was born on the 7th of October, Old Style.

blessings to mankind, and now one is taken away, and some part of your private care is thereby abated, I trust you will be so much the more of a public spirit, and lay out your life and talents to the best advantage for public usefulness, and that, as much as you can, in what relates to the interest of Religion as well as Justice. I am, with our tenderest regards to you both, and to the children, dear son,

Your most affectionate father,

S. Johnson.

His friends in England wrote him all the comforting words they could, and at the University of Oxford a memorial of the character of his son was drawn up, in which the Rev. George Horne, of Magdalen College, and the Rev. George Berkeley, student of Christ Church, had a share, and in which the hope was expressed that the guardians of the Church in America might find some expedient to "prevent future calamities of this kind, by rendering such long and perilous voyages unnecessary." Dr. Johnson used the event as a fresh reason for the establishment of an American Episcopate. In writing to Dr. Nicholls, December 10, 1756, and thanking him for his kindness to his deceased son, he urged this measure with great zeal, but despaired of seeing anything accomplished at present. He wrote in a similar strain to his other correspondents, and appeared to be as full of solicitude for the prosperity of the Church in America as of sorrow for the death of his beloved child. The following letter to the son of Bp. Berkeley may be taken as an example of the depth of his feeling on both subjects: —

KING'S COLLEGE, N. Y., *December* 10, 1756.

DEAREST SIR, — I have now before me three of your very kind and affectionate letters to acknowledge, which I most gratefully do. In particular I thank you for the very tender sympathy you express on occasion of the loss of my dear son, which is indeed a very heavy loss not only to me and my family, but to the poor people to whom he was to minister, and hath been most affectionately lamented by all who knew him. Your reflections on this unhappy occasion are both just and kind, and I thank God, under such considerations, He has enabled me to bear it better than I could have expected. And however hard it bears on flesh and blood, as I am deeply sensible that my Heavenly Father both always knows and does what is best, I heartily join with you in saying, Not my will, O my God, but Thine be done! And I gladly take this opportunity to render my most hearty thanks to you for the great kindness wherewith you treated my dear son, when he was at Oxford, and I beg you will give my humblest service and thanks to all those good gentlemen, as though named, into whose conversation you introduced him, and who treated him with so great kindness, and indeed to the whole Senate for the great honor they did him in his degree, of all which he had a most pleasing and grateful sense, as abundantly appears both from his journal, and a letter he wrote to me from London soon after. His satisfaction in his journey to Oxford was inexpressible, and particularly I beg you will give my humblest duty and thanks (lest my letter should miscarry) to my Lord of Oxford, whose treatment of him was like that of a father and friend, rather than a stranger and inferior, — for which I cannot be sufficiently thankful.

I am very much obliged to you for sending me a copy of your justly renowned and ever honored father's epitaph, for whom I had the most intense affection. It is extremely just and elegant. It was a mighty satisfaction that our friendship was like to be continued in our sons; but since God has been pleased to deny it in him that is gone, I wish it may be continued in my only surviving son, who though he is a lawyer, and (thank God) is in the best estimation in that profession, yet his chief affection is towards Divinity of the best sort, having read Hutchinson, etc., and would shine in that if he could have orders without such a dangerous voyage, which yet he would not much regard, if he had not a family. I beg, therefore, though unknown, he may be numbered among your friends. I desire, when you write, you will give my humblest service to that excellent lady your honored mother, as well as your brother, of whom I should be glad to hear, and assure her that I do most tenderly sympathize with her in her affliction, and do earnestly pray to God for the relief of your dear sister. I bless God who has infused your heart with a disposition to take Holy Orders in this degenerate, apostatizing age, in which a man had need to have the spirit of a confessor if not a martyr, and I shall not cease to pray earnestly that you may both have the grace and opportunity to act a worthy part in that capacity for which you are so excellently qualified.

And now it is time that I consider the subjects of your other letters, and particularly that I tender you my most hearty thanks for the most kind present of books you were so good as to send me, which I wish I could retaliate. I should have done this sooner but that they arrived not long before the sad news of my son's death, having lain so long with the Secretary that he had forgotten whence they were. Dr. Ellis' performance I am highly pleased with, so far as Religion is concerned, but I cannot say that I am satisfied with either Mr. Locke or him in that part. I cannot think sense the only source of our knowledge, and must conceive consciousness and the pure intellect another, without which instruction could take no effect, though it labor in the first materials. Bp. Berkeley, Dr. Cudworth, and Plato, should be well considered. I desire you would give my humble service and thanks to Mr. Holloway for his kind present, which is an excellent performance, but I am afraid of going out of one extreme into another, and so hurting the cause of our holy religion by carrying the humor of allegorizing too far, as some of the pious Fathers seem to have done ; and I have thought sometimes a handle has been groundlessly, at least it has been wickedly taken by the enemies of Christianity to set them in a very ridiculous light. Dr. Patten's, Mr. Wittar's and Mr. Horne's performances are exceeding good, and I am in particular prodigiously pleased with Mr. Horne's State of the Case, etc., which carries all before it. Would to Heaven all Hutchinsonians would write in that candid and powerful manner. Their cause, which I am persuaded is the cause of God, would at length, methinks, bear down all opposition. I long for those things he seems to hint as being upon the anvil. In short I am very much obliged to you for all those tracts, which are very excellent. I am heartily glad Mr. Hutchinson's works are so much esteemed at Oxford, and you may depend upon it, I shall do my best to make that University my pattern as far as may be, and particularly to induce as many as I can to study the Hebrew Scriptures, and to understand his writings. I thank God my College has at last got the victory of its enemies, having had an act passed this fall in favor of it by our Assembly, and all opposers stop their mouths. The foundation of the building is laid, to be carried on vigorously in spring. But as we shall want much assistance, I am very thankful for the forwardness you express to promote it, for the books contributed, and believe we shall soon empower somebody to put forward a subscription in England.

As to Tillotson, I have myself been heretofore a great admirer of his sermons, but for these several years have been sensible of the ill-effects of them in these parts, as well as of some others worse than they much here in vogue, — and done my best to guard against them ; but as he has long been in possession, it will not do here to speak against him with much acrimony except among Methodists. The Remarks on his life are doubtless but too just. However it is good to keep the golden mean and hold moderation, as far as can consist with a wise zeal and steadiness to the cause of God, and truth as it is in Jesus.

I am sadly grieved for the melancholy account you give me of some of the chief dignitaries, and the condition of the Church there, and little hopes of any establishment in our favor here. I confess I should scarce have thought my dear son's life ill bestowed (nor I believe would he) if it could have been a means of awakening this stupid age to a sense of the necessity of sending Bishops (at least one good one) to take care of the Church in these vastly wide extended regions. But alas! what can be expected of such an age as this! *O Deus bone in quæ tempora reservastis nos!* This is now the seventh precious life (most of them the flower of this country) that has been sacrificed to the atheistical politics of this miserable abandoned age, which seems to have lost all notion of the necessity of a due regard to the interest of Religion, in order to secure the blessing of God on our nation both at home and abroad. As to us here, as things have hitherto gone, we can scarce look for anything else but to come under a foreign yoke.

But it is now high time I should relieve your patience when I begin to have scarce any left of my own. I therefore conclude with my sincere thanks for your affectionate prayers for me and mine, the continuance of which I still desire; and be assured that both you and your relatives and friends shall always be severally remembered in mine, who am, dear Sir,

Your most affectionate friend and brother in Christ,

S. J.

The affairs of the College in the mean time went on prosperously, and Dr. Johnson applied all his energies to give form and effect to the plans of the Overseers. They appointed as Tutor, to take the place of his lamented son, Mr. Leonard Cutting, a gentleman who had been educated at Eton and the University of Cambridge, and was well qualified to fill the position. It was decided to locate the College building "in the skirts of the city," and the first stone, with a suitable inscription, was laid on the 23d of August, 1756, by Sir Charles Hardy, at which time the President made a short Latin address to the Governors, to Sir Charles, and Mr. De Lancy, the Lieutenant-governor of the Province, "congratulating them on this happy event, which was followed with an elegant dinner." But an interruption of his personal work soon occurred.

The appearance of the small-pox in the city at the setting in of the winter of 1756 obliged him to retire to West Chester, where he ministered to the poor people who had been disappointed in their expectations of having his son for their Rector. The thirty pupils in the three classes were left in charge of Mr. Cutting, to whom Mr. Daniel Treadwell, a graduate of Harvard College, was added as an assistant, having been appointed Professor of Mathematics and Natural Philosophy. Dr. Johnson himself did what he could in the way of advice and direction, but his long absence was felt to be a hindrance to the best designs of the Institution. At first he seems to have retired alone without his family, for he wrote to his son from West Chester on the 19th of December to say, "The kindness of everybody here is inexpressible. My Lord [Underhill] and his family think nothing too good for me, or too much to do, and everything I say is a law to them. The next day after you went away, he begged I would be perfectly at home and call for everything I wanted. I told him, when at home, I always had my family together morning and evening to prayers, and should be glad to do the same here. He was very glad at my motion, and is prodigiously pleased with the practice, insomuch that he tells all his neighbors of it, and if any of them are here, he will not let them go away before prayers are over.

"The snow looked terribly, but they intend, if it will continue, to make an advantage of it. My Lord and the Major have this evening, since church, engaged fourteen sleds to go to-morrow and fetch all up at once, so that I hope we may soon be together again, but it looks threatening for another storm."

The storm did continue, and some days elapsed before the removal was accomplished. In this retirement he found opportunity to refresh his mind with favorite studies, and to review some of the judgments which he had formed at an earlier period of his ministry. Writing to his son on the 30th of January, 1757, he said: "Your notion of those Oxford gentlemen is doubtless very right, and I hope we shall have more of their zealous labors to preserve Religion from sinking in this apostatizing age. I confess Dr. Clarke, etc., had led me far many years ago into the reasoning humor, now so fashionable in matters of Religion, from which I bless God I was happily reclaimed, first by Forbes and more perfectly by Hutchinson, whose system I have been now more thoroughly canvassing from the Hebrew Scriptures, since this retirement, in regard to the Philosophical as well as the Theological part, and, to my unspeakable satisfaction, am much convinced it is, in both, entirely right, and I could wish you to read both Forbes and Pike over and over again.

"But your dear brother yet lies very near my heart, and I cannot avoid yet daily and hourly following him in my thoughts, with the utmost tenderness, into the world of Spirits, whither he is gone before us. And when I pray for you and all of us, I cannot help remembering him, as I used to do, but in some such words as these: 'I humbly hope my dear departed son is accepted with Thee in Thy blessed Son, and that thou art still his God. O be the God of us also that survive, — our God and guide and chief good in time and to all eternity.' The expression you know is taken from that of the God of Abraham, etc., applied by our Saviour to the Resurrection; but we must remember it means in the original their *Elohim*, *i. e.*, their Father, Redeemer, and Comforter. No wonder then it includes the Resurrection. This custom of commemorating our departed friends obtained in the best and earliest times of Christianity, and by degrees degenerated to praying for them out of purgatory."

By the advice of his friends, he continued in his retirement at West Chester for upwards of a year, the prevalence of the small-pox in the city not making it prudent for him to resume his College duties. In the mean time he made a visit with his wife to Stratford, and spent several weeks of the early summer of 1757 among his old friends and parishioners. The journey was performed in a leisurely and private manner, and writing to his son on the last day of July, not long after the return to West Chester, he for the first time spoke of the illness of his wife. Her sickness proved to be the fever and ague, a complaint which then prevailed quite extensively in that neighborhood, and another member of his household was ill in the same way, — Mrs. Georgiana Maverick, — the widowed daughter of his wife by her former husband. No immediate danger attended this sickness, but persons afflicted with it, especially those of feeble constitutions, were often so shattered and reduced by its severity as never to recover. The following note, written to the wife of his son, shows his anxiety in the earlier stages of the complaint: —

West Chester, *September* 12, 1757.

Dear Daughter, — I am sensible my son is not at home, for which reason I write to you to let you know how it is with us. It is an exceeding sickly time in these parts, and we have our share of it, having all of us had the fever and ague, but your poor mother has a very bad fever. She had got well of the first turn so as to ride about several times, but yesterday a week ago she was taken bad again, and has been bad all the week and so continues, and God only knows what will be the event. It seems to be of the kind they call the long fever, but I hope it may have a comfortable issue. I mention our case that my son may know how it is when he comes home, but would not have him troubled with it where he is, and I hope I may be able to give him a better account of it by the time he returns. I was glad to find by his last letter that you were all in health, which I pray God continue. We all give our kind love to you and the children, and to him when he returns, and to Mrs. Beach.

I am, dear daughter,

Your most affectionate father and friend,

S. Johnson.

The next letter bore more favorable intelligence, but the signs of improvement were not lasting. Under the pressure of all his trials, his pen was employed whenever he could be of any service to the Church, and on the 3d of October, he excused himself from writing more largely to his son, because he had been obliged to prepare a long letter to the Rev. Mr. Wetmore, who had applied to him for his advice to be communicated to a meeting of the clergy which he was about to call at Stamford on the 13th at the instance of the Society "to look into the affairs of Mr. Beach's[1] sermon, and try to bring him to a better mind." "Truly," said Johnson, "things are come to that pass that he must make some submission to the Society or be discarded, or at least severely reprimanded, for Hobart[2] has procured a complaint from their Association against him to the Society, which has put them on these measures, though I wish this could be concealed, and that it could be rather represented as arising *ex proprio motu* from other information," which the Society possessed. Writing to his son a week later, he referred again to Mr. Beach playfully as one who "had always those two seeming inconsistencies, to be dying and yet relishing sublunary things." The reprimand, if given, seems not to have been very severe, and Mr. Beach subsequently in a measure atoned for his mistake by the publication of a sermon on "Scripture Mysteries," which received the sanction of his brethren, and was introduced to the public with a preface from the pen of Johnson himself.

Not deeming it prudent to return to New York in consequence of the small-pox, he moved into more comfortable quarters at West Chester, and for a good part of the winter was alternately hopeful and fearful about the result of his wife's illness. Occasionally his sorrow for the death of his son would break out

1 Rev. John Beach. The sermon was *An Inquiry concerning the State of the Dead*, which was misunderstood, and he regretted its publication.

2 Mr. Beach had very properly answered his "Addresses to the members of the Episcopal Separation in New England."

afresh, and any allusion to it by an English friend was sure to stir the depths of his feeling. He closed a letter to his son at Stratford, December 18, 1757, thus: "You tell me in your last you have had the *melancholy pleasure* of seeing Mr. Harison. It must be so, indeed; but though I have been very impatient for it, I have not yet had the opportunity. He sent me a short letter from Dr. Bearcroft, of July 2, by which it appears he had written to me the September before, which must have miscarried. It only relates to a scheme of the Society, to educate some Indian youths in my College as an expedient towards propagating Christianity among them. I want very much to see him, in order the better to know how to write my letters and what to do with these bills, and I fear I shall lose the opportunities.

Christmas is quite at hand, and if we may not have the pleasure of seeing you here (which though I long for, yet I durst not expect, however so much I desire it, it being such a tedious journey), I wish you may have a pleasant one and a happy new year, and many, many more."

He was induced to consult his old family physician at Stratford, Dr. Harpin, about his wife, who, as the winter wore on, became troubled with a cough and shortness of breath, and other symptoms of a consumption. She gradually improved under the use of new remedies, and by the middle of February, Dr. Johnson began to think of returning to his duties in town. The appearance of the small-pox at West Chester hastened this step, for in a letter to his son on the 4th of March, 1758, he said: "The young fellows here purposely take the small-pox so much, that I believe we cannot be any longer safer here than at town, so that I think to go within about a week, and the family will, I believe, hardly continue out the month before they follow me." Three weeks later he wrote again, but now from New York, where he had been nearly the whole of this time at the house of his step-son, and mentioned, "I have been but little abroad as yet, though I have some thoughts of venturing to church to-morrow. I have been and shall be very careful, but the small-pox is certainly very thin now, as neither doctors nor ministers, nor anybody else that I have seen, can tell where it is, of their own knowledge; but doubtless it is in some remote skirts of the town. However, I hope God will preserve me from it: the Freshmen have attended me every day at your brother's."

The family followed him to town early in April, and carried with them the fever and ague, which had afflicted his wife and daughter so long at West Chester. The change brought no real relief, and the letters of the father to the son spoke more and more discouragingly of the recovery of Mrs. Johnson. The crisis had been reached and all hope relinquished, when the following was written from, —

NEW YORK, *May* 29, Monday, 11 o'clock.

MY DEAREST SON, — God is now calling me to pass through another great revolution in my circumstances; another great change in my condition, which I hope may further contribute to prepare me the better for my last. I should have written by Philip Nicholls, but he called in the utmost hurry so early, that having sat up till 1 o'clock, I was not yet awake. He could give you, or at best my dear daughter, a prelude to what is now to follow. Your dear mother continued as she was, without seeming worse till about six o'clock last Friday evening, having rid out the day before, and conversed and walked about as usual, and would have rid out that day but the wind was too high. But about that hour she was seized all at once with a terrible shivering, not cold, but convulsive, which issued in a most terrible fever, and tormenting pains, except short intervals of dozing, which continued till midnight last night, since which she has been tolerably easy and slept a good deal, but is reduced to the lowest ebb of life, and cannot hold it many hours. She is perfectly resigned, and sometimes even longs to be released, with good hopes of a blessed immortality. May God give her an abundant entrance into his heavenly kingdom, and a happy meeting with your dear brother!

Had you been at Stratford, I should have sent an express for you to come, but the suddenness of the occasion, all the while threatening speedy death, together with your great distance, made us think it best to decline it, though I shall hope to see you as soon as may be, as you may chance to be here before her funeral. But you must be careful and inquisitive as you come along, as I hear the small-pox is much at New Rochelle, and about the half way to the Bridge, where you may do well to have some tar to smell to, and tobacco in your mouth. Yesterday I asked her whether there was anything she would have me say to you in particular. She bid me give her love and dying blessing to you and your children. Take care, dear son, you do not overdo yourself. You are now my all in effect. Your brother and sisters with me give our love to you all. *Lachrymans scribo*, being, dear son,

Your most affectionate, but very afflicted father,

S. JOHNSON.

She lingered till the Thursday evening after the date of this letter, and then expired, thus sundering a happy connection which had existed for more than thirty-two years. She was buried under the chancel of Trinity Church — the old edifice which was afterwards destroyed in the great conflagration that befell the city during the Revolutionary War.

It had been decided to hold the first commencement of the College on the 21st of June, and Johnson, who was desirous of making a good appearance, turned, in the freshness of his grief, to the work of preparing for this occasion. The graduating class numbered eight, and the two tutors, Cutting and Treadwell, with eleven other gentlemen, were admitted to the degree of Master of Arts. An "elegant entertainment" followed the public exercises, and such was the interest manifested in the Institution that a new impulse seemed to be given to its prosperity. Materials for completing the college building were at once procured, and then when the stone had been delivered, a delay arose from an unexpected cause. The difficulty of finding suitable workmen prevented any progress, so that nothing more was done till the winter had passed away and the spring opened. In the meantime Johnson, who had previously applied to the Archbishop of Canterbury and other friends in England for aid in behalf of the College, was not much encouraged by the answers which he received. A good philosophical and mathematical apparatus had been obtained, and the Rev. Dr. Bristowe, of London, who befriended his lamented son, intimated his purpose of procuring a large library for the infant seminary, a purpose which he afterwards executed by bequeathing to it his own valuable collection of nearly fifteen hundred volumes. But money to finish the building and endow the College was not readily given.

Having two good tutors, one to take charge of the

Classical and the other of the Mathematical department, he devoted himself chiefly to teaching the New Testament in Greek; and to Logic, Metaphysics, and Ethics, with lessons in Hebrew to those who desired to become acquainted with that language. He was interrupted for a time in his duties by sickness in the family, and was himself severely attacked with the measles in March, 1759, from which it was feared he might not recover. "God grant," he wrote to his son after all danger was passed, "that my life may have been spared to some good purpose, and that what remains of it may be more abundantly employed to his glory in the station I am in!"

A gloomy and anxious winter was not succeeded by a joyous spring, for Mrs. Maverick, upon whom, since the death of his wife, he had depended for the oversight of his domestic affairs, was in a precarious state of health, with decided tendencies to consumption. As late as the 28th of May, in reply to an invitation from his son's wife to visit Stratford, he said: "Your sister thanks you for your kind letter, but by reason of her weakness, begs me to answer it for her. She, as well as I, would gladly make you a visit, but she continues so infirm that I can neither bring her nor leave her; so that I must not have the pleasure of seeing you and my dear little girls this spring, but hope I may in the fall."

In less than a month from this date he had given up all hope of her recovery, and admitted to her friends that she was in a "fixed, incurable consumption." Her death came sooner than he expected; occurring on the 28th of June, thirteen months from the decease of her mother, and she was buried in the same grave above her, under the chancel of Trinity Church. "I am again," he informed his son, "bereaved, and now in a manner stripped. Your dear sister is gone and has left me very disconsolate." The event opened afresh his former griefs, and revived his inclinations to retire from the charge of the College and spend the remainder of his days in Stratford. But he was urged to remain, and the state of the Institution almost forbid him to leave it at this crisis.

The second Commencement had just been held and was private; one student only being admitted to the degree of Bachelor of Arts. The building was going on vigorously under his own eye, and his counsel and influence were much needed in the further steps to be taken for the advancement of the College. The following letter to Archbishop Secker shows that while he was deeply interested in the prosperity of the Church at large, and desirous of seeing another Mission established in New England, he was on the watch also for some suitable person to be his successor.

April 25, 1759.

MAY IT PLEASE YOUR GRACE, — In the beginning of last month I wrote an answer in part to your Grace's most kind letter of September 27. I hoped then by this time to have made a reply to the rest of that very important letter, but I have not sufficient information relating to some things, especially what concerns our frontiers. The occasion of my now writing is the desire and request of the clergy of Boston, that some letters of mine may accompany theirs that are going by this pacquet in behalf of Mr. Apthorp and a Mission at Cambridge near Boston. Indeed, that paragraph of your Grace's letter relating to Missions in New England, very much discourages me from writing anything relating to new Missions in these provinces. What I am now doing, therefore, proceeds purely from my friendship to those worthy gentlemen, to which I should be wanting, if I should refuse to write anything on this occasion. I therefore humbly beg your Grace will excuse me, if I only suggest that I am fully satisfied that a Mission would be of very good use to the interest of the Church and true religion so near that College, for the reasons they give, but what strongly sways with me is, that we want extremely to have as many worthy men as possible in this country, and Mr. Apthorp, by all accounts of him, is indeed a very superior young gentleman, having been bred at Cambridge, England, and merited a fellowship there, and that estimation and prospect of preferment that everybody wonders at his disposition to tarry in this, even though it be his native country, at all. And since it is so, I am very desirous to keep him, and the rather as he, having a considerable fortune of his own, may probably prove a fitter person than any we can ever expect to procure to succeed me in this station, and I am very desirous, if it may be, to be acquainted with my successor before I leave it, and that he may be some worthy person who has been bred at one of your Universities at home. However, whether the Society can think proper to make a new Mission in New England under the present condition of things, must be humbly submitted to the wisdom and goodness of the Board.

I remain, may it please your Grace,

Your Grace's most obliged, etc.,

S. J.

In writing to Dr. Bearcroft, the Secretary of the Society, two months after this, he expressed himself as having little expectation of a collection in England for his College, but it needed assistance so much, and he urged its claims with such zeal, that the board generously donated £500 sterling, — a gift which seemed to put new life into the hopes and energies of the somewhat tardy Governors. He defended at this period the Missionaries of the Society against the complaints of the Dissenters, who accused them of using undue means to gain the attention of their brethren and make converts. Secker had written him for information on the subject, and he replied repelling the accusations, and adding: "The quarrels of the Dissenters among themselves, especially, occasioned by the late enthusiasm, contributed vastly more to drive honest thinking people into the Church than any endeavors of the clergy to make proselytes. There is now a flagrant instance of this at Wallingford, a large country town in the heart of Connecticut." The "late enthusiasm" was the result of Whitefield's itinerancy, and a body of "shocking teachers followed him, who propagated so many wild notions of God and the Gospel, that a multitude of people were so bewildered that they could find no rest to the sole of their feet till they retired into the Church as the only ark of safety." The great want of the Church here was a Bishop, and he implored the authorities at home, in spite of the misrepresentations of their adversaries, to send one to America. "He need not," he said, "be fixed in New England, or in any part where Dissenters abound. He might be fixed at Virginia, where the Church is established, and only visit us northward once in three or four years. We should be content to ride three or four hundred miles for Holy Orders."

No objection was made at a meeting of the Society to the Mission at Cambridge, and to the appointment of Mr. Apthorp, with an annual stipend of £50. He met with a better reception at first among the Dissenters than was anticipated, and his temper, prudence, and abilities, gave him great advantage, if not influence, in that important seat of learning. But the Archbishop did not so complacently accord with Johnson in his plan of providing for his own retirement. "Your views," he said, "in relation to a successor, are very worthy of you; but I hope many years will pass before there be occasion to deliberate on that head." The change might bring with it no little discouragement, and put in peril the best interests of the Institution. At least it was too soon to give publicity to his intentions, and work with this end mainly in view.

CHAPTER X.

SMALL-POX AGAIN IN NEW YORK, AND RETIREMENT TO STRATFORD; MORE AFFLICTION; THIRD COMMENCEMENT; LETTERS TO THE ARCHBISHOP OF CANTERBURY; PUBLICATIONS ON PRAYER, AND DEFENSE OF THE LITURGY.

A. D. 1759–1761.

THE disease which had been the great horror of his life, drove him once more from his post. "Never" he wrote to his son, on the 15th of October, "was anything known like the present breaking out of the small-pox in New York. It seems as though it arose out of the ground. They are surprised at it and cannot account for it." He undertook to keep himself from exposure, and for a time heard the recitations of the classes in his own dwelling, but soon the disease appeared almost at his door, and fortifying himself as best he could, he hurried from the city to a farm-house in the suburbs, where he remained until all danger of having taken it was past, and then with a servant he proceeded to Stratford. Shut up in this rural retreat, he spent the winter with his son, more anxious than ever for the College, since one of the tutors — Mr. Treadwell — was in a decline, and could render very little assistance to his colleague. He died of consumption before the spring had much advanced; and thus the entire management of the Institution, in the absence of the President, devolved upon Mr. Cutting.

Dr. Johnson did not return to New York until the middle of May, and it was with some fear that he ventured at this time, for there were a few scattered cases of small-pox about the town, and he could not know when he might expose himself and become a victim of the distemper. A desolate feeling possessed him as he resumed his college duties. The city appeared to him as it never had before, almost a wilderness, for besides the loss of Mr. Treadwell, a place among the Governors had been vacated which he could not hope to see again filled by one of equal energy and influence. Benjamin Nicoll, the younger son of his deceased wife, whose education from childhood he had superintended, who had risen to the highest eminence as a lawyer in the city, and whose house had been his home as much as that of his own son in Stratford, sickened and died at the age of forty-two, in April, 1760, before he could return. It was said that "never in the memory of man at New York was any one so much lamented." His death was the severest misfortune which had befallen the College. It filled its friends with consternation, and to Johnson in particular it was a most painful bereavement, for of all the members of the governing board, none was more able, wise, and zealous than he, and upon none had he relied more confidently to carry him through his perplexities and trials, and enable him to place the College upon a broad and firm foundation.

His long absence and the sickness and death of his "best tutor" had been a serious detriment to the Institution. Several of the students withdrew, and the prospect for the future was surrounded with gloom.

These things made it the more necessary for him to apply all his energy and ingenuity to recover from the losses which had been suffered, and get back the confidence of those who had grown lukewarm or doubtful. The college building, one hundred and eighty feet in length by thirty, three stories high, erected in a delightful situation near the Hudson River, and "opening to the harbor," was so far completed that he moved into it and "set up housekeeping and tuition there, a little more than forty years after he had done the same at Yale College in New Haven." He wrote very earnestly to the Archbishop of Canterbury and begged him to send two good tutors — one that might be qualified in time to succeed him, and the other to take the department of mathematics and experimental philosophy, made vacant by the death of Mr. Treadwell. His Grace replied: "It grieves me that you should be without help so long. If any other person can procure it for you, I should be heartily glad. But I think you had better wait than have a wrong person sent you from hence. Could you not get some temporary assistance in your neighborhood?"

The selection was a difficult one in view of the requirements of Johnson. Among other names recommended to Secker was that of Myles Cooper, — a Fellow of Queen's College, Oxford. He had the reputation of being a grave and good man, and was "very well affected to the government; well qualified for the inferior tutor's place, but not inclined to accept it; not unskilled in Hebrew, and willing to take the Vice-President's office, but not of age for Priest's Orders" till the lapse of several months. This gentleman, as it will be seen, was afterwards appointed and made a useful and accomplished head of the Institution.

The third Commencement and the first from the college building, was now held, and the President delivered a brief speech in Latin to the governing body, congratulating them on the privilege of assembling in their new hall, and marking the event as the beginning of a fresh epoch in the history of the college. The degree of Bachelor of Arts was conferred upon six young gentlemen, and the eclat given to the occasion helped to bring the officers of instruction favorably before the public. The next term opened well, but as no assistance had been obtained, the President and Mr. Cutting were obliged to do double duty; and the whole year, as he himself said, "was remarkable only on account of hard services, which made him more and more weary of his station."

A preparatory school was projected about this time, and Johnson applied to the Rev. East Apthorp, the scholarly Missionary at Cambridge, referred to in the previous chapter, for his idea of what might be "executed at school and at college by a person of middling genius, persevering in a regular course of moderate study and assisted by good instructors." The very full answer which was returned, embraced what he was pleased to call an "excellent plan of education," and he would have been contented without seeking tutors from abroad, if he could have had the assistance of Mr. Apthorp in carrying it into execution throughout the whole course. "But since Providence," he wrote him, "seems to be ordering otherwise, I hope you are reserved for yet higher and better things. It may yet be a considerable time first, but as there is the greatest need of it, and the utmost propriety in it, that bishops should be sent into America, — for the accomplishing which I hope you will be continually using your influence in the manner the Archbishop advises, that the Church may enjoy in full her government and discipline here at least as well as the Dissenters theirs, — I hope the time is not a great way off before that most primitive and apostolical order may be established here, and I pray God you may be the first that may serve your country in that capacity."

His correspondence with the Archbishop of Canterbury turned upon matters which directly concerned the welfare of the Church. Sometimes, but rarely, he touched upon delicate questions of State policy, and during his retirement at Stratford in the winter of 1759–60, having little to do, and taking the advice of "several gentlemen of good understanding and public spirit," he drew up a paper with a view at first of publishing it in the "London Magazine," but upon reflection concluded to send it to his Grace and inclose copies to him for Lord Halifax and Mr. Pitt, with instructions to suppress or communicate his thoughts as he should see fit. Relying on his great candor he added in reference to the paper: "I humbly hope you will impute it to the feeble struggles of a well-meaning mind, that would be useful to the world if it could, but desires to be retired and concealed. I can only assure your Grace that it is the wish of many gentlemen in these two colonies, though but few know in confidence of my having taken this step."

It does not appear what the particular subjects were which he thus presented, but they related to America, and were written under the name of *Philanglus Americanus*. They met with no favor, for the Archbishop in his reply, November 4th, 1760, said: "I shall always be pleased with your notifying and proposing to me whatever you apprehend to be material; because I know it will always be done with good intention, and almost always furnish me with useful notices; and indeed will be of no small use, even when you may happen to judge amiss, as it will give me an opportunity of setting you right. In my opinion, the paper intended for the 'London Magazine,' and the letters for Lord Halifax and Mr. Pitt, are of the latter sort. The things said in them are in the main right, so far as they may be practicable; but publishing them to the world beforehand, instead of waiting till the time comes, and then applying privately to the persons whose advice the king will take about them, is likely to raise opposition and prevent success. Publishing them, indeed, in a magazine, may raise no great alarm; but then it will be apt to produce contempt, for those monthly collections are far from being in high esteem. And as soon as either of those great men should see that the queries offered to him were designed to be inserted in any of them, he would be strongly tempted to throw them aside, without looking further into them, even were he otherwise disposed to read them over; which men of business seldom are, when they receive papers from unknown hands, few of them in proportion deserving it. You will pardon the frankness with which I tell you my thoughts. Whatever good use I can make of your notions, I will. But the use which you propose is not agreeable to my judgment."

Johnson had mentioned in the same letter which accompanied his paper the sudden death of Mr. De Lancey, the Lieutenant-governor of New York, and suggested the importance of appointing in his place "not only a good statesman, but a friend to religion and the Church, and exemplary in attendance on her public offices, for want of which, religion had suffered extremely in that province." The suggestion was felt to be worthy of consideration. "I have spoken," said the Archbishop, "concerning a Lieutenant-governor, in the manner which you desired, to the Duke of Newcastle and Mr. Pitt, and also to Lord Halifax, in whom the choice is. They all admit the request to be a very reasonable and important one; and promise that care shall be taken about it. The last of them is very earnest for Bishops in America. I hope we may have a chance to succeed in that great point, when it shall please God to bless us with a peace."

Every letter written at this period was but a repetition of the wants of the Church in the American Colonies, and of his own desire for aid in carrying on the College. It was as difficult to find tutors as suitable persons to supply the vacant missions. After many diligent inquiries, the Archbishop had thus far been unsuccessful in meeting his wishes, and as a means of providing for the Church, he expressed the hope that good young men might be sent over from this country to receive ordination and be returned to fulfill the office of missionaries in the old parishes. The eye of Johnson was especially fixed upon the Church in Connecticut and New York, though he was depended upon in London for information to some extent, in regard to all the colonies. The Society looked to him for facts which it cost him much labor to procure, and frequently it was a long time before he could reply intelligently to all the inquiries received. He sent off by every packet something which was designed to put his English friends and patrons in possession of the state of American feeling, and transmitted, as they were issued, the pamphlets and publications that bore upon the concerns of the Church. The idea of the geography and extent of this continent was less understood in England then than now, — and it is not very well comprehended at the present time, — so that when the Archbishop of Canterbury in the same letter addressed questions to him for information concerning Missionaries from Newfoundland to North Carolina, he could not answer to his own satisfaction till he had obtained the data on which to proceed.

Quietly fixed at housekeeping in the College building, he passed the winter of 1760–61, and took great pains to preserve his health and avoid exposure to the dreaded contagious disease. He wrote his son at Stratford about the middle of November: "It would be an unspeakable satisfaction to see you here, but I would rather be denied it than you should be too much incommoded. I believe the small-pox will die away again, though perhaps never be quite gone. It would be one of the greatest satisfactions in life to me to have you well through it by inoculation, from which there are so good hopes that I should not care to oppose it, if you think it best to undertake it, and yet I dare not urge you to it, but would leave it to Providence and the dispositions of your own mind. It is indeed a wretched embarrassment to me in my present situation; so that if your case was as mine is, I should be almost ready to even advise you to it, and did I not think of retiring for good and all when it becomes general again, if I should live to it, I should be almost resolved to run the risk of it yet."

A few days before Christmas, when he was expecting a visit from his son, which the illness of his wife prevented, he wrote him again, a brief note in which were the words: "I hope by your account you are in no danger of the small-pox, as perhaps you would have been had you been here and gone much about, for there is a good deal of it about town. On which account I have been out only at Church and Mr. Barclay's these three or four weeks. Thank God, I continue in perfect health, and hope with this care I am in no danger."

The friends of the Institution were anxious to continue him at its head, and saw the importance of keeping him on the spot now that an effort was about to be made to renew the application for contributions from abroad. The times appeared more auspicious. The King of Great Britain had died suddenly on the 25th of October, 1760, and his grandson, George III., ascended the throne in the twenty-third year of his age, a sovereign of religious impulses and unspotted reputation. "The young king begins his reign, you see," wrote Johnson to his son, referring him to the public prints, "with a glorious proclamation in favor of religion and virtue, — the like to which I believe has not been before, unless in Queen Anne's reign."

The Episcopal clergy in this country transmitted addresses to him upon his accession, but that of the clergy in and near Boston was not presented to him, because it was thought to mention Bishops prematurely. "This is a matter," wrote Secker to Johnson, "of which you in America cannot judge; and therefore I beg you will attempt nothing without the advice of the Society or of the Bishops." He had written to his Grace, and with the advice of some of his clerical brethren, humbly suggested to him, whether there would not be good reason to hope from the declarations of the young king that upon the commencement of a peace he might be prevailed upon to settle Episcopacy in America, and whether the draught of an address to his Majesty something like the one which he inclosed, would not be expedient and contribute to this end.

The Governors of the College took occasion to add their congratulations in a formal way, and to manifest their loyalty as dutiful subjects of the youthful sovereign. Johnson was the author of this address, as he was of that which went from the clergy of New York, and the two neighboring provinces, but it does not seem to have awakened any new interest in behalf of his plans, and probably it was too soon after the coronation, to hope for benefits or changes. The most that it could do may have been to lead the King to inquire concerning the signers, and, as Secker suggested, "express himself in relation to them."

In the autumn of 1760 he published a discourse entitled: "A demonstration of the Reasonableness,

Usefulness, and great Duty of Prayer," which he dedicated to Jeffery Amherst, Major-general and Commander-in-chief of all his Majesty's forces in North America. The dedication was a graceful compliment to him for the "glorious success" which had attended his conduct in the reduction of Canada, "an event," he added, "of immortal renown, and a signal reward of your piety and virtue." The discourse was written at the earnest request of a person of note, who put into his hands a manuscript, undertaking to prove by reason, that Prayer, since it implies a petition to God to supply any wants of ours, is in effect, "an utterly impertinent and insignificant thing, and but a mere useless ceremony." Appended to it, was a letter to a friend in West Chester, relating to the same subject, with whom he had expostulated for not frequenting the public worship as usual, and whose absences sprung not so much from indifference, as from doubts and infidel speculations. He closed it in words as applicable to men of the present day, as to skeptics who lived a century ago.

I am grieved to hear you complain of endless doubts and perplexities in matters of religion, for it is indeed a miserable state to be worried with a spirit of skepticism, and dark suspicions and surmises about this, and that, and the other. *Nubila mens est hæc ubi regnant.* "It is a cloudy, doleful state of mind where these prevail." Pray sit down then and carefully distinguish and separate things certain from things doubtful, and abide by them, and give the doubts to the winds; but never doubt whether you ought diligently to attend on the public service of God. Attend, I say, in the first place, and above all things, to plain, evident, practical matters, and especially live in the constant regular practice of true devotion towards God in Christ, who is our only Supreme Good; and trouble not your head with curious disputes and speculations, and perplexing doubts and intricacies, many of which are only strifes about words, and others about things we have no concern with, and things quite beyond our faculties.

I will only add, that I am fully persuaded when you come to leave this world, it will be the greatest satisfaction to you, to be able to say with the royal Psalmist, "Lord, I have loved the habitation of thy house, and the place where thine honor dwelleth." I hope, therefore, you will this once excuse this long letter from a faithful friend, who is solicitously concerned for your best good, and I commend you to God's protection, conduct, and blessing.

To confirm the truth of his words, and give force to his reasoning, he subjoined a sententious extract from a sermon of his venerated friend Dr. Secker, the archbishop of Canterbury. "There must be public virtue, or government cannot stand; there must be private virtue, or there cannot be public; there must be religion, or there can be neither; there must be true religion, or there will be false. There must be attendance on God's worship, or there will be no religion at all."

This publication was followed by happy effects, and several months after he printed as a sequel to it a sermon, "On the Beauty of Holiness in the Worship of the Church of England," which he recommended to the attention of the good people of New England, and particularly of his former parishioners at Stratford and West Chester. It was a temperate defense of the Liturgy, and aimed to "show that in the Church of England we do most truly worship Almighty God, that our worship is a most holy worship, and tends to promote holiness in the best manner, and that it is a most beautiful worship, and is truly worshipping God in the beauty of holiness."

A passage under the last head, though somewhat quaint in its phraseology, may be cited as an example of the spirit of the whole discourse: —

Our worship is truly beautiful in its language, which is very weighty and expressive. It may, perhaps, be granted that in a few passages, it may be capable of some improvements, but in general this must be allowed to be the character of its language, that it carrieth a great force and weight with it, without either deficiency or redundancy, and is in the happy medium between an affectation of verbosity, and high flown figures, on the one hand, and obscurity and dullness, and a low vulgar meanness of expression on the other. It hath a grandeur and majesty in it, and, at the same time, a most easy, natural, intelligible simplicity; always fitted to the weight and importance of the matter, and the capacities of the whole body of worshippers. If it savors of antiquity, and on that account be thought not so polite to modern ears, yet this very thing giveth it an air of the greater gravity and importance, and there are but very few expressions that are at all the less intelligible, though it is nigh two hundred years old; and it adds much to its beauty, that it is expressed as far as it could well be, in the very language of Scripture, being an excellent collection from the very Word of God, which is ever full of majesty and grandeur. And as there cannot be a more decent and beautiful sight than to behold a great number of intelligent beings, the creatures and children of God, jointly conspiring to do all the honor they can to Him their common parent, in their united adoration of Him, so there is the greatest propriety and fitness in it, and consequently the greatest beauty that they should worship their heavenly Father in his own language, in the words which He hath put into their mouths. If, therefore, we love the Scriptures, we cannot fail to love the worship of the Church of England, which is for the most part taken from them, and entirely conformed to them.

But it adds to the beauty of our excellent Liturgy, that

there is an admirable proportion in all its parts; insomuch that no one part is so swelled or enlarged beyond its measure, as to jostle out or starve another. There is a just proportion of Devotions and Lessons, of Prayers and Praises, of Confessions and Deprecations, of Supplications and Intercessions, of Petitions and Thanksgivings for ourselves and for all men, for kings, and all that are in authority, and for all orders and conditions of men. And as all these parts of worship, without deficiency or redundancy, are thus so exquisitely fitted and proportioned one to the other, so they all aim at one end, to which they are no less aptly fitted and proportioned, namely, to advance the honor of God and the general benefit of mankind, and to promote universal holiness and righteousness among them, all which considerations abundantly speak their harmony and beauty.

And this beauty is further mightily improved by that grateful variety that appears among them, which renders our Liturgy like a beautiful garden, wherein there is a delightful variety of luxuriant nature intermixed with curious art, of other various plants with trees; of fruits with flowers of divers sorts, all ranged in a various and beautiful order. In like manner, in our Liturgy, devotions are gratefully intermixed with lessons, and prayers with praises. The people's part is generally intermixed with the minister's, and short responses, in the form of ejaculations, with set and continued prayers, in which there is an agreeable variety, and the prayers are each of them short, in imitation of the Lord's Prayer; and there is a correspondent variety of actions of the body, suited to this variety of the exercises of the mind; all wisely contrived to keep the congregations wakeful, lively, and attentive. This method is therefore vastly preferable to one tedious, long-continued prayer, without any variety, as is the case with our neighbors, in which the people's attention flags, and they grow dull and heavy, and the force of their devotion is extremely weakened. On which account nothing should tempt me to exchange our beautiful variety of short devotions, for their long, dull, and unvaried performances.

For such is our frailty at best, that we need all the wise precautions imaginable to be used to keep our minds vigorous, wakeful, and attentive, both by a variety of devotions and of bodily worship, which is the true intent of all that beautiful variety wherewith our worship is attended, and which, in proportion as it attains those ends, may be truly styled the beauty of holiness.[1]

An experience of nearly forty years had strengthened his love for these forms and given him an opportunity to test their value. From time to time he had seen in them fresh beauties, and the testimony which he bore to their excellence, in the evening of his days, was a proof that no trials, and hatreds, and adversities, had made him regret the step which he took when he broke away from the popular faith of New England. He felt that he was one in sympathy and fellowship with a great branch of the Church universal. "In the use of the Liturgy," said he, "I am offering up not the devotions of this or that assembly only, much less of this or that particular person or minister, but the prayers and praises of the whole English Church and nation, enjoined by lawful authority, and which every assembly is jointly offering up at the same time. And moreover, that I find I am worshipping God according to the ancient Scripture method, wherein it was the manner for all the people to lift up their voice with one accord, not only in singing, but in saying their devotions."

The sermon from which these portions are taken is closed with an earnest appeal to churchmen to adorn the religion they professed, by the "exemplary holiness" of their behavior. "We have lately had," are his words, "an adversary [Mr. Noah Hobart] who

[1] Pages 20–22.

pretends to show as an argument against us, *that where the Church prevails, all manner of wickedness prevails*." It was a groundless and abusive reproach, and he would have them confute it by living lives answerable to the mighty obligations their worship laid them under. A wicked churchman, in his judgment, was the most inexcusable of all creatures. Much as he loved the Liturgy, he was far more desirous that they who adopted it should be true to its teachings, and firmly resolved to bring forth those fruits of holiness whereby our Heavenly Father may be glorified.

Since the death of his wife and daughter, he had lived very much alone, and been little concerned about his domestic affairs. But they appeared to be suffering at this time "for want of a careful and disinterested housekeeper," and he began to turn over in his mind what he had thought of before, but dismissed without coming to a final decision. The following letter to his son will explain his views and feelings in regard to a second marriage: —

K. C., N. Y., *February* 16, 1761.

Dearest Son, — We cannot be sufficiently thankful that our health is so graciously continued, both yours and mine. Mine, I think, was never better, notwithstanding my confinement. For exercise I run frequently up garret, besides walking a great deal the length of my two rooms, by which I tire myself at least once a day; which with five recitations (lectures we call them), two of which are equal to two sermons, seem exercise enough to answer the end. Indeed, I am obliged to live very laboriously.

I thank you for explaining yourself so fully on the subject I mentioned, and with so much tenderness and filial affection, and I may add with much propriety and accuracy, considering your hurry and interruption. I was always with you, against second matches, especially in advanced years, for the reason you mention, on which account I bless myself a thousand times that I came off so well from my former views, which gave me great uneasiness on your account; and be sure I should never have thought of such a thing again, but in the present case, which can scarce possibly be attended with those ill consequences. Indeed, it seems very ridiculous, and I am really ashamed of the thoughts of matrimony at this time of day; but in truth it seems so doleful in old age to be destitute of a contemporary companion, that I am almost apt to think a man never wants one more, and that if he has a good one in his younger years, there is nothing in life he needs more earnestly to pray for than her continuance to the last. On these accounts, I don't know (since you approve of it, and I cannot for two or three years at least if I live, leave this station) but that I had best think of it in earnest. I should hardly come this spring, if it were not on this account, but if my life and health continue, I believe I shall go about the middle of May, if there is like to be an opportunity, or perhaps not till June, according as Commencement is. I doubt the difficulty will be to have a vessel ready immediately after Commencement.

I have got "Smollett," and with you do not quite like him. I fear he has no religion. Methinks he writes sometimes with a fleer. I am told he has written so freely about Lord Anson that he has prosecuted him and put him in jail. I believe there is but one volume of the continuation of it published. I shall send it when there is opportunity. I had another volume of sermons for a vehicle to this letter. With my love to Mrs. Beach and to you all, I remain,

Your most affectionate father and friend,

S. Johnson.

The practice of interchanging thoughts on the subject of their readings had been observed for a long time, and must have been as pleasant as it was profitable. Scarcely any new and important work upon theology, history, philosophy, or literature, made its appearance in England, which the father did not speedily procure, and possess himself of its contents before sending it to his son. In this way they benefited each other, and sharpened their moral and critical judgments. It was a period when the books published, especially those commanding attention, were not so numerous but that a diligent reader could easily find time to peruse them and weigh well their merits and tendencies. Johnson had a great dislike for any author who seemed to sneer at the Christian religion. He had no patience with infidels and scoffers, and believed Christianity to be not only the anchor of the soul and the safeguard of society, but the sublimest philosophy.

This feeling will account for his distrust of Smollett. "Infidelity" said Bishop Watson, in his reply to Thomas Paine, "is a rank weed, it threatens to overspread the land; its root is principally fixed amongst the great and opulent, — but you are endeavoring to extend the malignity of its poison through all the classes of the community."[1] It was a fear of this kind which made Johnson so careful to watch against the contaminating influence of irreligion. He would have the rising generation, — the merchants, manufacturers, and tradesmen of the British realm, preserved from the delusions of unbelief, and continued in that faith which is the foundation of happiness in this world, and of the hope of glory in another.

[1] *Apology for the Bible*, p. 176, American Ed.

CHAPTER XI.

FOURTH COMMENCEMENT; SECOND MARRIAGE; BENEFACTIONS TO THE COLLEGE; DR. JAY AUTHORIZED TO MAKE COLLECTIONS IN ENGLAND; ARRIVAL OF REV. MYLES COOPER; RELIGIOUS CONTROVERSY; AND FOREIGN CORRESPONDENCE.

A. D. 1761–1763.

At the fourth Commencement of King's College, which was held June 3, 1761, the first Bachelors proceeded to their second degree. Several graduates of other colleges were admitted at the same time to a like honor, and pains were taken to make friends for the institution among Episcopalians outside of New York. Johnson was now more hopeful than ever of its growth, and felt that its great want was the want of additional funds to continue its operations and extend the course of instruction. He needed both a tutor and a professor to aid him in his labors, and his correspondence with the Archbishop of Canterbury had led him to anticipate that one or the other might ere long come from England, and be found fit eventually to succeed to his responsibilities.

Immediately after this fourth Commencement, he proceeded to Stratford in a sailing vessel, and was there married on the 18th of June to Mrs. Sarah Beach, widow of his old friend and parishioner, William Beach, and mother of his son's wife. At the close of the vacation, he embarked with her for New York, and earnestly applied himself again to his duties in the College. Failing to procure assistance from England, the Governors appointed Mr. Robert Harpur, a gentleman who had been educated at the University of Glasgow, and was well qualified to be Professor of Mathematics and Natural Philosophy, and with his help, he had an easier time than in the preceding year, and the classes were more thoroughly instructed. Nothing occurred to disturb the even tenor of his course during the ensuing winter. His domestic affairs were every way agreeable, and he wrote his son in October that he "never was happier in his life than now." What added greatly to his pleasure, as he himself said, was: "That Providence has sent us a good teacher of Mathematics and Experiments from Ireland, bred at Glasgow," and the scholars were so charmed with him that he could not refrain from expressing his belief that the Institution was thus to receive a fresh impulse.

The increase of its funds was another stimulus to its prosperity. Those obtained to complete the building and provide for immediate necessities were already exhausted, and the Governors were beginning to spend a portion of their capital to carry on the Institution. Besides the sums early secured, and the donation from the venerable Society of five hundred pounds, a benevolent gentleman, Mr. Joseph Murray, had bequeathed his estate to the College, amounting to six or seven thousand pounds. But more was needed, and Dr. Johnson renewed his proposal to solicit a collection in England, and prepared the way for it by writing to his friends and asking their good offices. In a letter to the Archbishop of Canterbury dated January 6, 1762, after referring to his agency in procuring a suitable person for vice-president and to succeed him in case of his decease or resignation, he said, "Notwithstanding the exception made to his age, and the uncertainty whether he will answer as a preacher, he is desired, if he is willing, to come upon the terms, and with the views mentioned in our letters to your Grace. But as we have already been providentially provided for with an ingenious young gentleman, one Mr. Harpur, bred at Glasgow, who does very well in teaching Mathematics and Experimental Philosophy, Mr. Cooper will not need to bring one with him for that purpose. But the great difficulty is how to support these salaries which our stock cannot long do, unless we can by some means get an addition to it, and we see no way for this but by getting forward a subscription in England, and we have not yet any one here to go home on purpose to solicit one. So that unless some public spirited gentleman there would be so good as to undertake it, I see not what to do, though indeed I cannot excuse ourselves of too much indolence and inattention to the interests of the College."

A month before this he had written to Mr. Horne of Oxford, afterwards Bishop of Norwich, and author of the "Commentary on the Psalms," and sent the letter by a graduate of Yale College who went to England, recommended to the Society and the Bishop of London as a worthy candidate for Holy Orders and a Mission. After thanking him for the kindness he had shown to his deceased son, and mentioning favorably what he was pleased to call his "admirable state of the case between Sir Isaac and Mr. Hutchinson," Johnson said: —

I thought I would, though thus late, presume to trouble you with a few lines, to express my earnest wishes that some of you (and I hope you are about it), would give the world an entire methodical system of that sacred philosophy and theology in the same candid way to the best advantage. I say this because, though Mr. Hutchinson's Discourses, on the Hebrew Scriptures, are admirable, yet his way of writing is obscure and disagreeable, which together with his asperity of temper and expression, has been I believe, the chief, if not the only reason that his extraordinary works have been no more read and considered and so generally thrown by with contempt in this conceited and inattentive age. May I not hope that this is doing and will soon be done.

I have written several times to good Mr. Berkeley, but whether my letters or his miscarry, or his leaving Oxford be the occasion, I have heard nothing from him these five years. If you ever see or correspond with him please to give my most affectionate service to him.

I have heard a rumor that the Rev. Dr. Patten has lately published some excellent performance, but cannot hear what it is. I shall be much obliged to you to make my humblest compliments acceptable to him, whose excellent sermons as well as yours are much admired here.

It is uncertain whether the worthy youth, Mr. Treadwell, who carries this letter, will see Oxford. If he should I beg your kind notice of him. My College, I thank God, is now in a pretty flourishing condition, and the building finished, only we want a fund to support sufficient officers.

I am, Reverend Sir, with great esteem,

Your most affectionate obliged humble servant,

S. J.

He dispatched a brief note to his old friend Dr. Astry by the same gentleman, "who," he said, "will give you some account of the Church and of my College, and my labors and hopeful prospect of laying a good foundation for posterity. I pray, God be your staff, your support and your comfort in your declining years, and your exceeding great reward in a better world."

Letters of this sort served as an introduction to the movement which was in contemplation. An opportunity soon offered of soliciting subscriptions in England through the agency of Dr. James Jay; and the President of the College urged the Governors to accept his services and furnish him not only with the requisite authority, but with suitable addresses to the king, the two Archbishops, the Universities of Oxford and Cambridge, and the Society for the Propagation of the Gospel in Foreign Parts. All seemed ready to acquiesce in the proposal, and Dr. Jay was formally appointed; and took his departure from New York on the 12th of May, 1762. Of the letters and addresses put into his hand, which were all prepared by Johnson, it will be enough to select the one written to Archbishop Secker: —

To the Most Rev. Father in God, Thomas, Lord Archbishop of Canterbury.

May it please your Grace, — Your Grace is well acquainted with the labors and difficulties under which we have struggled in founding our College and carrying it on hitherto; and has been informed that we have erected an elegant building of one hundred eighty feet in length by thirty in width and three stories in height, which is now just finished and designed for one side of a quadrangle to be completed as we shall be enabled. But as we are not yet able to carry it any farther without assistance, nor have we a sufficient fund to support the necessary officers — the Master, Professors, and Tutors, — we are therefore constrained to beg the charitable contributions of such public spirited gentlemen as are generously disposed to promote so good a work, and have empowered the bearer hereof, Dr. James Jay of this city, who is an ingenious young gentleman, and a graduated physician of the University of Edinburgh, to ask and receive such benefactions as shall be contributed to this important undertaking.

And as your Grace is the first member of our corporation and has given abundant demonstration of your delight in doing good offices, and especially to this College, for which we are inexpressibly thankful, we humbly beg leave to recommend him to your Grace, and entreat you in addition to your former goodness that you will give him your best advice and direction for his carrying on a solicitation for benefactions; and if you think proper, that you will introduce him, or procure him introduced to our most gracious Sovereign for his favor; and also that you will be pleased to recommend him to his Grace, the Lord Archbishop of York and the Bishop of London, or any other of the nobility, clergy, or gentry as your Grace shall judge most expedient. In doing which you will unspeakably oblige, may it please your Grace, Your Grace's, etc.

On his arrival in England, Dr. Jay found a competitor for British charities in the Rev. Dr. Smith, Provost of the College in Philadelphia. He had preceded him to London and was engaged in soliciting subscriptions for his own institution. The Archbishop, who had warmly espoused the cause of King's College, feeling that separate collections at the same time would injure the claims of each, thought it would be best to unite them, and apply to the king for a brief to go through the kingdom in favor of both. This was accordingly done, and the proceeds were divided equally between the two institutions, except that a donation from his Majesty of six hundred pounds to the College in New York was adjudged to be not included in the general collection. The joint contributions yielded to King's College the net sum of nearly six thousand pounds sterling, which, with the legacy of Mr. Murray and other donations, constituted for the time a sufficient endowment. The son of Bishop Berkeley generously contributed ten guineas, and in answering Johnson's letter by Dr. Jay, said, "It gave great delight to my worthy mother, now at my house, to hear that you enjoyed your health and spirits; she bears a most sincere good will to that quarter of the world where your acquaintance with her took its rise."

The Governors were now enabled to furnish the assistance which had long been desired, and the Rev. Myles Cooper, the young Oxford graduate, whom the Archbishop had recommended as being well qualified to take part in the management of the College, came over to this country in the autumn of 1762, and was welcomed by the President, and immediately appointed Professor of Moral Philosophy. He proved equal to the duties of the position, in spite of the objection which had been raised against him that he was too young; and Johnson looked forward with satisfaction to the day when he himself would be allowed to retire. He worked zealously with his new officer, and sought in judicious ways to prepare him for the assumption of his own responsibilities, not expecting, however, that a Providential event would lead him so soon to sever his connection with the College.

Absorbed as he was at this time in matters of education, he did not forget the Church, or cease to take a lively interest in the prosperity of the parishes in his native colony. He longed to see a better and more learned clergy; and in a letter to his son who had referred to the subject, he said, December, 1762, "What you lament has occasioned in me many a sigh. But how to remedy it is the difficulty. I wish those we have, had better abilities, more inclination to books and more zeal; and if I am allowed to come again among you, I intend to try to animate them, and hope to do some good. But I doubt poverty is one chief remora, which I cannot remedy. But we must, as you say, take more care to have good candidates if we can get them, and not recommend poor ones. I hope you may have some good influence in getting a right choice for New Haven, which is of much importance. We have good hands here, Chandler and young Seabury, but I can't get them to write, nor indeed do they know enough of some affairs for this business, but might be informed. We must, as you say, leave it with God Almighty, with whom is the residue of the Spirit, to raise up instruments to defend His Church under His protection, and I hope and trust He will not desert it."

He had in his mind, while writing thus to his son, a pamphlet which had recently been published anonymously, and circulated to the injury of the Church of England, especially in Massachusetts and Connecticut, and to which the Archbishop of Canterbury had called his attention, and desired that it might be answered. Johnson fixed upon the Missionary at Newtown as the most competent person to do this, and wrote again to his son, "I shall be very sorry if Mr. Beach does not answer that base pamphlet. Tell Mr.

Winslow, let the clergy give him no rest till he is persuaded. I would undertake it myself rather than fail, if writing were not so tedious to me. I fear how the Church will do when her old champions are gone. If he fails I know of none anywhere equal to it. I knew nothing before of that Boston act. I wonder with the Archbishop none of the Church's friends had been earlier in their notice."

It was a time of sharp theological controversy. The bitter hostility of the Independents to the introduction of Bishops into this country, and to the work of the Society for the Propagation of the Gospel, was the origin of the pamphlet, and a few of the Episcopal clergy, in view of its ironical character, were inclined to regard it as unworthy of the least attention. The younger Johnson, in a letter to his father, dated January 7, 1763, said: "Mr. Beach, I am now assured, is writing, as he has sent to me to procure an account of the settlements and salaries of some of the Dissenting ministers; and I hope with you, he will do it well. I have written him to encourage the thing and to suggest some few things. Mr. Caner, it seems by a letter to Mr. Winslow, thinks the piece too low and scandalous to answer; but I cannot agree with him. As our enemies avail themselves so much of it, I am not content to let it pass."

The answer was prepared and submitted to the examination of Dr. Johnson through his son, into whose hands the manuscript first came, and he, after running it over, wrote to his father: "I durst not pronounce upon it from this hasty reading, and am sorry I have not more time to consider it, but hope you and Mr. Cooper and others there will consider it carefully before it is published. I fear it is too severe in some expressions, though they deserve it all." With a few words referring to his own suggestions, he added, "Perhaps it would have been well if Mr. Beach had not so often mentioned Messrs. Hobart and Dickinson as the authors of the pamphlet, as it is very uncertain who they were,[1] though I believe he is right, that all their clergy are pleased with it. You will critically examine the whole. Notwithstanding the opinion of Mr. Caner, Mr. Winslow, etc., an answer must be published; I think I every day see more and more occasion for it."

Dr. Johnson had determined by this time, to retire from his position in New York, and was shaping his plans with reference to such a step. There was some prospect that Mr. Winslow might be transferred to another station, and an opportunity given for restoring him to his old parish. But if this should not be effected, his son wrote him to have no anxiety about his temporal concerns. "Your determination," said he, "to leave the conduct of your affairs to me is kind and does me honor, but it is too much, as I am very liable to mistake. Only be assured that you will always have my best judgment, and that I shall never think anything I can do a burden, or too much to render your

[1] The author was Mr. Noah Welles, a Congregational divine in Stamford, Ct. The irony extended through 47 octavo pages, and justified Johnson in using the expression "base pamphlet." The title page ran thus: "The Real Advantages which ministers and people may enjoy, especially in the Colonies, by conforming to the Church of England; faithfully considered and impartially represented, in a Letter to a young Gentleman, printed in the year 1762." It opened with these words: "I received your's by the worthy Mr. ———, in which you inform me that pursuant to my advice, you went to Church on *Christmas Day*, and was so greatly pleased with our worship that you have some thoughts of conforming, and going home for orders next spring. You may be sure this gave me the greatest satisfaction, as I am firmly attached to the *Apostolic* Church of England, that *great bulwark* of the Reformation."

life comfortable. I know not why it is not equally a duty, at least to provide for parents as for children. But use your own judgment (of which we have both had so long and so good experience) with mine for the best means to attain that end. Be not concerned for me or mine so as to give yourself any uneasiness; if I or they have less fortune, it may be less temptation to go astray, and redoubled diligence may make amends for it. Those who are not content to be diligent have no title to the goods of fortune, and those who are really so, will very seldom want a competency. If you can stay there with ease, satisfaction, honor, and credit I can be content; if not, do not hesitate to retire, whatever becomes of every other consideration, for all others are inferior to them. Providence will not desert us."

A domestic affliction prevented him from giving much attention to Mr. Beach's pamphlet before its publication; and soon the minds of Churchmen were turned to the controversy as renewed and carried on in Boston. In 1763 appeared a vindication of the Society by the Rev. East Apthorp, entitled "Considerations on the Institution and Conduct of the Society for the Propagation of the Gospel in Foreign Parts," to which a Dissenting divine, Dr. Jonathan Mayhew, replied in a much thicker pamphlet, and contended that the managers were either deceived by the representations of their Missionaries, or were governed more by a regard to Episcopacy than to the interests of true religion. Replies and rejoinders followed, and the republication in England of Dr. Mayhew's "Observations on the Charter and Conduct of the Society," led the Archbishop of Canterbury to prepare an answer and print it that the truth might be known to the British public. The following letters, though anticipating a little the chronological order of events, will let the reader into a pretty full history of the whole controversy, as well as shed some light on the affair of American Bishops: —

GOOD DR. JOHNSON, — I heartily thank you for your letter of August 10, particularly for the concern which you express about my health. It is frequently disordered; but I can for the most part pay some attention to business. When I fail, as I am now within a few days of seventy, an abler person in all respects, I hope, will succeed me.

Mr. Beach's book is not come to my hands; I wish it had received your corrections. I am as desirous that your answer to Dr. Mayhew should be published, as I can be without having seen it; because I dare say it is written with the temper which I told you I wished Mr. Beach might preserve. But indeed I fear the world will think we have settled too many missions in New England and New York; and therefore it may be best, not absolutely to justify, but to excuse ourselves in that respect, as prevailed on by entreaties hard to be resisted, as having many applications, and resolved to be hereafter more sparing in the admission of them, instead of making it our business to *Episcopize* New England, as Dr. Mayhew expresses himself. Our adversaries may be asked whether they have not made as great mistakes in some points, as we in this; and whether bitter invectives against them would not be unchristian. There was a company incorporporated by Car. 2, in 1661, *for Propagating the Gospel amongst the heathen nations of New England and the adjacent parts*, which still subsists, and the affairs of it are managed by the Dissenters. Queen Anne, in 1709, incorporated *The Society in Scotland for Propagating Christian Knowledge*, and empowered them to propagate it not only there, but *in Popish and infidel parts of the world*. Accordingly they had correspondents and Missionaries in New England above thirty years ago; and in Long Island, Pennsylvania, North Carolina, and Georgia above twenty years ago; and probably they have still. It may be useful to inquire, whether these two Societies have observed their charters better than ours hath. If not, their friends should think and speak mildly of us. The new projected Society at Boston is about sinking itself into the latter of these, as I am informed. I know nothing of Dr. Barclay's "Defence against Smith," nor of Aplin; possibly this last word was a slip of your pen for Apthorp.

What will be done about Bishops, I cannot guess. Application for them was made to Lord Egremont, who promised to consult with the other ministers, but died without making any report from them. His successor, Lord Halifax, is a friend to the scheme; but I doubt, whether in the present weak state of the ministry, he will dare to meddle with what will certainly raise opposition. I believe very little is done or doing yet toward the settlement of America; and I know not what disposition will be made of the lands belonging to the Popish clergy in the conquered provinces.

I am very glad to hear the money is paid to Mr. Charlton. I have heard nothing of any design of a Degree for Mr. Chandler, but from you. If any person here is engaged in it, I should know, that we may act in concert. But I think we should have a more formal recommendation of him from you and Dr. Barclay, and any other principal persons, clergy or laity.

Your account of Mr. Cooper gives me great pleasure. In a late letter to me, he expresses good hopes about the College; but complains of some disappointment in regard to his income, which I do not distinctly understand. I have written to him, to recommend patience; and to Dr. Barclay, to desire that the Governors will be as kind to him as with propriety they can. Mr. Caner hath sent over one Mr. Frink for a new mission at Rutland, about sixty miles from Boston, without any previous mention of the matter to the Society, which is irregular; and I do not think we shall appoint him to it; perhaps to some vacant old one we may, if such there be. The Mission of Braintree is offered to Mr. Winslow, in order to make room for you at Stratford. Whether it be worth his acceptance I know not. But the Society are very desirous of restoring you to your old station; and if this proposal doth not succeed, they will be glad to have any other method pointed out to them.

Since I wrote thus far, the Society hath appointed Mr. Frink Missionary at Augusta. It seems he was inoculated a few days before. I hope he will get safe through the distemper.

God bless you, good Dr. Johnson, and His Church in your parts. I am, with much esteem,

Your loving brother,

THO. CANT.

LAMBETH, *September* 28, 1763.

Answer: —

December 20, 1763.

MAY IT PLEASE YOUR GRACE, — I humbly ask your Grace's pardon for writing so soon again, which I hope you will excuse, as I should be extremely wanting in my duty to your Grace, if I did not most gratefully acknowledge your very kind letter of September 28, which I lately received. I am very glad and thank God that your health is not so much impaired as to forbid your giving some attention to business, and I earnestly pray that it may be yet again confirmed and lengthened out to the utmost, and the rather as I am extremely afraid that in these times no gentleman can be found that will go near to make good your Grace's ground. I am surprised Mr. Beach's book is not come to your hands; I sent a copy which was promised me to be sent you from Boston seven months ago; and I have again urged it, and Aplin's (a lawyer), for so is his name. Mr. Caner (as it is privately said) has made, I think, a pretty good answer to Mayhew, with which mine, such as it is, is printed; but I hear Mayhew has replied already, still in his own way. Mr. Caner has remarked upon these Societies much as your

Grace mentions. I trust it will soon come to you, and that you will not dislike it.

Did our benefactors know the real state of things in New England, they would allow that missionaries are as much needed here as in other parts of America. The wildest notions are propagated here both on the side of enthusiasm and infidelity; but I wish to God more could be done there as well as here. Dr. Barclay's Defense was sent to the Society, and I have advised him to send your Grace a copy, and also to write in behalf of Mr. Chandler, whose character truly is that of a most faithful Missionary, and one that hath made much proficiency in learning, and especially in divinity. I know of none so much to my mind that loves books, and reads so much as he. It would be for the honor and interest of the Church and religion, if there were at least one in each province of that degree, and he a Commissary. I wish Mr. Caner had a D. D. degree, who well deserves it, and the rather as there is none in that province now but Dr. Cutler, who has done. By a letter lately from Mr. Cooper it appears that the Governors of the College have enlarged his salary to his content.

It is truly a miserable thing, my Lord, that we no sooner leave fighting our neighbors, the French, but we must fall to quarrelling among ourselves. I fear the present state of our ministry is indeed very feeble; so that I doubt we must, after all our hopes, lose the present juncture also for gaining the point we have long had so much at heart, and I believe must never expect another. Is there then nothing more that can be done either for obtaining Bishops or demolishing these pernicious charter governments, and reducing them all to one form in immediate dependence on the king? I cannot help calling them pernicious, for they are indeed so as well for the best good of the people themselves as for the interests of true religion. I would hope Providence may somehow bring it about that things may be compromised respecting the ministry, and would it not now be a proper juncture for some such general address from the provinces here to the King as I once mentioned to your Grace? or is there not probability enough of success left with regard to both Bishops and government to make it worth while for a gentleman or two, who I believe might be procured to go from hence for the purpose of gaining these points? for I doubt nothing will do without solicitation from hence. I should be greatly obliged to your Grace for your opinion and direction in respect to these things as soon as may be. It is indeed too much to trouble your Grace with these affairs in your present infirm state. I therefore humbly beg your pardon that I am thus importunate. I remember you once mentioned his Grace of York as having extraordinary talents for business; could not he be engaged to be active in these affairs? I am greatly obliged to the Society that they are very desirous to restore me to this station. Mr. Winslow is gone to Braintree, to see whether it will do for him to accept it, and I am prone to think he will. If he does I shall do my best, but I shall soon need some assistance.

I am, with the greatest veneration, etc.,

S. J.

The reply of Archbishop Secker to this letter gives the reason for his own share in the controversy, and suggests a conciliatory course to attain the great object in view.

Good Dr. Johnson, — Since my last of September 28, 1763, I have been favored with two letters from you, dated Ooctober 20, and December 20. The first did not seem to require an immediate answer, and about the time that I received the second, the gout seized both my hands and both my feet. It made several attacks on my right hand, and disabled me from making almost any use of it for two or three months. I am now, God be thanked, nearly as well as usual, and have received all the pamphlets which were designed for me from America. When Dr. Mayhew's

"Observations," etc., were reprinted here, it was thought necessary that an answer to them should also be printed here; which was done before the "Candid Examination, and Letter to a Friend," came to my hands. An hundred copies of the answer were sent by the Society to the Colonies, and I hope you have had one of them. It was believed that they would do no harm amongst you, and might do some good, though the "Candid Examination," etc., was undoubtedly sufficient for your part of the world. If you see any mistakes in the Answer, or hear of any objections to any part of it, that seem to be material, be pleased to send me an account of them, with such remarks as you think proper. I have Dr. Mayhew's "Defence of his Observations." He manifests the same spirit as before, and runs out into many things of little consequence to the Society. The case of Mr. Price and Mr. Barrett, page 125, etc., is new to me; and if it be truly represented, the former seems to have been blamable. If any reply is made, I hope it will be short and cool. Some angry Dissenter hath published a pamphlet, entitled, "The Claims of the Church of England Seriously Considered, in a letter to the author of the Answer to Dr. Mayhew." There is but little in it relative to the Society, and nothing that requires confutation.

The affair of American Bishops continues in suspense. Lord Willoughby of Parham, the only English Dissenting Peer, and Dr. Chandler,[1] have declared, after our scheme was fully laid before them, that they saw no objection against it. The Duke of Bedford, Lord President, hath given a calm and favorable hearing to it, hath desired it may be reduced into writing, and promised to consult about it with the other ministers at his first leisure. Indeed, I see not how Protestant Bishops can decently be refused us, as in all probability a Popish one will be allowed, by connivance at least, in Canada. The Ecclesiastical settlement of that country is not made yet, but is under consideration, and I hope will be a reasonable and satisfactory one. Four clergymen will

[1] Samuel Chandler, a Presbyterian divine of London.

be appointed for Florida, with salaries of £100 each, and four school-masters with £25 each; and the Society have been desired to provide them. This I consider as a good omen; yet much will depend on various circumstances, and particularly on the opinion, or persuasion concerning the opinion of the Americans, both Dissenters and Churchmen.

The Bishop of London died last week; poor man, he was every way unequal to that station. His successor, Dr. Terrick, is a sensible and good tempered man, greatly esteemed as a preacher, and personally liked by the king, as well as favored by the ministry. Therefore I hope he will both have considerable influence, and use it well. He was Residentiary of St. Paul's Church, when I was made Dean. I had no acquaintance with him before, but we have been very good friends ever since; and I doubt not but we shall remain such, and consult together about American affairs.

We must not run the risk of increasing the outcry against the Society; especially in the present crisis, and so perhaps lose an opportunity of settling Bishops in our Colonies, by establishing two or three new Missions in New England. Our affairs are not to be carried on with a high hand, but our success, if we do succeed, must arise from conciliating the minds of men. And this ought to be labored very diligently abroad as well as at home.

The Society hath agreed, in pursuance of a proposal made by Dr. Smith, to establish a proper number of corresponding Societies, with an agent or president for each of them; to give information and advice concerning all needful affairs, and act for the Society in all requisite cases. But this general scheme cannot be brought into due form for execution, till we see whether Bishops can be obtained and how many.

The Archbishop of York is very active in our business, as well as able. He hath brought the estate of Codrington College out of a most lamentable condition into a very hopeful one, and he hath done a great deal with the ministers in our ecclesiastical concerns. But these, and particularly what relates to Bishops, must be managed in a quiet, private manner. Were solicitors to be sent over prematurely from America for Bishops, there would come also solicitors against them; a flame would be raised, and we should never carry our point. Whenever an application from them is really wanted and become seasonable, be assured that you will have immediate notice.

I have heard nothing yet of Dr. Barclay's Defence; nor hath he mentioned to me the propriety of a Degree for Mr. Chandler, though I had a letter from him, dated January 20. I desire to know what College degree Mr. Chandler hath, and of what standing he is in that College; and the same of Mr. Caner.

Concerning the other particulars in your letters, I presume the Secretary hath written to you; and therefore I shall only add that I heartily pray God to give you every blessing needful for you, and earnestly desire your prayers in return for Your loving brother,

THO. CANT.

LAMBETH, *May* 22, 1764.

These letters show how much Secker relied upon the judgment of Johnson to guide him in his efforts for the Church in the American Colonies. A wide ocean rolled between them and there was often opportunity for ministerial crises and important political events before they could interchange views. But they kept each other well posted, and if Johnson could not discern the wisdom of the state policy which hemmed in the zeal of his "loving brother," he would not cease to plead for the Episcopacy in America, and to hope that it might be secured before his probation ended.

He had written to Mr. Apthorp very freely on this and other subjects growing out of the controversy with Dr. Mayhew, and among the letters which he received in reply was one that spoke of the influence which his son might have, if employed to present the application for Bishops. The letter should be given in full for the information it contains: —

CAMBRIDGE, *May* 7, 1764.

REVEREND AND GOOD SIR, — I have before me two of your favors, for which I make my earliest acknowledgments. The great affliction of our family in the death of Mrs. Wheelwright, who was extremely dear to us all, has hardly given me leisure or spirits, for some time past, to attend to any but the most necessary business.

I had a long conversation with Mr. Bennet on his affair. His public spirit leads him to project things that I fear cannot be effected, for want of the same spirit among those who alone can execute them. I have however undertaken to do all in my power; which is, to solicit our Governor and Lieutenant-governor to patronize him, and to receive four Indian youths at Boston, and in England. I shall use the influence of my friends with the Society to fix Mr. Bennet on their list, and to obtain, if possible, the appointment of two missionaries for the Mohawks. I hope something was done for him at a meeting of the Episcopal Society in Boston, to whom I recommended the support of his good undertaking. He proposes to make me another visit in a fortnight, when everything that can be done at Boston will be attempted.

The affair of soliciting the settlement of Bishops among us, is, I perceive, a matter of too great consequence and difficulty for me to engage in singly. What I wrote so hastily was rather expressive of my good will than of my settled thoughts. I soon after received a permission from the Society, and an invitation from my friends to make a voyage to England, which I hope to accomplish, by God's blessing, this year. I shall gladly exert myself in promoting that great national measure you speak of, as far as shall be proper for me. And as the subject is of much importance,

I will write my thoughts to you with freedom and simplicity. It is an affair that would be solicited by a layman with less aversion and opposition than by a clergyman. And I believe there can hardly be a properer person employed than Mr. Johnson, whom I heartily wish well recovered of the small-pox. If he should engage in that service, I think his instructions from hence ought to be of weight and authority. If he was himself, in person, to collect the sense of the principal governments, not only of the clergy, but of the Governors and persons of property and character among the laity, it might have a good effect. But I think the letters you mention, signed by a few of the clergy in each province, would be ineffectual. If the whole application both here and in England was conducted with firmness, spirit and dignity, I am apt to think it would succeed, as the Archbishop, and (it is said) the King himself approves of it. My opinion is confirmed by an answer to Dr. Mayhew published in London last winter, and wrote with admirable strength and temper. But this I suppose you have seen.

I know nothing of the article of news relating to Dr. Tucker of Bristol; nor do I think it is at all to be depended on.

What I write on this subject is with the most entire confidence in your wisdom to suppress any thoughts which you may not approve, and to accept my good intention. In this view I transcribe the quotation I mentioned, on the opposite page, and beg leave to declare myself,

Very respectfully, Reverend Sir,

Your most humble servant,

EAST APTHORP.[1]

[1] Though the son of a wealthy merchant of Boston, he did not return to this country again, but spent the remainder of his days in England, being first presented by Archbishop Secker to the Vicarage of Croydon. He was subsequently collated to the Rectory of St. Mary-le-Bow in London, with other benefices annexed, and still later became a Prebend in St. Paul's Cathedral. It is said he was actually offered the Bishopric of Kildare, but having lost his sight, he was obliged to decline, and finally retired to Cambridge among the scenes of his early education, for he was an alumnus and fellow of Jesus College, "honored and loved not only in his immediate circle, but by many of the great and good beyond it." He died April 16, 1816, in the 85th year of his age.

CHAPTER XII.

THE SMALL-POX IN NEW YORK; DEATH OF HIS WIFE; RESIGNATION OF THE PRESIDENCY AND RETIREMENT TO STRATFORD; CORRESPONDENCE WITH FRIENDS IN ENGLAND; RE-APPOINTMENT TO HIS FORMER MISSION; ADDRESS TO THE BISHOP OF LONDON; THE STAMP ACT; CONTINUED INTEREST IN THE COLLEGE; AND CLERICAL CONVENTION.

A. D. 1763–1766.

For some time it had been known that the disease which Johnson so much dreaded was more or less prevalent in town. He had not chosen to avail himself of the stipulation made with the Governors that he might retire into the country on its appearance, but had remained at his post, and used additional caution, to avoid the contagion. When the last Commencement was held (1762), he was carried to the Chapel in a close carriage; and in all the letters to his son for the rest of the year, he expressed his thankfulness to God for the continuance of good health, and seemed to be cheered with the hope of soon getting away from a situation of such peculiar anxiety. He began to think of having accommodations provided for him in Stratford, and his son, writing to him in Christmas week, said, "If you determine absolutely to remove in the Spring you will let me know by-and-by, whether I shall prepare to enlarge my house, or endeavor to hire one for you, if any should offer."

By this time the small-pox had appeared in several dwellings near the College, and he and his wife were obliged to keep as close as possible in the building, and with this precaution they hoped to be safe. Towards the end of January, however, Mrs. Johnson became very ill with what was thought to be only a bad cold, but alas! on the first day of February her real disorder developed itself, which proved to be the small-pox. She received the information with composure, and, from a tender regard for the welfare of her husband, desired him to leave her with his prayers in the hands of God, and withdraw to a place of less danger. For two days he occupied a room in the other end of the College building, and then his friends, thinking him too much exposed, he retired three miles distant to the country seat of Mr. Watts, and there waited in painful suspense the result of his wife's sickness. He had not long to wait, for on the 11th of February, overwhelmed with grief, he wrote to his son, "The thing that I feared is come upon me, God's will is done. Your good mother died on Wednesday evening, the 9th," and he added that they were probably then "carrying her to her grave, to lie by his own mother," under the Chancel of Trinity Church.

This bereavement was a crushing blow to him, and he resolved at once to resign the presidency of the College and go into retirement. He tarried a fortnight longer at the country seat of his friend, wrote his letter of resignation to the Governors, and then committing his affairs to Mr. Cooper and a lay-gentleman, "hired an able hand with a sleigh" to take him to Stratford, where he arrived February 25, 1763.

He was now in the 67th year of his age, blessed with good health, but having natural infirmities which called for a less anxious and active life. His connection with the College had been a sacrifice to him in a pecuniary sense, and in resigning the charge of it, he modestly hinted that he might be entitled to some consideration for his many hardships and losses. That it had not prospered more was not owing to any fault of his, but to "providential misfortunes or to the Governors themselves, in not providing a good Grammar school; for," said he, "till provision is made both for a better classical and English education, the College can never flourish."

The following correspondence has a meaning that is more than simply official: —

NEW YORK, *March* 2, 1763.

REVEREND SIR, — At the meeting of the Governors of King's College yesterday, your letter addressed to them was laid before them. They are sensibly touched with your late misfortune, and the immediate occasion of your retiring; and that vein of benevolence, which runs through your letter, could not but very much affect them.

I have the pleasure to be the instrument of returning their thanks for your faithful service as President, and your good offices for promoting the interest of the College hitherto, and your affectionate wishes for the future prosperity of it, gratefully accepting your kind offer of continuing your endeavors on all occasions for the advancement of that good work; and they wish you health and happiness.

As for the rest, the Governors have resolved to take your case into consideration at some future meeting. In the mean time be assured that I am,

Reverend Sir, your very affectionate friend and
very humble servant,
DANIEL HORSMANDEN.

Answer: —

March 30.

Gentlemen, — I very humbly thank you for your kind answer to my letter to you, communicated to me by the Honorable Judge Horsmanden, and for your affectionate sympathy with me under my truly compassionable circumstances; and that you take in so good part my past faithful endeavors to serve you, and my persevering solicitude for the prosperity of the College. This, I trust, is a pleasing prelude to that friendship which I hope will always subsist between the Corporation and me, and a further engagement to any good offices in my power for the furtherance of its wants.

I am particularly thankful, gentlemen, for your kind resolution in my favor, to take my present depressed condition into your benevolent consideration at some future meeting, and shall gratefully acknowledge whatever kind dispositions you shall at any time express towards me. With my continued fervent wishes for the prosperity of you and yours, and that dear College,

I remain, Gentlemen, with great regard,

Your most affectionate friend and obed't humble serv't,

S. J.

It was a time of war during the whole of his Presidency, and the expenses of living in town had been so much greater than was expected, that the Governors could not well refuse a gratuity, and finally voted to settle upon him a pension of fifty pounds per annum. This was secured chiefly through the influence of the Rev. Mr. Auchmuty, who did not think it enough, but was glad to have some recognition of the sacrifices and self-denials of his venerable friend.

Johnson was resolved not to be idle in his retirement. His son "built him an elegant apartment," attached to his own mansion, where, surrounded with his books and his grandchildren, he devoted himself to quiet study and was happy in the enjoyment of his domestic privileges. His literary and theological correspondence was not slackened but rather increased; and the introduction of the works of good authors into this country continued to be an object near his heart. A letter of his to the Rev. Mr. Horne of Oxford, from which an extract was given in the previous chapter, brought forth a reply which must have reached him in the freshness of his sorrow for the death of his wife.

Reverend Sir, — I am greatly obliged to you for the good opinion you are pleased to entertain of me and any trifle I have published; and rejoice to have an opportunity of recommending a work of real merit and solidity on the subject of the sacred philosophy, by my learned friend Mr. Jones, who is proceeding on the same plan, with ability and erudition adequate to the work, as fast as his health will permit him. Dr. Patten's controversy with Heathcote, some time since at an end, I presume hath found its way to New York. The Doctor hath published nothing more except an excellent sermon on "Natural Religion." Dr. Newton, Bishop of Bristol, hath lately put forth an admirable work on the "Prophecies," in three vols. octavo. I expect Dr. Jay every minute, to whom I shall deliver this with a letter from Mr. Berkeley; and am with best wishes and prayers for the prosperity of King's College and the worthy President thereof,

Reverend Sir, your most affectionate servant,

G. Horne.

Magd. Coll., *November* 29, 1762.

Answer: —

Stratford, in Conn., N. E., *June* 1.

Reverend and worthy Sir, — I am very much obliged to you for your most kind letter of November 29, and the very excellent things that accompanied it, which are all entirely to my mind, and I want words to express my gratitude for them. Mr. Jones's Essay is exactly such a thing as I have long wished to see, and I am the more pleased with it as coming from the author of the "Catholic Doctrine of the Trinity," which I had before been highly pleased with. These are indeed the true primitive original philosophy and divinity of the Holy Scriptures, made evident and intelligible. You will please to give him my compliments and thanks for these good works, which I shall earnestly recommend to our booksellers to have always by them, and to my College to be always there taught and inculcated, where your state of the case has already been of good use. I earnestly pray God to give Mr. Jones life and health to finish what he designs; and to you also, good Sir, as well as Dr. Patten, that you may go on to bless the world with your most useful writings, that this unholy age may if possible be reclaimed from its apostatising turn. I had received from Mr. Cooper a high notion of Dr. Morton and ordered my bookseller to procure it, and grow impatient till it comes.

It is of vast importance to us at this distance to have good authors pointed out to us by good judges. I shall therefore be highly obliged to you, if you will be so kind as to communicate to me and my successor such as at any time excel; and indeed it would be happy for us if really good authors could be induced from time to time to present our Library with their productions in every kind.

I date, you see, Sir, from this place, whither I am retired to spend with my only and most tender and dutiful son the little declining remainder of my time, being near sixty-seven, and wanting retirement, though, thank God, in perfect health except somewhat paralytic. I did not indeed intend quite so soon to leave the College, but so it pleased God. I was suddenly driven from it by the small-pox breaking out in my family and depriving me of the dear partner of my life. But I hope it will immediately be well governed and instructed by Mr. Cooper, who is well esteemed and appears to be an ingenious, industrious, and prudent young gentleman. I have still the same care for it as ever so far as can be at this distance — about seventy miles, — the post weekly passing, and I hope now and then to visit it. If you do me the favor to write again, please direct to me here, to the care of the Rev. Mr. Auchmuty of New York.

I am, Reverend and dear Sir, with great esteem and regard,
Your most obliged and affectionate friend and servant,
S. J.

He wrote to Dr. Burton, the Secretary of the Society, in the autumn of 1763, to express his thanks for the proposition to transfer Mr. Winslow to a Mission near his friends in Boston, that he might himself be reappointed to Stratford. He had not had much thought of doing more in his advanced years than to direct the theological studies of a few young candidates for Holy Orders, and send them with commendatory letters to England. But this opportunity of resuming parochial duty was too attractive to be disregarded. It met with favor from Mr. Winslow, who for many reasons was desirous of a change. "I have communicated the proposal to him," said Johnson, "which he was fond of, as it would place him near his friends. He had indeed had thoughts of it before, but some of his friends had discouraged him about it. However, upon this offer of it, he is now thinking in earnest about it and is treating with the Wardens and Vestry of Braintree, to see whether it may prove to his advantage, and he will soon let the Society know whether he accepts, as I am apt to believe he will."

Mr. Winslow's name was suggested at one time as a suitable person to take the Rectorship of Trinity Church, New York; and the son of Dr. Johnson, writing April 9, 1764, from that city, whither he had gone to be inoculated for the small-pox, said to his father, " Good Dr. Barclay made me a visit yesterday though he was but illy able to get up-stairs; he has had a bad week of it. He returns his affectionate compliments to you, but is at present by no means fit to undertake such a journey as you propose, as he cannot ride above three or four miles in a day, and durst by no means be out of the way of his physicians. The Doctor's illness has occasioned the Church to think of looking out for another clergyman. Mr. Auchmuty has desired my opinion of Mr. Winslow, whom I have recommended as the best preacher I know of, but as I have not his liberty to mention it, I must beg you will say nothing of it at present, and perhaps he will write to you himself on the subject."

Letters were addressed afterwards directly to Mr. Winslow, but he seems not to have favored a settlement in New York, for he was shortly transferred to Braintree, and the venerable Doctor took his place and returned to pastoral work among a people who had not forgotten his fidelity, though for ten years they had only heard his voice occasionally. With the assistance of a student at times in reading the service, he found little difficulty in fulfilling his duties, and his residence in the Colony again became a tower of strength to the Church in Connecticut.

The following letter to the Archbishop of Canterbury, in answer to one which appears in the previous chapter, shows how earnest he was at this juncture for the complete establishment of the Church in America: —

September 20, 1764.

It grieves me that your Grace must be so persecuted with that tormenting distemper for which nothing can atone, but what were good Bishop Berkeley's opinion and hopes, that it might prevent more fatal maladies in the decline of life, and tend to lengthen one's days. This I do at least earnestly pray may be the happy event with respect to your Grace's precious life, which is of so much importance to the present age.

I was almost overjoyed after our feeble efforts here to find one, who I did not doubt was the ablest hand in the kingdom, had condescended to undertake our mighty giant, and in the opinion of our people had utterly disarmed him; nor had any of the Dissenters, that I can hear of, a word to say, except Mayhew himself, who, upon its being immediately reprinted here, directly advertised an answer preparing, contrary to the advice of his best friends. I had it from a good hand that a man of the best sense among them told him he was completely answered, and advised him by no means to attempt a reply. But undaunted, he would not be dissuaded, and in a few days published it; but I am told, in a letter from Boston, that "to his mortification very little is said about it." . . . . In a word, I am verily persuaded it will do much the most good here as well as at home of anything that has yet been published. It is doubtless now in your hands, and you are the fittest judge whether any reply is necessary.

Neither had I, my Lord, ever heard of the case of Mr. Price and Barret, in which there might be too much truth, as I remember Mr. Price was too intemperate for the sake of his farm, in his endeavors to propagate the Church there.

I beg your Grace's pardon that I seemed perhaps a little too impatient in my last with regard to the settling Episcopacy in these countries, where I know that all the Church people (except a few lukewarm persons and free-thinking pretenders to it, and sometimes attendants on it, but are really enemies to any establishment) are very desirous of it;

and that all moderate Dissenters, who, I believe, are the most numerous in the whole, and who know what is really designed, have little or no objection to it; and that the number of such bitter zealots against it is comparatively few, and chiefly in these two governments, either such loose thinkers as Mayhew, who can scarcely be accounted better Christians than the Turks, or such furious bitter Calvinistical enthusiasts as are really no more friends to monarchy than Episcopacy; and against people of both these sorts Episcopacy is really necessary towards the better securing our dependence, as well as many other good political purposes.

Your Grace's quiet, private, and conciliating method, is doubtless best if the point can be gained, as it ought to be, in that way; but as I knew of no steps taken or like to be, and as your Grace was so infirm, I was afraid nothing would be done without some general and strong solicitations from hence, without which indeed I feared the ministry would hardly think anything about it themselves, or that we were at all solicitous for it here. I am therefore greatly rejoiced that something is doing, that the two chiefs of the separation have no objection to it, and that your Grace is assisted by two such great, worthy, and active gentlemen as the Archbishop of York and the Bishop of London; and that they have so good an interest; and that so great a minister as the Duke of Bedford has given so favorable attention to it and promised to promote it. These are very hopeful beginnings, and from these, together with the other considerations your Grace mentions, it should seem scarce possible that it should miscarry; so that I hope our first news in the spring will be that it is done, and that our governments all depend immediately on the Crown. May God Almighty grant a happy success to your Grace's faithful endeavors that his Church here may at length at this crisis be provided with worthy Bishops, without which, according to the original constitution of the Church (in my humble opinion), no Church can be perfect; which if it should please God to grant,

I could then cheerfully sing my *nunc dimittis!* but if He should not, the best thing that could be done would be to go into Dr. Smith's proposal, which we have long wished for.

The reason for not increasing missions here might be allowed good at this juncture; the young men[1] are safe returned, and will doubtless be very useful. I hope Mr. Jarvis may do tolerably for several years, as his people are much more able. But Mr. Hubbard must in two or three years be otherwise provided for, if the Society cannot help Guilford, which for the reasons I mentioned to your Grace, I earnestly hope they may by that time safely do.

What hindered good Dr. Barclay from mentioning the two things your Grace tells me he neglected, I am not able to say, unless it was the great infirmity he then began to labor under, which soon disabled him for public duty, and last month put a period to his very valuable life, to the inexpressible grief of his church, and indeed all the churches. The worthy and faithful Mr. S. Auchmuty was soon unanimously chosen in his place, and one Mr. Inglis in his, whom I know not, but I have good reason to think that Mr. Auchmuty will prove a worthy incumbent, and I wish for the honor of the Church and his station, that being of nigh twenty years' standing of our Cambridge, he might also succeed the Doctor in his degree. As to Mr. Caner, he was bred and graduated at our New Haven College, but was also created M. A. at Oxford, March 3, 1735, on the recommendation of Archbishop Potter; and Mr. Chandler of the same College proceeded M. A. in 1748, and had a diploma from Oxford, June 4, 1753, I believe, by your Grace's influence. And now I am upon the subject of degrees,[2] as I can't but retain a great affection for Oxon. and am desirous of continuing my connection with it, will your Grace forgive me if I mention my only son, who is a lawyer, for whom I am desirous of a Doctor's degree

[1] Rev. Abraham Jarvis, afterwards Bishop of Connecticut, and Rev. Bela Hubbard, for forty-five years Rector of Trinity Church, New Haven.

[2] Those for which Johnson asked in this letter were all conferred in 1766.

in that faculty? His name is Wm. Samuel. He is M. A. of seventeen years' standing in both our Colleges, and after a laborious study of the law he has been above ten years in the practice of it to good acceptance, and is studious in Divinity as well as in Law, and much engaged in the interest of the Church and true religion. He is well known to the bearer, Mr. Harison, from whom your Grace may have a further account of him if you think it needful. Mr. Apthorp's affairs suddenly calling him home, I beg your Grace's particular regard to him as a very worthy young gentleman. As I continue to pray earnestly for your Grace's health and long life, I humbly beg the continuance of your prayers and blessing in behalf of, etc., S. J.

The hope of obtaining Bishops, which now appeared so bright, was not realized. The ministry disappointed all the friends of the measure by neglecting the case of the Church and directing attention wholly to the civil affairs of the Colonies. Great confusions and tumults soon after followed both here and at home in consequence of the passage of the Stamp-act, and advantage was taken of this state of things to raise a fresh clamor against the establishment of Bishops in America. It was claimed that nineteen twentieths of the American people utterly opposed the scheme, and no correction of such a statement was ever accepted by the ministry. Dr. Johnson and the clergy of Connecticut sent congratulatory addresses to Bishop Terrick on his advancement to the See of London, and a correspondence ensued which must have opened his eyes, though he was powerless to effect a reform. Johnson wrote to him as follows: —

July 15, 1765.

I take this opportunity with the utmost gratitude to acknowledge your Lordship's most kind and condescending letters of February 22, both to the clergy and me, — theirs I sent to them at their Convention, which I could not attend by reason of the distance and badness of the roads, and I hear they have also most graciously acknowledged it in a joint letter to your Lordship. I am glad your Lordship is pleased with the worthy Mr. Harison's account of the clergy in this Colony, which I hope they will be more emulous to deserve.

It is, my Lord, a kind condescension that you are pleased to desire of me an account of the state of religion in these parts of the world. It is with much difficulty that I write, having a trembling hand, and therefore I can be but brief.

The true state of religion in America, with respect to the several denominations, is this: The Independents or Congregationalists, as they call themselves here in New England, especially in the Massachusetts and Connecticut Colonies, without any regard to the king's supremacy in matters of religion, have got themselves established by law and are pleased to consider us as Dissenters, but are miserably harassed with controversies among themselves, at the same time that they write against the Church. One great cause of their quarrels is the Arminian, Calvinistical, Antinomian and enthusiastical controversies which run high among them and create great feuds and schisms; and these occasion the great increase of the Church, at which they also are enraged, though themselves are the chief cause of it.

As to the Presbyterians, my Lord, they chiefly obtain in the Southwestern Colonies, and have flourishing presbyteries and synods, especially in New York, New Jersey, and Pennsylvania, in their full vigor; while in all these parts the poor Church is in a low, depressed, and very imperfect state for want of her pure primitive Episcopal form of government. We do not, my Lord, envy our neighbors, nor in the least desire to disquiet them in their several ways. We only desire to be upon at least as good a foot as they, and as perfect in our kind as they in theirs; and this we think we have a right to, both as the Episcopal form was the only form of government at first universally established by the Apostles, and is the primitive form established by law in our mother country; and therefore cannot but think ourselves extremely injured in not being provided for, and in a state little short of persecution in our candidates being forced, at a great expense of both lives and fortune, to go a thousand leagues for every ordination, as well as destitute of Confirmation and a regular government. So that unless we can have Bishops, especially at this juncture, the Church, and with it the interest of true religion, must dwindle; while we suffer the contempt and triumph of our neighbors under this neglect, who plume themselves with the hope that the Episcopate is more likely (as from the lukewarmness and indifference of this miserably apostatizing age they have too much reason to do) to be abolished at home, than established abroad. And indeed, my Lord, they are vain enough to think the civil government at home is itself really better affected to them than to the Church; and even disaffected to it; otherwise it would establish Episcopacy here as it is there. *Pudet hæc opprobria commemorare.*

I humbly thank your Lordship for saying so much in our behalf in your excellent sermon before the Society. Would to God a due notice might be taken of it; I do also most humbly thank you for your kind prayers and blessing, and beg the continuance of them; nor shall I cease to pray earnestly for the long continuance of your Lordship's very important life and health, being truly, my Lord, with great veneration, etc., S. J.

The Stamp-act threw the country into such a ferment and the opposition to its enforcement was so great that steps were early taken to procure its repeal. A Congress of the Colonies met at New York, and the son of Dr. Johnson was chosen to represent Connecticut in that body, and drew up the remonstrance to the King and Parliament against the measure, asserting taxation by themselves and trial by jury as among the inherent privileges of the subjects of the British realm in all her dependencies. The President of the Congress — Ruggles of Massachusetts — would not sign the document; and James Otis, a colleague of his, writing to Johnson after reaching his home in Boston, spoke of the attempt of the Massachusetts Assembly to censure him for his refusal, which he himself prevented, and then added: "The people of this Province, however, will never forgive him. We are much surprised at the violent proceedings at New York, as there has been so much time for people to cool, and the outrages on private property are so generally detested. By a vessel from South Carolina we learn that the people were in a tumult at Charleston and terrible consequences apprehended. God knows what all these things will end in, and to Him they must be submitted. In the mean time 'tis much to be feared the Parliament will charge the Colonies with presenting petitions in one hand and a dagger in the other."[1]

The Stamp-act was repealed just one year after its passage, and the venerable Missionary, who from his retirement in Stratford had looked with sorrow on the public discontents, was once more hopeful that the establishment of Bishops in this country might receive the attention of the ministry. He had not ceased to be interested in the College at New York, and Mr. Cooper, his successor in the Presidency, had been in the habit of spending more or less of his vacations with him, that they might consult together

[1] MS. Letter to Wm. S. Johnson, November 12, 1765.

and devise good things for its welfare. He paid a visit to New York in May, 1766, and was present at the annual Commencement held on the 20th of that month in Trinity Church. It afforded him unspeakable satisfaction to find the College in a prosperous condition, and the graduating class the largest hitherto sent forth.

But there was another matter which interested him at the time quite as much as that of education. The day after the Commencement, fourteen clergymen, two from Connecticut and the rest from the provinces of New York and New Jersey, held a Convention at which Johnson presided and Dr. Auchmuty preached a sermon. The most important business transacted was the adoption of an address to the Society on the extreme hardships the Church in America labored under for want of Bishops. It added to the moral force of the address that two young men, Mr. Giles of New York, and Mr. Wilson of Philadelphia, who had been to England for Holy Orders, had just been lost on their return in a ship that was dashed to pieces near Cape Henlopen. These made ten, whose precious lives sickness or the sea claimed, out of fifty-one who had gone from this country for ordination in a little more than forty years. It was an awful sacrifice for the sake of the Church, and they implored that it might be ended. "It is a greater loss," said Johnson, "to the Church here in proportion than she suffered in the times of Popish persecution in England."

While the clergy were holding this Convention, a Synod of about sixty Presbyterians met at New York with the design, it was said, of asking the General Assembly of Scotland to apply to the Parliament of

Great Britain for an act of incorporation in their behalf. Reference was made to this Synod in communicating the address of the clergy, and a letter from the Archbishop of Canterbury, which is among the last, if not the very last that he wrote to his venerated friend, met the considerations urged then and previously, and touched upon another point of great importance: —

LAMBETH, *July* 31, 1766.

GOOD DR. JOHNSON, — I am much ashamed, that I have delayed so long to answer your letters, and still more grieved that I cannot do it now to my own satisfaction or yours. It is very probable, that a Bishop or Bishops would have been quietly received in America before the Stamp-act was passed here. But it is certain, that we could get no permission here to send one. Earnest and continued endeavors have been used with our successive ministers, but without obtaining more than promises to consider and confer about the matter; which promises have never been fulfilled. The King hath expressed himself repeatedly in favor of the scheme; and hath proposed, that if objections are imagined to lie against other places, a Protestant Bishop should be sent to Quebec, where there is a Popish one, and where there are few Dissenters to take offence. And in the latter end of Mr. Grenville's ministry, a plan of an ecclesiastical establishment for Canada was formed, on which a Bishop might easily have been grafted, and was laid before a Committee of Council. But opinions differed there; and proper persons could not be persuaded to attend; and in a while the ministry changed. Incessant opposition was made to the new ministry; some slight hopes were given, but no one step taken. Yesterday the ministry was changed again, as you may see by the papers; but whether any change will happen in our concern, and whether for the better or the worse, I cannot so much as guess. Of late indeed it hath not been prudent to do anything unless at Quebec. And therefore the Address from the clergy of Connecticut, which arrived here in December last, and that from the clergy of New York and New Jersey, which arrived in January, have not been presented to the King. But he hath been acquainted with the purport of them, and directed them to be postponed to a fitter time. In the mean while, I wish the Bishop of London would take out a patent like Bishop Gibson's, only somewhat improved. For then he might appoint commissaries; and we might set up corresponding societies, as we have for some time intended, with those commissaries at their head. He appears unwilling, but I hope may be at length persuaded to it.

Requests have been made to me and other Bishops, first for countenance, then for contributions to Mr. Wheelock's Indian school. My answer was that we heartily wished success to it; and intended to set up one not in opposition, but in imitation of it; that we hoped the Dissenters would sufficiently support Mr. Wheelock's undertaking; but could not hope that they would contribute anything to a similar one of ours; and therefore it seemed requisite, that Churchmen should do their best for ours; though if any would be kind to theirs also, we should not blame them. They seemed pretty well satisfied. My first notion was, that we might maintain Indian boys at Mr. Wheelock's school, who should afterwards take Episcopal Orders. But Mr. Apthorp was clearly of opinion, that they would all disappoint our expectations in that respect. Now if only most, or many of them would, it will be absolutely necessary, that we should set up an Episcopal Indian school; else we shall both neglect our duty and lose our reputation. But we shall need the best advice of our friends, in what place or places, and under what masters and regulations, it will be most proper to attempt this. And the sooner we have such advice the better; for the distance between the Society and the scene of their business is extremely inconvenient. Mr. Barton of Lancaster hath conversed on this subject with Sir William

Johnson, who hath desired to be proposed for a member of our Society, and earnestly recommends the Indians to our care at present. We have sent to ask further information from both these gentlemen; and shall be glad of it from all who are capable of giving it.

I have mentioned our late and former losses of missionaries to the King, as one argument for Bishops. He is thoroughly sensible, that the Episcopalians are his best friends in America. There seems no likelihood that the Scotch Presbyterians will obtain any further privileges from our Parliament for their American brethren. Nor do I think there is any considerable increase of vehemence against Episcopacy here. Declaimers in newspapers are not much to be minded; nor a few hot-headed men of higher rank. I entreat you to write often and fully to me concerning all the Church affairs of America. I have not indeed been tolerably regular in my returns to your letters. Gout and business, and principally the delusive hope that a little time would produce good news, have hindered me. I will endeavor to do better, if God spares my life. But at least your informations and advice will be always highly acceptable and useful to

Your loving brother,

THO. CANT.

CHAPTER XIII.

REVIEW OF HUTCHINSON'S PHILOSOPHY; STUDY OF HEBREW AND PUBLICATION OF GRAMMAR; INDIAN SCHOOL; DEPARTURE OF HIS SON FOR ENGLAND; CHANDLER'S APPEAL; CORRESPONDENCE WITH HIS SON; ENGLISH ANCESTRY; AND DEATH OF ARCHBISHOP SECKER.

A. D. 1766–1768.

THE nest of Hutchinsonians, which his younger son found at Oxford in 1756,[1] was by this time well-nigh broken up; but he had neither relinquished their philosophy, nor ceased to read their books. He found leisure in his retirement to review the studies of former years, and reëxamine the conclusions which he had reached on philosophical and theological subjects. It gratified him that he was under no necessity of essentially changing his opinions; and while he could not approve the tendency towards extremes in some things, he still leaned to the side of Hutchinson in the controversy which arose upon his writings, and generally accepted them as teaching the truth. He thought he saw in the respectable scholars at Oxford[2]

[1] Mr. Berkeley, "the very worthy son of his great father, introduced us to a very valuable set of Fellows of several of the Colleges, Hutchinsonians, and truly primitive Christians, who yet revere the memory of King Charles and Archbishop Laud; and despise preferments and honors when the way to them is Heresy and Deism." — *MS. Letter of Wm. Johnson, May* 25, 1756.

[2] "I am sorry to find that the Bishop of Oxford [Dr. Lowth] is not a very good friend to Dr. Horne, but you will readily suppose that the Hutchinsonians are not out of countenance when you see Horne is head of Magdalen, and Wetherell of University College, Jones in a good living, and Berkeley with two, and in the high road to preferment by the patronage of his Grace." — *MS. Letter of Wm. Sam'l Johnson, March* 15, 1768

who favored that author's views, an earnest effort for the revival of Hebrew literature, and as this was a branch of study upon which he prided himself, he was glad of anything in the shape of new light, to guide his inquiries and help to a proper understanding of the original tongue.

It was about this time, or a little earlier, that he composed a small English Grammar for use in conducting the preliminary education of his two grandsons, and having revised his Catechism hitherto issued, he published them both together, in the hope that they might serve a good purpose to others.

But the study of Hebrew was the chief delight of his quiet hours. For many years he had entertained a strong opinion that as this was "the first language taught by God himself to mankind, and was really the mother and fountain of all language and eloquence, so in teaching, it would be, on many accounts, vastly advantageous to begin a learned education with that language," which lends to all others and borrows from none. He set himself, therefore, to the preparation of a Hebrew Grammar to go side by side with his English Grammar; the structure of the two languages bearing in his view a close resemblance. While engaged in this work, a new Hebrew Lexicon, by the Rev. John Parkhurst, was sent to him, and the value which he attached to this publication is best seen by quoting the letter which he addressed to the author from

STRATFORD, CONN., N. E.

REV. SIR, — I humbly hope your candor and goodness will pardon the assurance and liberty that so obscure, remote, and unknown a person as I am, takes to address you in this manner; as it proceeds from a well-meant zeal to promote the interest of religion and learning, and especially the study of the Hebrew Scriptures in this my native country. I labored for ten years in founding a College in New York, and I hope with good success; but it growing too tedious for my years, I have lately retired hither into a delightful country parish, where I had before served the Society for Propagating the Gospel for above thirty years. And having great health and leisure (thank God), I am still pursuing the same design of promoting the study of the Hebrew Scriptures, to which but very few here are addicted, and I could think of no better project than to get the Grammar of it studied with a Grammar of our own excellent language as the best introduction to what is called a learned education.

While I was pursuing this design, I was most agreeably surprised with your admirable "Lexicon," calculated in the best manner to promote my favorite views; and I take this opportunity to offer you my most hearty thanks for that excellent work which I hope will be a very great blessing to this as well as to our mother country. And since I must send my little performance home to be printed, as we have no types here, I humbly take the liberty to beg the favor of you to take the trouble of perusing it, and if you judge it may be of any good use to the purpose I aim at, to correct whatever mistakes I have made in it, and to recommend it to your printer to print it. The bearer hereof is Mr. Giles (who has transcribed it for the press). He goes well recommended by the clergy here to my Lord of London and his Grace and the Society for Holy Orders and a mission, and is very desirous of being a factor for the sale of as many as we can get of your "Lexicon" and this Grammar, in these parts of the world. I am, Reverend Sir, etc.,

S. J.

The work was printed by W. Faden, London, in 1767, and four years afterwards a second edition of it, "corrected and much amended," was published by the same bookseller, with the title, "An English and Hebrew Grammar, being the First short Rudiments of those two Languages, taught together." Its receipt was acknowledged with approbation by Robert Lowth, then Bishop of Oxford, a scholar whose "Prælections on Hebrew Poetry" interested Johnson, and gave him a high opinion of their author as introducing a new era in sacred literature. The publication was remarkable for its simplicity, and attracted the attention of several men of letters. He had been known before as one of the best Hebrew scholars in the country, and when Dr. Kennicott undertook to collate all the Hebrew manuscripts of the Old Testament, in England and other parts of Europe, he sent an inquiry to Johnson through Franklin, who was then in London; and he, in communicating it, said, "I have but little expectation that any ancient Hebrew manuscripts of the Bible may be found in America; but if such have possibly strayed thither, I think you, who are so well skilled in that language, are most likely to know of them."

The General Assembly of Connecticut, at the May Session, 1766, "Upon the memorial of the Rev. Eleazar Wheelock," revived a brief throughout the Colony, for the support and encouragement of the Indian Charity-school under his care at Lebanon. Printed copies of the act were delivered to the several ministers of the Gospel, who were directed to read the same to their congregations and fix a time for contributions. Johnson, who had always felt a compassion for the poor Indians, and tried, on various occasions, to make God's way known among them, showed his Christian and catholic spirit when, upon publishing the brief to his people, he urged them to contribute cheerfully and generously to promote so good a work. "If any," said he, "are reluctant because Mr. Wheelock is not of our communion, we should remember St. Paul's blessed temper which he expresses on the like occasion, 'whether the Gospel be preached of envy or of good will — I therein do rejoice, yea and will rejoice;' and this we may the rather do as this gentleman seems to express a truly Christian temper. And he has certainly fallen upon the right method for converting the heathen, by civilizing their children and teaching them husbandry, and the arts and manufactures, while he teaches them Christianity. I hope, therefore, you will liberally promote this good work, according to your ability, by coming prepared next Lord's day after service, to make your offerings to that purpose."

In acknowledging the "generous contribution," Mr. Wheelock was pleased to compliment him for his English Grammar and Catechism, and was so impressed with the value of the latter that he proposed to the author a slight change in the answer to one question, which, if he would make, he promised to use his influence to have the whole reprinted for the benefit of children, particularly in the Indian schools. The change involved a nice doctrinal point, having reference to a new heart and a new life.

Dr. Johnson agreed with Archbishop Secker in the opinion that the Society should establish an Episcopal Indian school, and thought that with a Bishop placed at Albany or Schenectady, such a one might be carried on under his eye and direction vastly to the credit and reputation of the Church. He even wrote to Sir William Johnson, Bart., the British agent for Indian affairs in New York, who was a Churchman and a member of the Society, to consult him about the best place in which to set up a school after the general plan of Mr. Wheelock,[1] but his suggestion was eventually overlooked in the consideration of other things.

The Colony of Connecticut was deeply interested in the title to a large tract of land, which one Mason had raised a dispute about in behalf of the Mohegan Indians. Twice it had been determined here in the Colony's favor by disinterested Commissioners, acting under the appointment of the King and Council; but still the great question was unsettled; and Dr. William Samuel Johnson was selected as a special agent to the Court of Great Britain to manage the case and bring it to a righteous conclusion. "I know not," said the father in a note introducing him to Archbishop Secker, "by what fate it is, but quite contrary to all my expectations, the people of this Colony, notwithstanding their aversion to the Church, have chosen my son a member of their Council, and appointed him their agent to defend them in a cause of great importance before the King and Council." He departed from New York the day before Christmas, 1766, and arrived in Falmouth harbor on the 30th of January. The letters which he carried with him gave him access to the highest dignitaries of the Church, as well as to the highest officials in the Government, and he used his pen freely in communicating to his father whatever he saw and heard that might interest him personally, or tend to affect the progress of Christian-

[1] The Indian Charity-school at Lebanon was incorporated with Dartmouth College, New Hampshire, in 1771, and Dr. Wheelock made President.

ity and the welfare of America. "Yesterday," said he in his first letter to him after reaching London, "I went to Lambeth, and was introduced to his Grace, and happily met there the Bishops of London and Bristol. The Archbishop received me very kindly and inquired very kindly as well as minutely after your health. He assured me he would, if possible, attend the hearing of the Mohegan cause when it should come on, and hoped to find it as just as I had represented it."

The next letter mentioned his presence at the Anniversary Sermon of the Society for the Propagation of the Gospel, preached February 20, 1767, in the Church of St. Mary-le-Bow, by Dr. Ewer, Bishop of Llandaff. Owing to a bad delivery and his own bad hearing he "could take up very few sentences," but he knew he dwelt "largely upon the subject of American Bishops."[1]

The following extract is from the same letter: —

Last Sunday I had the pleasure to hear the Archbishop preach, and to receive the Sacrament with him. He is truly an excellent preacher, even yet full of life and vigor; uses no glasses, and speaks with great ease; he has a fine voice, a decent, emphatical gesture, and an affectionate manner which engages the closest attention. His language is pure and correct, his sentiments just and masterly, yet adapted to the meanest capacities; he enters very little into speculative points, but exhorts to the practice of religion with great force, warmth, and energy. After service I dined with his Chaplains, Dr. Stinton of Oxford, and Dr. Porteus of Cambridge, both of them very worthy men. I then received an invitation to dine with his Grace the next day, which I com-

[1] This was the celebrated sermon which excited the hostility of Dr. Charles Chauncy of Boston, an able Congregational divine, who thereupon renewed the war of pamphlets in this country, which had recently been closed.

plied with, and found at his table only Mrs. Talbot and her daughter, who live with the Archbishop, Lady Carter, the Bishop of St. David's, Dr. Moss, and Dr. Porteus. The entertainment was very elegant, and the Archbishop extremely facetious, easy, and agreeable. He carves himself, helps everybody, and does the honors of the table with an extreme good grace. This is telling you trifles, but I imagine every circumstance with respect to the Archbishop will be agreeable to you. You cannot imagine how much I wished you had been there. The conversation turned much upon American affairs, and from the course of it, I am convinced that such is the situation here at present that you must not expect anything can be soon done relative to the important object you have so much at heart.

This "important object" was the American Episcopate, and a new effort was now made to remove, if possible, all opposition to it in both countries. So early as September, 1766, Dr. Chandler of Elizabethtown wrote thus to his venerable friend at Stratford: "By a letter from Mr. Cooper of a late date, I find that you continue to think that something should be published on the subject of American Bishops, and that I ought to undertake it. As to the former of these points, I have for a long time been convinced of the necessity of it, in order to bring the Dissenters and some of the Church people, and perhaps, *horresco referens*, some of our clergy into a just way of thinking on the subject. But as to the other point, as I am conscious of my own unfitness for the task, I have never been so happy as to be able to join with you in opinion."

The matter took definite shape afterwards when at a "general Convention" of clergymen from New York and New Jersey, with a few from other provinces, Chandler was appointed to prepare an appeal to the public, and he assured Johnson, who but for a tremor in his hand would have written it himself, that not a page should be printed until it had been submitted to his examination. He was indebted to him for a plan of the pamphlet, which he worked up by degrees, and furnished early in the spring of 1767. For on the 15th of April in that year, he wrote, announcing a proposed visit of President Cooper to Connecticut, and said among other things, —

Mr. Cooper will bring you my papers concerning American Bishops. I am ashamed that they should be offered for your inspection in so rough and imperfect a state; but my absolute inability to gain time to write them over again and give them a general correction, must be my apology. Before they go to the press, which will be some time in June, I must transcribe them; and by that time I shall be able to improve them much by the assistance of friends. Even without any such assistance, I think I could make them less unworthy of the notice of the public, by straightening the crooked places, and smoothing the rough ones, besides other amendments. But I begin to be disturbed in proportion as the time of publication draws nigh; and I must beg the favor of you to be on this occasion, what you have ever been on all occasions, my *fidus Achates*, my mentor, my guardian, and conductor. Every instance of your severity I shall esteem as a proof of your affection; and should your pen be as sharp as the point of a javelin, it would give me not pain, but pleasure.

You will therefore not be sparing in your animadversions, for the credit's sake of a young adventurer, who has been pushed forward by your own impulse, and for the sake of the cause, which must considerably depend on the success of this publication. I am sorry the papers cannot be left longer in your hands than Mr. Cooper is with you; but when I was appointed by the Convention to draw them up, I insisted upon a Committee to assist me; and as Mr. Seabury is one of that Committee, and has never had an opportunity of seeing them but in a very cursory manner last week in New York, I promised him, that after Mr. Cooper's return from Stratford they should be left in his hands. In my opinion the most blundering part of them at present is in the passage relating to Sir W. Johnson, of whom something is said that ought by no means to be said without his particular permission. And yet his testimony in favor of the usefulness of an Episcopate towards the conversion of the Indians is of too much weight to be omitted.

The publication of the "Appeal" did not at first fulfill the expectations of its author. He was disappointed that the clergy were not more active in circulating it, though he knew previously that those southward would regard it with little favor. Shortly before it appeared Dr. Chandler made a journey into Maryland, and in a letter to Johnson, giving a humorous account of the agricultural skill of the people, and a deplorable one of the state of the Church, he said, "Of about forty-five clergymen in the province, five or six are of good character, whose names should be mentioned with honor, ... but to hear the character of the rest, from the inhabitants, would make the ears of any sober heathen to tingle. You may be sure that they are much averse to having an American Episcopate, and they are averse to their numbers being increased, or their vacancies supplied from the northward."

The "Appeal" was reprinted in London, and sharply attacked there, as it had been here by Dr. Chauncy and other Dissenters. A passage from a letter of its author to Dr. Johnson, written at the close of the summer of 1768, will show the nature of these attacks. "You see," speaking of the reprints, "that it has been answered by a Presbyterian there; and I find that the 'London Chronicle' has introduced the subject to the view of the populace; several pieces having been published therein, but all of them by Chauncy's friends. In one of them an account is given of the answer made by the very learned Dr. Chauncy to a piece written in favor of American Bishops *by one Chandler*. In another, it is asserted that Dr. Chandler says that an American Episcopate is upon the point of being established, and *that a tax is to be laid on the Americans for the support of it*. It is astonishing that such falsehoods as these can be suffered to go unanswered, and that no methods are taken by the guardians of the Church to prevent the propagation and growth of them."

It was difficult for Dr. Johnson, at this period, to write long letters to his son, but he managed to keep him well informed of the state of political and religious feeling on this side; and weighed thoroughly what was communicated to him in reply. In a letter from Stratford dated June 8, 1767, he expressed his pleasure at hearing that temperance was so much in fashion in England, and added, —

I wish you could have said the same of religion and all other virtues, but upon the whole I doubt the times are very deplorable, especially on account of the rage of avarice, ambition, and lust, which seem to threaten a dissolution. What else can be expected from such an unsettled state of the ministry, owing to such a perpetual and violent justling about *in* and *out*? What can a Pitt do in such a state, even if he mean ever so well, which after all is, perhaps, as well to be doubted of him as other men? If they cannot agree to do us any mischief, so they can neither, for the same reason, agree to do us any good; and that will be a great mischief, especially since what concerns the interest of religion here is totally neglected and despised.

I am extremely glad you heard and communicated with my great and good friend the Archbishop. Your character of him as a preacher and at his table is extremely beautiful and amiable. I wish with you I could have been with you. I must believe him to be one of the first characters of the age. I am indeed glad if he took in good part my last long letter. I was afraid it would be of hard digestion.

The Society have truly done you a great honor, in making you their agent in the Hampshire affair, and I am glad you have so good hopes of that, and that you have audience with the Earl of Shelburne. It is said here with triumph that he told one Stockton of New Jersey, who I see has been in Scotland, and I suppose is the Synod's agent against Bishops, that there is no occasion for Bishops in America. I wish you may be able to convince him to the contrary, as I hope you will by Dr. Chandler's "Appeal," which I will send you as soon as printed.

The son, in his next letter, observed: "I doubt not Lord Shelburne said as you have been told. I wish he was the only one amongst the ministers of that opinion. I fear it is universal, and the common sentiment of all the leaders of all parties, and that, perhaps, of all others in which they are most agreed. The 'Appeal' you mention, however well drawn up, will, I fear, have very little effect. Perhaps the more you stir about this matter at present, the worse it will be." In the same letter, he took occasion to speak of Archbishop Secker, characterizing him as certainly one of the best of men. "I can clear up," he said, "whatever has seemed dubious in his conduct or character, and shall do it when I return to America. But the Court is not a scene for such good men to act in, and he wisely keeps himself to his own province; his diligence and condescension would surprise you; he excuses himself from no labors, assiduities, or attendance where he has the least prospect of doing good; he is beloved most by those who know him best; even the most profligate reverence him."

Besides attending to the business of his agency, which was protracted beyond his expectation, and having interviews with British Lords, who were occupied far more with material comforts than religious questions, the son found time to make several journeys into the country; some for the benefit of his health, and others for the sake of observation and historic culture. In returning to London from one of these, he went out of his course to visit at Bray the family of the late Bishop of Cloyne. His friend, the Doctor, was not at home, but his mother, the widow of Berkeley, made amends in some degree for his absence, whom he described to his father thus: "She is the finest old lady I ever saw; sensible, lively, facetious, and benevolent. She insinuates herself at the first acquaintance into one's esteem, and begets a high opinion of her virtues. She received me very affectionately, and remembered America, and you in particular with great regard, and was pleased to say that the Bishop and she had more pleasure in your acquaintance than any other person's while they were in that country."

In October, 1767, he made a tour into Yorkshire, and the agreeable letter which he wrote after reaching his destination has more than a family value: —

YORK, *October* 17, 1767.

HONORED SIR, — I received yours of the 11th of July the day before I left London, on my tour this way, and as I have been in motion ever since, could not write before. I am surprised that there should be so long an interval as three months between my letters, which I repeat very often; however, I hope it was not many days after you wrote, before you had intelligence, and that you will not again have so long a delay, unless it be in the depth of winter, when it may indeed be expected. The favorable account you give me of your own and my family's health gives me the greatest pleasure, and I bless God for it as I do for my own, which I find much confirmed by my ride here, which I was advised to take for that purpose, both the exercise and the country air having been very beneficial to me, and perfectly recovered me from my late indisposition.

. . . .

It gave me concern to find you were in danger of some trouble in Church matters, and especially that my old friend Jabez Hurd should have any hand in it, who I hoped would use all his influence to preserve peace and quietness; by this time, however, I hope matters are settled again; and indeed what can you fear with such a weight as the newly acquired friendship you mention must bring with it?

I see nothing amiss in the letters you inclose me, and shall deliver them as soon as I have opportunity for it; when I came out, those to whom they are directed were all out of town. I spoke to Faden the morning I came away to get Foster's Bible, which he said he would do, but chose to take Mr. Parkhurst's opinion of it first, which he would have against my return; and as to the second part of the "Introduction," etc., it is not yet brought to the press, being the composition of a gentleman for the benefit of his own school, who delays the publication till his own pupils are ready to make use of it.

I thank you for sending your bill, and will get the pictures you mention if to be had, but fear there is no plate of the

Bishop of Oxford or Lord Lyttleton, if there be of the Bishop of Carlisle. The latter are two as indifferent faces as are to be seen in the House of Lords, especially Lord Lyttleton, who is a lean, long-visaged, crooked, shriveled old gentleman; you would think him in a consumption; his voice too is very bad, but when he speaks, as he does pretty often, it is always very sensibly, and he is heard with great attention.[1]

When I came to Kingston-upon-Hull, I found Mr. Bell, with the Mayor and Corporation of the town at a turtle feast, at the inn I put up at. I introduced myself to him, and he me to the Mayor, etc., and after some time to his lady, who was very well pleased to see and acknowledge me as a relation. She is a worthy, sensible woman, but has few memorials of the family; both her parents having died when she was not two years old. Her father was a lawyer and died at the age of thirty-two. Her grandfather lived upon his estate (without any profession), which I find was very considerable. Her great uncle was a Doctor of Physic, eminent in his profession and by his monument in Cherry-Burton Church (which I visited as well as the family seat there), it appears he died the 1st of November, 1724, at the age of ninety-four, having survived his wife, and seven out of nine children, who all died without issue, and the two which survived him being females never married, by which means the whole estate came to Mrs. Bell. This old Dr. Johnson retained his memory, etc. to the last, and as he remembered the transactions of almost a century, had you happened to have met with him, when you were here in 1723, he could doubtless have told you the circumstances of the emigration of our ancestors, no traces of which can now be discovered

1 "Since you wanted Lord Lyttleton's picture, I got an acquaintance of mine to mention it to his Lordship and know of him whether he had any plate; and your being an American who had a value for his writings, he desired his compliments to you and thanks for taking so much notice of him, but said there never had been any picture taken of him, though his bookseller had requested one to prefix to his *Life of Henry II.*, and perhaps he should consent to it when he had finished that work." — *MS. Letter, February* 6, 1768.

here. The arms are not the same with those we have assumed. I have taken a note of them, and shall examine at the "Herald's" office when I return to London. If, at this distance, any evidence of our relation could be imagined to arise from similarity of countenance, Mrs. Bell and I might pass very well for brother and sister, except that her eyes are very black. Her eldest child, a daughter about thirteen, is exactly our Polly, with a little longer face, and the other very like Betsey. Their son I did not see, being at a distant school. Whether we are related or not, they were really very civil, and as much so as they could have been with the clearest proof of it, and desired me to present their affectionate compliments to you and all the family.

Nothing very material has occurred here, unless it be the death of the Duke of York, who is not very greatly lamented (except by the Royal family and his own domestics), though we are all obliged to go into deep mourning for him.

I congratulate you on the anniversary of our birthdays, and hope the next we may celebrate together, in agreeable remembrance of my present rambles. I shall set out in a few days on my return to London, and shall write again by the first conveyance after I get to town; and in the mean time am, with the tenderest love to my dear wife and all the children,

Honored Sir, your most dutiful son and humble servant,

WM. SAM'L JOHNSON.

The trouble in the parish, referred to in this letter, was not very serious, and appears to have grown out of a desire on the part of Dr. Johnson's friends to furnish him with some aid in his ministrations. His infirmities had become so great that at times he was unable to discharge his public duties, and a "soreness in his legs," the result partly of breaking one of them about twenty years before, confined him to the house several weeks, in the winter season. Mr.

John Tyler, a graduate of Yale College and a theological student of his, who was about to proceed to England for ordination, was thought of as a permanent assistant; but opposition was raised to him on the ground that he was not a very good reader and did not promise to make much of a preacher, and a few of the parishioners therefore did not wish to see him in a position where, according to the natural course of things, he would succeed to the Rectorship.

Dr. Johnson, not less than the Church of England in the Colonies, lost a firm and noble friend in the death of Archbishop Secker. They were kindred spirits. They were "loving brothers," as far as two men of nearly the same age could be so, without having seen each other face to face, or known each other only in a long and affectionate correspondence. The letter of his son which brought the intelligence of his decease was one of the saddest that could have come to him at that crisis. It is worthy of being spread upon these pages, for the facts it contains and the counsels it gave: —

LONDON, *August* 12, 1768.

HONORED SIR, — I must not fail by this packet to acquaint you (though I imagine Mr. Tyler did not leave the Downs before the melancholy intelligence reached him) of the death of our great and good friend, the Archbishop of Canterbury, in whom religion in general, and particularly the Church in America, have lost their best friend in this country. His physicians and friends flattered us with hopes that he might recover from this disorder, and continue yet some time; but for my own part I have been, ever since I saw him last, about a month ago, satisfied he was drawing near his end. The immediate occasion of his death was the misfortune of breaking his thigh bone, which happened on

Sunday evening the 31st of July, as he was endeavoring to raise himself hastily from his couch; it was immediately set by the king's surgeons, and he was easy and more comfortable than could have been expected after such an accident, but soon grew worse, and on Wednesday, the 3d inst., he expired. When his body was opened, it appeared that his thigh bone was extremely decayed, and the physicians expressed their astonishment, that he could have lived so long under so much pain as he must have endured, for some time past with the gout, rheumatism, and gravel, by all which he was sorely afflicted, and his constitution quite worn out. He was interred privately, according to his own orders, in Lambeth churchyard.

Thus we must bid adieu to one of the best of men. God's will be done! He can and certainly will take care of His own cause and interest in the world, but in truth I see no prospect at present that anybody here will make good the Archbishop's ground. Several of the Bishops are indeed very worthy men, but none of them in my opinion by any means so well qualified for that high station as the late Archbishop. It does not yet appear who will succeed him; almost every Bishop has been named; at present the Bishop of Lichfield and Coventry, Dr. Cornwallis, is most talked of, and he and the Bishop of London seem to stand the fairest chance; but interest may give it to another, and it is difficult to say who, at present, is most in favor at Court.

But from none of them, I fear, may religion in America expect that attention and aid which it has formerly had. The Church of England there should in fact think more of taking care of itself. The Society will indeed, I trust, still continue to afford their friendly assistance, but even that is a precarious dependence, and I wish my countrymen not to rely too much upon it, but prepare themselves as far as possible to stand upon their own ground. The affection between that country and this seems to be every day decreasing, and the growing jealousies on both sides threaten the destruction of all our harmony and happiness; already there is hardly any other cement left between us beside the interest founded in trade, and even that is declining. Let us look forward and see where these things must end, and consider what must probably be soon the state of that country and this. I was going to imagine it with respect to religion. But in truth I dare not pursue these reflections farther upon paper. Let them remain for the subjects of future, but alas! distant conversation, for I see little prospect that I may spend next winter with you at Stratford, or that I can leave this country before next spring. I almost say with David, "Woe is me that I am constrained to dwell with Mesech, and to have my habitation among the tents of Kedar;" but we must submit and leave it to Providence, which orders all things for the best.

I am just now happy in receiving your favor of the 10th of June, by which I find you were all well at that time. God be thanked for it, and for the perfect health I enjoy. I shall forward your letter to Dr. Berkeley, who is now at Canterbury, and will bring Pike's "Lexicon," as you advise, for Billy, who, I rejoice greatly to find, proceeds so rapidly in his studies. With my tenderest love to him, my dear wife, and all the children, and compliments to all friends,

I remain, honored Sir,

Your most dutiful son and humble servant,

WM. SAM'L JOHNSON.

August 13.

I inclose you this morning's paper, by which it appears that the Bishop of Lichfield is nominated Archbishop of Canterbury; you have also some account of the late Archbishop's will, and a list of his charities.

Yours, W. S. J.

CHAPTER XIV.

STRUGGLE FOR AMERICAN BISHOPS CONTINUED; FOREIGN CORRESPONDENCE; BISHOP LOWTH AND HEBREW GRAMMAR; ASSISTANT MINISTER; MARRIAGE OF GRANDDAUGHTER; AND PROLONGED ABSENCE OF HIS SON.

A. D. 1768–1770.

THE opponents of the Church of England in this country were restless under the continued efforts to secure American Bishops. As often as the clergy applied for this boon, they repeated their representations to the Government and Dissenters at home, that it was uncalled for, and, if granted, would be followed by outbursts of popular indignation. It has already been mentioned that the Southern Provinces were opposed, or rather not inclined to the scheme, and attempts were made to bring them over to its support. Johnson, writing to the Rev. Mr. Camm of Virginia, before the death of Secker, said: "We have been informed from home that our adversaries, who seem to have much influence with the ministry, endeavor, and with too much success, to make it believed, that nineteen twentieths of America are utterly against receiving Bishops, and that sending them, though only with spiritual powers, would cause more dangerous disturbances than the Stamp-act itself; insomuch that our most excellent Archbishop, who has been much engaged in this great affair, and has greatly condescended to exchange many letters with me upon it for several years, has lately informed me that he has not been able to gain the attention of the ministry to it; though his Majesty is very kindly disposed to favor and promote it. I am therefore very apprehensive that our solicitations will fail of gaining the point unless we could bring it to a general cry, and prevail with the Southern Provinces to join us in a zealous application to the Government at home in the same important cause."

The attacks upon Chandler's "Appeal" led the author to prepare an elaborate defense, and particularly with a view of replying to Dr. Chauncy, who was his most formidable antagonist. The outlook for the Church at this time was anything but encouraging. Passion took the place of argument, and hostile pens ran beyond the limits of reason, so that what Johnson wrote to his son was true: "These violent asserters of civil liberty for themselves, as violently plead the cause of tyranny against ecclesiastical liberty to others." The "Appeal Defended" was followed, at a later day, by another publication, entitled "The Appeal Farther Defended," and this was the last of the pamphlets in favor of the American Episcopate, though the idea could not be dislodged from the minds of the true friends of the Church. Chandler, in congratulating his venerable adviser at Stratford on recovering from a severe illness, expressed the hope that his health might hold out, by the blessing of Heaven, till he should "have the pleasure of seeing a Bishop in America."

The effect of the controversy was not felt to any good purpose in England. Other things absorbed the public attention, and the ministry was so much engaged with political measures, that no time was taken for deliberate consultation upon the interests of religion in the Colonial dependencies. Johnson, the agent, wrote to his father in midsummer, 1769, when it was almost over: "I cannot but say, I am rather pleased that your controversy about American Bishops seems to be near its close, since I am afraid it can have no very good effects there, and it certainly produces none at all here. It is surprising how little attention is paid to it." The struggles of party were violent, and the uneasiness and discontents of the people at home needed watching and allaying not less than the troubles and disquietudes of the Colonies; and in this way the great and important design of an American Episcopate was kept in the distance. "While the state of affairs, both with us and with you, continues just as it now is, I am afraid," said Dr. Lowth, then Bishop of Oxford, "we may not expect much to be done in it." One is reminded in this connection of the sarcastic observation of Sir Robert Walpole, the prime minister, when Dean Berkeley solicited in Parliament an act in favor of his scheme for the Bermuda College. He had gained the good will of the King, and he requested Walpole, in presenting the measure, only to be silent; he was so. After it was passed, a courtier remonstrated with him against the proposition of the Crown, and he replied, "Who would have thought anything for promoting religion or learning could have passed a British Parliament?"[1]

Dr. Johnson did not cease, under all the discouragements of the times, to cherish some good hopes

[1] MS. of Wm. S. Johnson, 1767.

for the future. He was now the oldest of the clergy in America, and felt at liberty, as he had always done, to write very plain things to his English correspondents. He began, however, to foresee the storm gathering in the political horizon. He could not be blind to the determination of all parties to give up neither the parliamentary authority nor even the right of taxation in the Colonies. "I thank you," he said to his son in the spring of 1769, "for sending the Resolves, etc. What dreadful things they are! They are like so many thunderbolts upon poor Boston, and it is well if they do not actually turn into great guns and bombs before they have done; for these Oliverians begin to think themselves Corsicans, and I suspect will resist unto blood. But if it should come to this, I doubt Old England and New will fall together, and both become a prey to the House of Bourbon. *Deus avertat omen!*"

His foreign correspondence grew more irksome with the increase of his infirmities, and he relied upon his son to do for him in England what he could not so well plead for by letter. Several of his friends in turn were pleased to communicate with him through the same medium. A domestic rather than a literary or theological interest is attached to the following letters: —

MY DEAR SIR, — I write these lines with your good son sitting by me. He has been so obliging as to give me his company (when at this place in last December) as often as he could conveniently. It was matter of great concern to me that he called on me at Bray last summer during my residence at my other parish, twenty-five miles distant, and my mother, who, to her no small joy, received him, totally forgot to ask his address; so that I had it not in my power to return his visit.

I have, on the strength of an hereditary friendship, opened my mind to your worthy son on every subject without reserve. His Grace of Canterbury receives him always with the regard due to him on his own account, and on that of his excellent father, to whom I beg leave to return my best thanks for a valuable token of regard which had not thus long escaped my notice.

I have the happiness of telling you that my good mother (who remembers you with the truest respect) is very well, and likely to bless her family for many years. I am also, I thank God, very happy in my wife and two sons. My choice in matrimony gave the highest satisfaction to my mother, and therefore you will believe that it was not an unwise one.

I earnestly pray for the continuance of your valuable life, and that a long stay on earth may lead you to a longer happiness. These lines are written, as you perceive, in a hurry, as Dr. Johnson must carry them away with him.

I remain, my dear Sir,

Your most faithful and affectionate friend and servant,

GEORGE BERKELEY.

LAMBETH PALACE, Thursday, *March* 10, 1768.

Answer: —

June 10, 1768.

MY VERY DEAR AND WORTHY SIR, — It gave me the greatest satisfaction to receive your affectionate letter, and to be informed of your welfare, and of the health of that most excellent lady, your mother; and moreover of your great happiness in so excellent a consort as she must undoubtedly be to have the approbation and esteem of so good a judge. I also rejoice with you in your two sons, and am glad that the great and good Bishop whom I am proud to call my friend is like to live in so hopeful a posterity, and I heartily pray God that all those joys and many more may long, very long be continued to you. I beg you will make my most affectionate compliments acceptable to your honored mother (and your lady, though unknown), together with my hearty thanks for the very kind manner in which she received and treated my dear and only son, who has the highest sense of her amiableness and benevolence. I bless God that the friendship I had the honor of with your renowned father still subsists between our children, and am very glad that on the score of it you have so particularly opened your mind to my son on the most important subjects.

I am greatly grieved at the dark account he gives me from you of the ill-health of the most worthy and excellent Mr. Jones, and let him know, with my compliments when you have opportunity, how great satisfaction I have in his excellent performance in Philosophy as well as the Trinity, and how earnestly I pray for his life and health, that he may bless the world with other labors![1] I bless God that such excellent men as Drs. Horne and Wetherell are preferred to be heads of those important houses in the University, and when you have opportunity give them my compliments and joy.

I am inexpressibly obliged to his Grace of Canterbury for the great honor he does my son, and thank you for the candor with which you accept such a trifle as my little Grammar, in which I had no other view than to be useful to young lads in America, where I am extremely desirous, if possible, to promote the study of Hebrew, as it is very little known here. I thank you, my dear Sir, for your affectionate prayers in my behalf, and remain with great esteem and regard,

Your most affectionate friend and brother,

S. J.

[1] Wm. Samuel Johnson, writing to his father May 14, 1768, and speaking of Archbishop Secker, said: —

"I dined with him about ten days ago, when he was able to sit at table, but had no use of his left hand and arm. I had the pleasure to meet there Dr. Berkeley, and the very worthy and learned Mr. Jones, who is much better in health than he used to be, and told me he was still pursuing his *Principles of Natural Philosophy*, and hoped he should ere long be able to publish something upon that subject. He remembered my brother with much affection, and desired his compliments to you, as did Dr. Berkeley. His account of the state of Hutchinsonianism is much the same with what I have before mentioned to you."

It alleviated the grief of his son's long absence that he received from him frequent and agreeable accounts of interviews with his old correspondents and with men of distinction in literature as well as in the affairs of the government. "For the sake of the name," he wrote in November 1769, "and because I think him one of the best of the modern writers, I made an acquaintance, some time ago, with Dr. Samuel Johnson, author of the 'Dictionary,' etc. He was very well pleased with the attention I paid him; had heard of you, and presents his compliments. He has shining abilities, great erudition, and extensive knowledge; is ranked in the first class of the literati, and highly esteemed for his strong sense and virtue; but is as odd a mortal as you ever saw. You would not, at first sight, suspect he had ever read, or thought in his life, or was much above the degree of an idiot. But *nulla fronti fides*, when he opens himself, after a little acquaintance, you are abundantly repaid for these first unfavorable appearances."[1]

The Rev. Dr. Johnson had intimated to his son that seeing so much grandeur, and being conversant with the luxuries and refinement of the Old World, he might be tempted to look down upon America, or that his home, when he returned to it, would appear mean and despicable. But great minds are never thus affected. "I will not have the vanity," he replied, "to impute it to my philosophy; but it is my good fortune,

[1] It has been told that when he introduced himself as an American, the great sage and moralist treated him, at first, somewhat rudely, and spoke harshly of his countrymen, saying, among other things: "The Americans! what do they know and what do they read?" "They read, Sir, the *Rambler*," was the quick and polite reply; which so pleased him that he took the statesman into his confidence, paid him many civilities in London, and, after his return to this country honored him with kind and courteous letters. See Appendix A.

that though I am pleased enough with seeing these things, yet they take little hold of my affections. I like to look behind the gay curtain, but when I do, I find little to admire and less to be attached to." And he added still more: "My wishes, were they indulged me to the utmost, would be very limited, and all centre in a little ease and independence in the tranquil vales of America. The worst of it is, that I am not likely to be very soon gratified even in such humble hopes, and the best way (to which I hope to bring myself by and by) is to have no wishes for anything in this world but what we actually possess, or have certainly within our reach. This however cannot be till I return to Stratford."

Ever since the publication of his "Hebrew Grammar," he had been desirous of issuing a second edition corrected and improved. It was his last contribution to Christian education in America, and he would leave it, as far as he had the means of making it so, in a perfect state. For this purpose he consulted several Hebrew scholars and solicited their opinion of the merit of his performance. To Bishop Lowth he suggested the idea of laying a broad foundation for the study of the language in this country, and giving to it a prominent place in collegiate instruction. "I wish," said the Bishop, "it were as much in my power, as were there an opportunity it would certainly be in my inclination, to promote your useful proposal of establishing a Hebrew Professorship in North America. We must leave to God's good providence this and many other improvements in that country, and I doubt not of their being in due time accomplished." The Bishop had given him to understand that the learned were beginning to think in earnest of a new translation of the Scriptures, "as a thing not a great way off;" and writing November 1, 1771, to Mr. Parkhurst, the scholar who carried his "Hebrew Grammar" through the press in London, Johnson expressed the wish that all helps might be made available in such a work, even the discoveries of Hutchinson, for whose learning, with some exceptions, he still retained a high respect.

Among others whom he consulted was Mr. Sewall, Professor of Oriental Literature in Harvard University; and through him he desired the opinion of a colleague, Mr. John Winthrop, about Hutchinson's "Scripture Philosophy." The answer returned is too good to be excluded from these pages: —

CAMBRIDGE, 24*th July*, 1769.

REV. SIR, — An answer to your obliging favor of March 1, 1768, I acknowledge hath been long due. The only reason of delay was the want of a private conveyance. For I could not persuade myself an epistle of this nature was worth the postage for such a length of way.

My thanks are due, Sir, for those favorable sentiments you are pleased to express of the Oriental Professor at Cambridge. He wishes his poor, but honest endeavors may be followed with those happy consequences you mention.

The union of the whole Christian Church, in the bonds of peace and love, is an object much to be desired. In the mean time, however we may differ in certain external modes and forms, I trust we shall each bear an undissembled affection to all, of whatever denomination, who love our common Lord Jesus Christ in sincerity.

Mr. Professor Winthrop, Sir, is a firm believer in the Newtonian system. It cannot, therefore, be supposed he should entertain a very high opinion of a scheme so opposite to that as the Hutchinsonian is.

The Hebrew language is certainly the most simple of any; and the grammars of it (setting aside the incumbrance of points), may be reduced to a smaller compass than that of any other language upon earth: it may, consequently, be learned with greater facility and expedition. Upon these accounts, and others that possibly might be added, I cannot but think it claims priority in a learned education. The progression ought always to be from the easier to the more difficult.

Your Grammar, Sir, in my humble opinion, is upon a very good plan, and may answer very valuable purposes. You are the best judge whether it may be improved. It hardly becomes the modesty of one who is comparatively but a youth to point out to a gentleman of Dr. Johnson's learning and experience what improvement, if any, may be made in his own composition.

I am, Rev. Sir, with great respect,

Your very humble servant,

STEPHEN SEWALL.

Something more than a lay-reader was now needed to aid Dr. Johnson in his parochial duties. Mr. Tyler, who had been with him above a year, pursuing the study of Hebrew and Divinity, was desirous of proceeding to England for ordination, and of being appointed to a mission within the colony. Guilford and Norwich were both vacant, and as the former was the birthplace of Johnson, he procured him an invitation to read there for several months before embarking, and then gave him commendatory letters to the Archbishop and the Society.

The Rev. Ebenezer Kneeland, a graduate of Yale College in 1761, three years in holy orders, and a chaplain in the British army, appeared in Stratford and rendered acceptable service to the parish.

He wrote to his son, January 15, 1768: "My

health, D. G., is perfectly good, but my legs much as they were. Mr. Kneeland, whom I much like, is here till March, and nearly adored: the people have subscribed £30 per annum, and he has agreed to quit his regiment and come next summer. Mr. Tyler is invited and gone to Guilford, and the Church is very happy and increasing." He described Mr. Kneeland at the same time as a good scholar and an excellent speaker; but letters and other memorials will hardly sustain the description. They indicate neither depth of learning nor polished culture, and subsequent and more intimate relations must have led him to qualify his opinion. He was chosen associate minister, however, and took the more laborious duties which had become so burdensome to the aged Rector. It was a welcome and timely relief, and the people were glad to provide it.

Eighteen months elapsed, and his son in England was surprised to learn that Mr. Kneeland had formed an acquaintance with his eldest daughter (Charity), and desired to be united to her in marriage. The approbation of her mother and grandfather was obtained before his consent was asked, which appears to have been reluctantly given, with some good advice about the happiness and responsibility of the married state. This connection brought the assistant minister and his superior more closely together, and made their interests in working the parish one. It left no room for jealousies, and Dr. Johnson was now gratified with the prospect of being succeeded by one of his own affinity in a charge especially dear to him, and which he had held for nearly forty years.

What gave him the greatest anxiety at this period

was the prolonged absence of his son in England. From year to year he had looked for his return, and lived upon the hope of seeing him again restored to his family, but his expectations were continually disappointed. He often begged him, for the sake of his domestic affairs, to relinquish his agency, if the business intrusted to him could not be speedily accomplished; and in December, 1769, he wrote to Governor Trumbull of Connecticut, congratulating him on his advancement to the head of the government; and at the same time expostulating with him on the subject of his son's being so long detained in England. "I am told," said he, "the Lower House voted to direct him to come home in the spring at all events; but that the Upper House, led by, I know not what expressions in his letters, prevailed on the Assembly to conclude to instruct him by all means to continue longer, leaving, however, a discretionary power with your Honor to direct otherwise, if you should see reason for it, or something to this effect."

The Governor, in acknowledging his "pathetic expostulation," did not admit that any such discretionary power was lodged with him, but rather that the General Assembly fully relied on the purity of the agent's intentions to serve the interests of the colony, and to return whenever it should be consistent with his sense of duty. He lamented the public confusions, and the "paltry injurious Indian cause," which had led to the long separation from his "dearest and tenderest connections;" and then added, what was quite true, "his observations and intelligence will be of lasting advantage to the colony, and his services there at this critical juncture peculiarly great."

The agent, writing to his wife on New Year's Day, 1770, said: —

The present situation of our affairs is this. On the 22d ult. the Lords of the Council were moved to assign a day for hearing a motion we intend to make for dismission of the Mohegan cause, when their Lordships were pleased to appoint the first day of their next sittings for that purpose, and to assure us it should be before the expiration of this month. Should this motion on our part succeed, the cause is at an end. I shall then be disengaged from this tedious affair, and shall have only to see what Parliament will do with the colonies in the course of this session, and may certainly leave England as soon as it is over, which will probably be sometime in May. Should we fail in this motion, we shall then indeed have to try the merits of the cause at large, but still have good reason to expect that it may be got through with in the course of the winter or spring; so that either way I have the strongest hopes of seeing you some time next summer, at farthest, and you may rely upon it, it shall be as soon as possible.

His strong hopes were not realized, and a vexatious delay again filled his friends with disappointment. He wrote his father late in the summer of this year that he had not only been unable to get his business dispatched, but had for a month past been extremely ill with a serious fit of the gout in both his feet; and he intimated that if no probability existed of the Mohegan cause being tried in five or six months, he should not hesitate to come away as soon as his health would permit, though to return again, should it be thought necessary, to attend the trial. Once the case was nearly finished, June, 1770, when the sickness of the attorney general intervened and led to a postponement. Every way this was a sad misfortune to him, and speaking of his detention on this account in the same letter, he said: "One mitigating circumstance, however, attends it; that one can bear with more patience those ills which are the immediate inflictions of Providence than those which are occasioned by the faults of men. Had this delay been occasioned by anything less than sickness or unavoidable necessity I should have had no patience left. But nobody is to blame; it was the act of Providence."

It has already been mentioned, as some compensation for this protracted absence, that the father was favored with such graphic and admirable letters from his son. Nothing but talking over experiences at the fireside in Stratford could exceed the interest with which he read the descriptions of what he saw and heard in England, and his brief account of interviews with men high in Church and State. The son was present at some of the most important and exciting debates in Parliament, and at a period too when great minds were occupied with great national subjects. He listened to the most eloquent defenders of the British Constitution, and gathered up every word that was spoken in vindication of measures which bore upon the welfare of America. The caution with which he communicated his observations to his father showed how critical the times were, and how solicitous he was that his countrymen should not be unprepared for the perils and hardships that lay in their path.

In a letter to him on the 4th of January, 1769, he spoke of what seemed to be the fixed resolution of the Administration not to repeal immediately those acts which the Colonies complained of, but to maintain the right of Parliament to impose duties and taxes in America, and to enforce obedience to its laws in the most effectual manner. "The tide, in fact, at present," he added, "sets strongly enough against us, and I fancy will continue to do so while Lord Hillsborough administers our affairs, who is extremely inflexible." Four months later he wrote again to his father with scarcely happier forebodings: —

I am very much obliged to you that you accept so well my apology for this long, tedious absence, which, as I have said, I greatly hope will not be prolonged through another winter, though I cannot determine its period. Your obliging compliment upon my defense of the charter against Lord Hillsborough's objections is very flattering. I am sensible of the danger we are in with respect to all our rights, and particularly the evil eye they have upon this charter especially; yet I should be particularly sorry to have that event take place while I am here, and shall therefore, as it is my duty, continue to defend both that and all our other just rights, in the best manner I can while I continue in the service of the colony. It is extremely unhappy that we cannot on both sides come to a better temper in the unfortunate dispute now subsisting between this country and that. If we once get into blood, your conjecture will undoubtedly be but too soon fatally verified: we shall destroy each other, and become an easy prey to our enemies. Prudent men, on both sides, are aware of this danger, and will, I hope, by degrees gain so much influence as to prevent it. Administration have, since the rising of Parliament, given out that the duty-act shall be repealed next year, if the Colonies remain quiet, but one can hardly depend much upon the declarations of ministers.

When the year came round and the address from

the Throne had been issued, he inclosed a copy to his father, and wrote, among other things: —

Lord Chatham appeared again (after three years' absence) in the House of Lords, and declared himself the friend of America. He said he had not altered his ideas of the proper mode of governing the Colonies, wished for moderation and lenity, but would not go fully into the subject. "I have," says he, "a strong propensity towards that country, and love liberty wherever it appears. That country was settled upon ideas of liberty. It is a vine, to use the allusion of Scripture, which has taken deep root and filled the land. May it long flourish! But I am the friend not the flatterer of America; they have done wrong in some things, but let us inquire coolly and candidly before we censure as the address does."

On the 7th of February, 1770, he wrote him a long letter, reciting his hindrances, and gravely repelling an insinuation which seems to have been mischievously made, that he was becoming alienated from his family; and then he proceeded to things less personal, and described a debate in Parliament, the memory of which must have lingered with him to the end of his days.

I hardly know how to write upon any other subject, but I must just tell you that we have had many changes of men, both by deaths and dismissions (which the papers, I presume, will have acquainted you with), without any changes of measures. Lord North, for the present, succeeds the Duke of Grafton as prime minister, and seems to intend to pursue the same system of politics. Parliament have been much retarded in their proceedings by these changes, and the rest of their time has been taken up with the Middlesex election, which has been repeatedly debated with great vehemence and acrimony, both by the Lords and Commons; but the ministry have still carried their point in favor of the decision of last year, on several divisions, by a majority of about forty in the Commons, and in the Lords of about fifty. The Lords in the minority have signed the most spirited protest that is perhaps of record. The opposition intend still to pursue the point in every shape they can devise.

Lord Chatham told the Lords that while he lived it should never rest, nor would they cease to bring it before Parliament in every possible method, till the wound in the Constitution was healed. His last speech upon this occasion (about two o'clock last Saturday morning) was amazingly fine. Neither Greece nor Rome, I believe I may venture to say, ever heard anything superior to it. Roused with indignation at some unfair proceedings of the ministry, as well as warmed by the universal ardor of the debate, he displayed his utmost powers of eloquence, and with astonishing ability and energy even vanquished Lord Mansfield, who is certainly one of the first of mankind, and worthy of such an antagonist. He obliged him to change his ground even in a point within his own profession, — the law. The conflicts of these two great men are such as would have been seen between Demosthenes and Cicero, had they been opposed to each other, warmed by emulation and heated by opposition. They excel each other in different manners of eloquence, but are equally superior to all others. This dispute so engrosses the attention of all the politicians that they can hardly think of anything else. Hence it is that American affairs have not yet been taken up, though we expect they will be soon entered upon. There seems to be but little hope, at present, that we shall obtain more than the repeal of the duties upon glass, paper, and painters' colors, which will answer no purpose to America. On the contrary, they threaten us with some severe resolutions, or perhaps a penal act, against agreements not to import goods. Lord Chatham, we are told, wishes the repeal of the whole of this Revenue act, but I fear he will not have influence enough to effect it.

CHAPTER XV.

DESIRE FOR AMERICAN BISHOPS UNQUENCHED; LETTERS FROM DR. BERKELEY AND THE BISHOP OF LONDON; JOY AT THE RETURN OF HIS SON; WISH FOR A PEACEFUL EXIT; DEATH AND BURIAL; CONCLUSION.

A. D. 1770–1772.

THOUGH the war of pamphlets was about over, and formal appeals from the clergy in this country were ended, yet Dr. Johnson could not cease to be interested in the effort to obtain American Bishops. He still felt that it was a want which must be supplied, and whenever he wrote to his English correspondents, which was not often now, he pressed it upon their attention. The Bishop of London, Dr. Terrick, appreciated his feelings, and expressed a willingness to favor the design on first coming to his London see. But objections were raised which he was not able to remove. They were the same which had hindered the attempts of his immediate predecessor, Bishop Sherlock, and deterred him from repeating his memorials to the throne upon the subject. They centered in the policy of statesmen, and gathered strength from the uneasiness and remonstrance of the Dissenters.

Dr. Berkeley, not always perhaps with the best discretion, was a strong advocate of the scheme so persistently opposed. At one time he seriously meditated a visit to America with his wife, and went so far as to take steps towards purchasing a farm in the colony of Connecticut. "I should much like," he wrote to the Rev. Dr. Johnson, from Cookham near Maidenhead, April 21, 1770, "to pass one year in a country for which I have inherited no slight affection from both my parents." In the same letter he mentioned: "Mr. Dalton is settled on a little farm near me, and enjoys very good health; he often talks of America with great regard." And then he added, with a mixture of playfulness and seriousness: —

> If you Americans are not betrayed by your wives and daughters, you may transmit the invaluable blessing of liberty to your posterity; but if your females conspire with short-sighted merchants (who are too lazy to become farmers), you may in half a century be enslaved as the Irish are at this day, where the list of court-pensioners (mostly English) consumes more than ninety thousand pounds sterling annually; all of which money is granted without Parliament, by virtue of the Privy Seal. And after it has been so granted, Parliament is applied to for ways and means, which if the Irish Parliament should refuse to afford, the English Parliament would claim a privilege once surreptitiously obtained, and raise a revenue by taxation without representation.

The design of visiting America was relinquished, partly owing to a preferment which kept him at home, but his interest in the country continued. He was a warm friend of the American Church, and appears to have anticipated for it a great future. His intimacy with Dr. Johnson, the Colonial agent, increased with every year of his stay in England, and his regret at parting with him was deeper than words could express. That gentleman under date of

Tuesday, June 11th, 1771, entered in his private journal: "Attended at the Cock-pit the final hearing of the Mohegan cause;" and having disposed of other trusts and business committed to him, and taken leave of his many friends, he bade adieu to London, and sailed from Gravesend for New York on Saturday, the 3d of August. Among the letters which he brought with him addressed to his father, was the following: —

CANTERBURY, *Monday, July* 29, 1771.

REVEREND AND DEAR SIR, — God grant that you may speedily receive these lines from the hands of your excellent and very amiable son. His deep distress at being thus long unavoidably detained from his worthy lady, yourself, and his beloved olive-branches, has sensibly impaired his health. We, who love and regret him, as he deserves, hope that the effect will cease with the cause.

I wrote to you a long letter immediately on the receipt of your last favor. In that letter I opened my mind to you with great freedom on some important subjects, and I have now reason to suspect that (by the carelessness of a servant) those breathings of my soul have miscarried. This accident would have been much more grievous to us if Dr. Johnson's return did not now anticipate my reflections on the state of learning, church discipline, and religion in America. Mr. Temple of Boston visited me here a few days ago; he styled his friend, Dr. Johnson, the flower of America.

My expectations of receiving one more visit from the beloved bearer of these lines are, alas! now to be given up. This morning, a person just arrived from London, has brought me a most unwelcome message from him, and my letter will be but barely in time.

It happens, by what we mortals call chance, that the Dean of this church is an amiable and religious man; he is to be elected Bishop of Lichfield and Coventry as soon as he shall have completed his thirtieth year, *i. e.*, before the end of next week. Dr. North is much fitter for the office of a Bishop than any *old* man (without exception) that I remember to have seen appointed to that office. Your good son knows as much of the real political and ecclesiastical state of England as any man in it; I need not add, more than all the Americans I ever knew put together.

Mrs. Berkeley, your old acquaintance, and Mrs. George Berkeley, who would be very glad to become your acquaintance, join in every possible kind wish for you. May a long and happy life lead you, through Redeeming mercy, to a longer happiness!

My time is short, and my spirits are depressed by the consideration of the loss I am to sustain. Dr. Johnson indeed was so good as to come on purpose to Canterbury to take leave of us, but unfortunately I was then on a visit to my parishioners.

I am, with the truest respect, dear Doctor,

Your faithful and affectionate brother,

G. BERKELEY.

P. S. I have the comfort of being able to say that Dr. North is not ashamed of the Gospel of Christ in his sermons; if there was a vacancy, I should be happy to see him our Metropolitan to-morrow.

Dr. Johnson reached his family in Stratford on the 1st of October, having been absent from the country for nearly five years. He found his aged father full of infirmities and bending to the grave, but ready to welcome him with a warm heart and a clear intellect. He had begun to feel that he might not live till his return, and therefore his joy was all the greater when he came and renewed with him the scenes through which he had passed, and the personal interviews with distinguished men, known to him hitherto only through the medium of their correspondence, their works, or their statesmanship.

His measure of earthly happiness was now full, and he had no more for which to look forward in this life. He continued a little longer to use his pen, and write to his friends; but his letters were those of one who seemed to be conscious that he was closing up his stewardship. The Bishop of London had sent him a brief communication by his son, which, though not inspiring him with any new hopes, was gratefully received and resolutely answered. Its burden was the old obstacles to the American Episcopate.

Reverend Sir, — I cannot let your son leave this part of the world without taking the opportunity of writing a few lines to you in answer to your letter delivered to me by Mr. Marshall.[1] The Society, entirely satisfied with the testimonial he has brought with him, and with the assurances of a sufficient allowance from the inhabitants of Woodbury, has recommended him to me for orders. And, as I am always unwilling to keep the candidates from America longer than is necessary, especially as their stay is attended with expense, I shall lose no time in ordaining Mr. Marshall, provided he is found, as I trust he will [be], properly qualified for the profession. The character you give of him, with regard to his morals and behavior, will entitle him to some indulgence, if he has not made that progress in languages which we wish to find, though sometimes obliged to excuse, in our candidates.

I feel as sensibly as you can wish me to do, the distress of the Americans in being obliged, at so much hazard and

1 Rev. John R. Marshall, bred a merchant, and afterwards turning his attention to theology, pursued his studies under Dr. Johnson, and was licensed for Woodbury, Conn., by the Bishop of London, July 28, 1771. He received the degree of M. A. *honoris causâ*, from King's College, N. Y., 1773.

expense, to come to this country for orders. But I own I see no prospect of a speedy remedy to it. They who are enemies to the measure of an Episcopacy, whether on your part of the globe or ours, have hitherto found means to prevent its taking place; though no measure can be better suited to every principle of true policy, none can be more consistent with every idea I have formed of truly religious liberty. We want no other motive for declaring our sentiments and wishes on the subject, but what arise from the expediency, I had almost said, the necessity of putting the American Church upon a more respectable plan by the appointment of a Bishop. But whatever are our sentiments or wishes, we must leave it to the discretion and wisdom of Government to choose the time for adopting that measure. Whether we shall live to see that day, is in the hands of God alone. We wish only that we could look forward with pleasure and enjoy the thought.

Accept, sir, my best wishes for everything which may contribute to your health and happiness, and assure yourself that I am, with great truth and sincerity,

Your affectionate brother,

RIC. LONDON.

FULHAM, *July* 22, 1771.

In replying to this letter, Johnson affirmed that no one could be more concerned than he that the Church should always, as far as possible, have a learned ministry; but in such a country as America then was, much learning could not ordinarily be expected. He was glad his Lordship felt so sensibly "the distress of Americans" on being without Bishops, and apologizing for the importunity of his brethren in Connecticut, who, contrary to his advice, had made another address for them, he asked: "Is the case incurable? Is there no remedy? Must we forever go a thousand leagues for every ordination? Can it be that the English Government should suffer such an encroachment upon Christian liberty to the English Church in any part of its dominions? I foresee," he continued, "fearful consequences, political as well as religious, that will inevitably follow it." If there was no prospect of relief, if all hope and dependence on England must be relinquished, he thought that a number of the clergy would be disposed to apply to some other Episcopal Church — perhaps the Moravian — to give them Bishops, "being conscientiously persuaded that Episcopacy, such as it was in St. Cyprian's time, was the only form of government that the Apostles established in the Church."

The following reply to Dr. Berkeley, if not his last letter to England, was his last to that devoted friend of his son and of the American Church. It shows the depth of his feelings, and the great thought which ever rose in his mind as he turned to survey "the branch of God's planting" in this land.

November 10, 1771.

Reverend and most dear Sir, — I am most intensely thankful to our good God that he hath so graciously preserved my dear son to me and his family, and us to him through his long absence and many dangers, and at length restored him to us and given us to rejoice together in all the great goodness of his kind Providence both towards him and us. And now I return my most affectionate thanks to your very excellent mother and lady and dear sons for the great kindness and affection wherewith you have treated him in his absence from us. May my God abundantly reward all your goodness and beneficence.

I was much grieved for the miscarriage of your kind answer to my last letter, wherein you opened your mind with so much freedom. I thank you for it, though I had it not, and I could wish you yet to give me a short recapitulation of it. I am unwilling to give up all hopes of seeing you in America, at least of your being our first Bishop, for then I could trust that we should set out upon the foot of true, genuine, primitive Christianity; and if you be not yourself the man, I beg of you through your whole life strongly to interest yourself in our affairs, and so far as is possible to influence that we may have one or more Bishops, and that they be true, primitive Christians; otherwise, if they are mere men of this world, we are indeed better without them.

I rejoice and bless God that there is one such in these abandoned times as Bishop North, and he so young, too, and that of a noble family. Such an one is a phœnix indeed. I desire you, if you think proper, to give my dutiful compliments to him, and let him know that, as I am the oldest of the clergy here, I humbly beg he would pity our deplorable condition in being obliged to go a thousand leagues for every ordination, and use all the influence in his power without ceasing, till we are provided with a Bishop to ordain and govern the clergy here. I earnestly pray God to bless you, my dear sir, and that worthy lady your mother, together with your lady and dear offspring, with all the blessings of this life, and that we may all at length be happy together in a better world, I am, etc.

Nearly forty years before, when Dean Berkeley was promoted to the see of Cloyne, Johnson wrote to a London friend, expressing his joy at the appointment, but regretting that it had not been an English Bishopric, for then, he said, "he would have been in the way of being more useful to the Church in these parts of the world." The zealous son was untiring in his efforts to prosecute what the father could really do nothing towards accomplishing, and, at a later day, was of personal service to Dr. Seabury in securing his consecration to the Apostolic office from a church north of the Tweed, where there were no State oaths to hamper the little college of bishops, and no silken cord binding together the crown and the crosier.[1]

The waning year brought peace and quietness to Johnson. He left his parochial duties chiefly to the care of his assistant, and while he lived in the scenes and recollections of the past rather than in the distractions and political uncertainties of the present, he did not forget the nearness of the end, much less contemplate it with indifference. He often wished for a peaceful exit, and prayed that his death might resemble that of his good friend, Bishop Berkeley. Though apparently little indisposed, yet finding his strength to be failing him, on the morning of January 6, 1772, he conversed calmly with his family upon the subject of his departure, said that he was "going home," and then sank to rest quietly, so as the "Lord giveth his beloved sleep." An extract from the letter which his son wrote to Bishop Lowth a week after the event, furnishes a good description of his last moments.

STRATFORD IN CONNECTICUT, *January* 13, 1772.

MY LORD, — I did myself the honor to write your Lordship a short letter on my arrival in this country, acknowledging the honor of your favor of the 29th of June, from Cuddesden, which I received just as I left London; and presenting to your Lordship mine and my good father's duty.

I have now the misfortune to inform your Lordship of the departure of my father, who left us the morning of the Epiphany full of faith and hope, and we doubt not has entered into the joy of our Lord. He died as he had lived, with great composure and serenity of mind, and had just such a

1 Rev. Samuel Seabury, D. D., was publicly consecrated Bishop of Connecticut at Aberdeen, on Sunday, the 14th of November, 1784.

transition as one would wish for his best friend. He often wished, and repeated it the morning of his departure, that he might resemble in his death his friend, the late excellent Bishop Berkeley, whose virtues he labored to imitate in his life, and Heaven heard his prayer; for, like him, he expired sitting up in his chair, without a struggle or a groan. It would be very inexcusable in me to trouble your Lordship with this minute account, were it not also my duty to acquaint your Lordship, that from the great satisfaction and improvement he had received from your writings, my father had often assured me since my return that he had the greatest respect, veneration, and esteem for your Lordship, of any man now living. That respect and esteem, give me leave to say, will live in his family and among all his acquaintance, upon whom he sought to inculcate it. . . . .

The funeral of Dr. Johnson took place at Stratford two days after his decease, and the clergy from the neighboring towns were present; one of whom, the Rev. Jeremiah Leaming of Norwalk, delivered a sermon in commemoration of his acquirements and Christian character. His long tried and particular friend, the Rev. John Beach of Newtown, had been selected for this office, but want of health prevented his attendance at the funeral, though the sermon which he prepared was afterwards preached and published. It dwelt largely upon the wisdom of diverting the stream of our thoughts from this visible world to eternal things, and contained tributes to the memory of the great man, which were neither fanciful nor undeserved. "With much satisfaction," said he, "and the recollection of many advantages I have received, I call to mind the acquaintance which I have had with this excellent divine for more than fifty-five years; and without an hyperbole, I may say it, I know not that ever I conversed with him without finding myself afterwards the better for it. He had from his youth devoted himself to the sacred ministry, and the studies which qualify for it he followed with unwearied application, which a firm constitution enabled him to pursue even in old age." He closed a description of his intellectual attainments with these words: "The sum is this; he was the most excellent scholar, and most accomplished divine, that this colony ever had to glory in, and what is infinitely more excellent, he was an eminent Christian."

Other memorial sermons were preached, one by the Rev. Mr. Inglis in Trinity Church, New York, where his name was held in grateful remembrance for services rendered to the parish, and to the college with which the parish was in a measure identified. The loss of such a guiding light was felt by the depressed Church of England in this country, especially in the Northern colonies, and no pen of equal zeal, ability, and influence, was ready to take up the correspondence which he had so long conducted with British minds interested in the progress of Christianity on the American continent. The times grew more eventful, and soon the troubles which produced the Revolution interrupted communication, and sadder than all the days before were those which came to the supporters of Episcopacy.

"As to Dr. Johnson's person," says Chandler, "he was rather tall, and, in the latter part of his life, considerably corpulent. There was something in his countenance that was pleasing and familiar, and that indicated the benevolence of his heart; and yet, at the same time it was majestic, and commanded respect. He had a ruddiness of complexion, which was the effect of natural constitution, and was sometimes farther brightened by a peculiar briskness in the circulation of his spirits, brought on by the exercise of the benevolent affections." [1]

Frequent reference has been made in this volume to his autobiography, which he began in the seventieth year of his age, and completed after the return of his son from England. It was written in the third person, and is entitled, "Memoirs of the Life of the Rev. Dr. Johnson, and several Things relating to the state both of Religion and Learning in his Times." This manuscript with other papers was confided to the Rev. Dr. Chandler of Elizabethtown, and liberty given him to use them freely in preparing a more elaborate account of the life and character of his ever honored friend and patron. The colonial disturbances thickened, and even before the work was ready for the press, the son wrote to Dr. Chandler expressing his fears about publishing: "I am at a loss what to say upon the subject. On the one hand, I should be extremely glad to have anything published which would subserve the general interest of the Church of England, and tend to do honor to the memory of my father, and I know you will render whatever you publish as perfect and unexceptionable as possible. On the other hand, the age is so captious and so glutted with publications of every kind, and we have so many malicious adversaries working and watching for every circumstance of which they may take advantage, and upon which to ground a controversy or excite a clamor, that I am sometimes in doubt whether it be best to publish anything of this kind or not."

[1] *Life of Johnson*, p. 126.

Prudent friends advised delay, — among them Mr. Beach of Newtown, who, in September 1774, wrote to the hesitating son, who had placed the manuscript in his hands, and asked his opinion: "I should think that it might be obvious to the slightest observer, that this day of rage and madness is not the most favorable for publications of this nature." [1]

He had full liberty to communicate this opinion to Dr. Chandler, and in doing so he expressed his own concurrence in it, and added: "I am further confirmed in this idea from the insolent spirit which is lately excited against the professors of the Church of England, particularly throughout New England, from an apprehension that we are not sufficiently zealous in the cause of American liberty. A publication of this kind would on that account, I have no doubt, be particularly obnoxious at this juncture, and had better be postponed to some more favorable opportunity. For these reasons, I have not read the papers with a view to any corrections or additions, as I should have done, had I conceived it advisable to publish. As you proposed to transcribe the work again, I have returned the original memoir."

Dr. Chandler was soon after forced by the outbursts of popular fury to quit his parish, and with Dr. Cooper of New York sailed for England. Probably he never found time to transcribe his manuscript, and the wonder is how it escaped the many perils to which it was subjected on his journeys.[2] It fell at length into the hands of his son-in-law,[3] who published it more than thirty years after its preparation,

[1] See *History of the Episcopal Church in Connecticut*, vol. i. pp. 296, 297.

[2] See Appendix B.

[3] Rt. Rev. John Henry Hobart, D. D., third Bishop of New York.

in a small duodecimo volume of one hundred and fifty pages, besides an appendix containing a few letters; and he took care to mention in his preface that "however humble may be the early annals of his country, they should be interesting to every American, and whatever tends to throw light on them should be deemed worthy of preservation."

The little volume embraced the substance of the autobiography, and is at best but a meagre sketch which did slender justice to the intellectual eminence and personal worth of Johnson. Had he lived in these times, he would have been distinguished among men of learning, and recognized by them as an honest and patient lover of truth and justice. That he attained to such excellence under all the disadvantages of the period in which he was a conspicuous actor, is remarkable. He dared to think for himself, and if his keen penetration discovered defects in theological and philosophical systems, he was careful not to accept any new views until he had fairly examined the opposing arguments and tested them by the strongest proofs within his reach. It was in this way that he "gradually exchanged the principles of the old philosophy for those of the Newtonian system," that he relinquished the rigid predestinarian tenets for what appeared to be more rational and Scriptural doctrines, and that he gave in his adhesion to the Church of England while there were many worldly motives leading him to cling to "the provincial standard of orthodoxy."

As a preacher, Dr. Johnson, in the golden prime of his years, had attractive qualities. He himself said to his grandson towards the end of his days, that if he had been eminent for anything, it was for his eloquence. But eloquence has different forms of expression, and may not necessarily consist in studied rhetoric and passionate declamation. The power to interest and edify an audience, to move the heart and produce conviction, is a high intellectual quality, and the divine who possesses it, is in the truest sense of the word, eloquent. With a mind rich in theological lore, with clearness of method and plainness of speech, and with an earnest desire to promote the salvation of souls, Johnson was a minister in the Church of Christ whom neither the learned nor the unlearned could hear without pleasure and profit. The people followed him for the Word's sake, and it is upon record that at Christmas and other high festivals, his house was thronged for successive days with worshippers from the adjacent towns, who came to Stratford to enjoy the benefit of his public and private ministrations.

If he was great in pulpit eloquence and parochial duties, he was greater in his library and as an educator in systematic divinity and the laws of ecclesiastical polity. The Church in the northern portion of this country is largely indebted to him for training a generation of clergymen, who, with rare exceptions, adorned their vocation, and left the impress of their characters upon the communities in which they were appointed to labor. It is something to be thankful for, that in its headless condition there was one who knew so well how to instruct and guide the young candidates for Holy Orders, and to send them forth with his own passport on their perilous voyage across the Atlantic. He had a profound sense of the grandeur of the profession of a clergyman, and felt rightly enough that he could not be mistaken in educating those who came under his care, never to forget how their names were to become historic as pioneers of the Church in a new country, where all models of Christian character that did not approach the perfect ONE, would be despised or discredited.

It was a frequent expression of his to speak of the age as "abandoned and apostatizing." He used it in reference to the tendency of the times to infidelity, and seemed to have no patience with those who were ready to exchange the beauty of the Christian life and the vitality of the Christian faith for the cold dreams and theories of men of reprobate minds. Up to his decease, there had been no writers against Divine Revelation in this country worthy of note, but there had been large importations of skeptical books, and not a little mischief had been wrought by their circulation. He made it his business to acquaint himself with all publications of this nature, that he might know how to disarm the enemy and meet the demand for unreasonable and impossible conditions of belief. The brightest minds among the Dissenters, however much they might differ from him on doctrinal points and questions of ecclesiastical polity, made common cause with him in the defense of the foundations of our faith, and shared his anxiety to clear away the clouds of infidelity. They respected him for his learning and logical skill, and welcomed his system of philosophy as a most commendable effort in the interests and direction of the truth.

A century has passed by and the new atheism of this day needs to be met with something besides the older works on Christian evidence. Bishop Butler, who spoke to the mind of the English nation, in his celebrated "Analogy," has never been answered, nor have the testimonies collected by Leland and Leslie; but they are little read now, for modern infidelity addresses itself not so much to men of culture and refinement, as to the popular imagination, weaving itself into a miscellaneous literature, and at best presenting a masked portraiture of Christianity to blind the eyes of the unwary.

Dr. Johnson trusted firmly in the Divine promises, and did not believe that "the motley crew of Deists, Socinians, Arians, and factious unbelievers" of his time, as the son of Bishop Berkeley termed them, could demolish what is founded on a rock. He defended the faith heroically, and trained others to imitate himself, and be ready to "banish and drive away from the Church all erroneous and strange doctrines contrary to God's word." His name will ever have an important place in American history, and the more his character is studied, the more it will be seen how he applied his learning and Christian philosophy to the good of his country, and the advancement of the "one Catholic and Apostolic Church," in whose bosom the Lord "has promised his blessing and life forevermore."

APPENDIX.

APPENDIX A.

THE following letter, an accurate copy of the original, appears with slight variations in Boswell's "Life of Johnson." A foot-note credited to the "Gentleman's Magazine," states that "several letters passed between them, after the American Dr Johnson had returned to his native country; of which, however, it is found that this is the only one remaining."

It is "the only one" to which an answer has been found, and the answer is here printed for the first time from the original draught. He is known to have written one other letter, but probably the outbreak of the Revolution interrupted the correspondence. This was sent under cover, as appears from the filling up of the superscription, to Rev. Mr. White, afterwards Bishop of Pennsylvania, to whom the English Dr. Johnson wrote the same date, saying: "I take the liberty which you give me, of troubling you with a letter, of which you will please fill up the direction."

So highly did he esteem his American friend, that he presented him, before leaving England, with an elegantly bound copy of his large folio Dictionary, third edition, 1765; and an engraving of himself, from a painting of Sir Joshua Reynolds, which he considered his best likeness.

TO DR. JOHNSON: —

Sir, — Of all those whom the various accidents of life have brought within my notice, there is scarce any one whose acquaintance I have more desired to cultivate than yours. I cannot indeed charge you with neglecting me, yet our mutual inclination could scarce gratify itself with opportunities; the current of the day always bore us away from one another, and now the Atlantic is between us.

Whether you carried away an impression of me as pleasing as that which you left me of yourself, I know not; if you did, you have not forgotten me, and will be glad that I do not forget you. Merely to be remembered is indeed a barren pleasure, but it is one of the pleasures which is more sensibly felt as human nature is more exalted.

To make you wish that I should have you in my mind, I would be glad to tell you something which you do not know, but all public affairs are printed; and as you and I had no common friends, I can tell you no private history.

The Government I think grows stronger, but I am afraid the next general election will be a time of uncommon turbulence, violence, and outrage.

Of Literature no great product has appeared, or is expected; the attention of the people has for some years been otherwise employed.

I was told two days ago of a design which must excite some curiosity. Two ships are [in] preparation, which are under the command of Captain Constantine Phipps, to explore the Northern ocean, not to seek the Northeast or the Northwest passage, but to sail directly north, as near the pole as they can go. They hope to find an open ocean, but I suspect it is one mass of perpetual congelation. I do not much wish well to discoveries, for I am always afraid they will end in conquest and robbery.

I have been out of order this winter, but am grown better. Can I ever hope to see you again; or must I be always content to tell you that in another hemisphere,

I am, Sir, your most humble servant,

SAMUEL JOHNSON.

JOHNSON'S COURT, FLEET STREET, LONDON, *March* 4, 1773.

STRATFORD, *June* 5, 1773.

DEAR AND RESPECTED SIR, — I am perfectly unable to express the grateful sense I have of the singular honor you have done me by your favor of the 4th of March. There was no man in England whose acquaintance I so much wished to be honored with when I first embarked in my late voyage. Your excellent writings had given me the highest veneration and esteem of your character. I waited some time for some accidental or favorable introduction to you, but when none offered, I presumed so much on the idea I had formed of you, that I at last ventured to introduce myself to you in the abrupt manner you remember. The kind and obliging reception you then and ever after gave me, when I waited upon you, confirmed and increased my respect, and your kind remembrance of me now lays me under such obligations as I must never hope to repay. To be remembered by one of the first characters of an age in which there are so few whose remembrance is not rather a reproach than an honor, is, I assure you, to me one of the highest pleasures that I am capable of.

I bless God that at the date of your letter you were returning again to health, which I hope will be very long continued to you not only for your own sake, but of human nature, which will be benefited by your labors, for you live not for yourself, but for all mankind.

It will, I hope, be some satisfaction to you to know that your writings are in the highest esteem and are doing much good in this extensive and growing country, and will, I doubt not, continue to do so to very late posterity, for which reason, as well as for the increase of your reputation, which I assure you is very dear to me, I hope you will be still preparing something for the public, who will read with the utmost avidity whatever appears under the sanction of your name.

It gives me great pleasure to learn from so good an authority that Government grows stronger. You had indeed convinced me that the alarm which the factious and the desperate had excited was false, but I hardly expected when I left England that Government would have obtained so speedy and so manifest a superiority over the friends of confusion, as, if we may credit the printed accounts, it seems to have done. From them it would seem as if the cause of opposition was almost desperate. It must be expected, however, that every effort will be made to revive it against the next general election, and I wish your apprehensions may not be verified: but still I hope there is no great danger of their gaining so great advantages as to enable them to do much mischief to the public. Upon the stability of Government will depend also in a high degree the felicity of this country. The Government have much to do here when the opinion that has been maintained by the Boston Assembly [in] a late dispute with no opposition to their Governor, that the Colonies are independent of the Parliament of Great Britain, gains ground, and will require their attention unless they mean to acquiesce in the idea and give up their authority over us, which I presume they will not be inclined to do.

The design you mention of exploring the Northern Ocean, is an experiment of great curiosity, and I shall be impatient to know the success of it. I have ever entertained the opinion you seem to have adopted that the Pole is the empire of frost and snow, which will effectually forever stop the gains from those evils which, as you justly remark, have generally been the consequence of discoveries. Neither ambition nor avarice, I fancy, will there have any opportunity for gratification; we shall only acquire an innocent and perhaps useless acquaintance with an unknown part of our globe.

I wish I could gratify you with any intelligence from this side of the Atlantic; but nothing occurs to me worthy of your notice. I have lost since my return to America my venerable father, who, to his other good qualities, added a sincere respect and esteem for you, and was extremely minute and particular in his inquiries concerning you. We had the happiness to spend three months together after my return, when he expired full of days, satisfied with life, with hopes full of immortality, and without a groan or any apparent previous pain.

For myself I am again engaged largely in the busy, and in this country not very profitable profession of the law, which, however, answers tolerably well for the support of the numerous young family with which God has blessed me. That you may enjoy every felicity, and long, very long continue as you have done to bless mankind, be useful to the world, is and will be the sincere and ardent prayer of, dear Sir,

Your most obedient and most faithful humble servant,

WM. SAMUEL JOHNSON.

TO DR. SAMUEL JOHNSON.

Johnson's Court, Fleet Street, London.

APPENDIX B.

ELIZABETHTOWN, *June* 20, 1774.

MY DEAR SIR, — The not seeing you on your return from Philadelphia last winter, was a considerable disappointment to me, as I partly depended upon your spending a day here, that we might have time to read over, while together, the "Life" of your father which I had compiled a year before. If I could have consented to send it to the press without your inspection and examination, it would have been published long ago, but I have all along been impressed with a strong sense both of your right to be consulted, and of the advantage which the work would receive from your correction, and perhaps from your addition, which has hitherto, and will still cause me to suppress it, till it can be honored with your *Imprimatur*. With a view chiefly to this I have proposed from time to time, to take a journey into New England; but difficulties have as often arisen to interrupt me. Once indeed, I could have come, but I recollected that you must then be engaged in attendance upon the General Court at Hartford, and consequently would not be at leisure, nor at home to consider matters of a literary nature. As, therefore, I have no prospect of going your way, and hear not of your intending to come this way, during the present summer, I have determined to *send* you, as I am like to have no opportunity of *bringing*, the rough copy of the "Life;" requesting you to examine it very closely, and to make such corrections upon any parts of it as may occur upon a careful perusal. I expect Mr. Beach to call upon me in an hour or two in his way to New England, by whom I propose to send it; and if you can be ready to return it by him,[1] it will be so much the better.

I shall send with it your father's MS. that you may compare them together. On that comparison you will find that I have used it only as a guide, preserving the facts in their chronological order, adding many anecdotes collected from other quarters, and some of them recollected from what I formerly knew, and expressing the whole in my own language. This I thought would better answer the general design than confining myself more strictly to the MS. I have concluded the whole with a portrait of the character of my beloved patron and friend. I could wish to do it justice; in order to which I would neither say too much nor too little. As I find that private affection is apt to predominate, I have endeavored to be on my guard, in this part, which is by far the most difficult of the whole. Be so good, therefore, as to bestow a particular attention to this part, and advise and assist me in it with all freedom.

In transcribing for the press, I fancy I can make some considerable improvements, especially by way of notes. I have, as you will see, made some references to authors, extracts from which are intended for that use.

As soon as you return the "Life," I think of issuing Proposals to see what encouragement can be procured for a publication of this nature. New England, and especially Connecticut, I flatter myself, will subscribe liberally to the work. New York may be expected to do something, and the Colonies to the southward of it but very little. With right management I should imagine a pretty large subscription may be procured; in which case I may save myself here, although I have lost money by every former publication I have been concerned in. If you think proper, I will try what encouragement can be had for a volume of your father's sermons, towards which but little can be expected this way. When I have done what I have to do, I will return you all the papers,

[1] Rev. Abraham Beach, then Missionary of the Church of England at New Brunswick, and afterwards assistant minister of Trinity Church, New York.

letters, etc., which you were so good as to transmit to me· but while anything is depending, it is best that they should remain in my hands ; for which reason I must desire you to send back the original MS., from which the "Life" is chiefly compiled.

By so good an opportunity I shall send a copy of my "Free Examination," etc., of which I request your acceptance. A few copies were subscribed for, and five or six paid for in Connecticut; but as strange as it may seem, I have not been able to get them sent. Gaine says it has not been possible to procure a binder to do them up in New York, as every person of that occupation was previously engaged in other business; however, he now promises that they shall be forwarded very soon. A copy arrived in England about the beginning of April; and the Bishops, etc., ordered the subtance of my "Free Examination," together with Sherlock's "Memorial," to be immediately reprinted there, imagining it might be of service at that critical time when a plan was under consideration for the future regulation of the Colonies. Lord Dartmouth took up the cause of the Church, and appointed to meet, and consult with the Bishop of London about the Episcopate requested. He thought of bringing the case immediately before the Parliament; but the Bishop of Oxford was of opinion that the Parliament had no business with it, and that it was best to wait for the event of the Boston Expedition.

With compliments to Mrs. Johnson, Mr. Kneeland, and your families,

I am, with great truth and sincerity,

Your very respectful and obedient servant,

THOMAS B. CHANDLER.

DR. JOHNSON.

After the Revolution and the settlement of the Government, he wrote again in answer to a request for the return of the papers as follows: —

ELIZABETHTOWN, *December* 28, 1785.

MY DEAR SIR, — Although I do and always shall think myself honored and obliged by every line I may receive from you, yet I am ashamed that I have given occasion for that of the 21st instant, by not sending you, or at least, not giving you some satisfaction concerning the papers of your most excellent father, my ever honored friend and patron. I am ashamed too, that I have not sooner returned the "Journal" of the Convention in Virginia, which you kindly put into my hands on my first arrival in New York. These neglects will not admit of a full justification, yet I beg you to allow as much as you can to the following apology.

To a person of my disposition, and in my situation, it was impossible, for a considerable while after I got home, to attend to any matters of business excepting that kind of business mentioned by Sir T. Moore; *nempe reverso domum, cum uxore fabulandum est, garriendum cum liberis, colloquendum cum ministris. Quæ ego omnia inter negotia numero.* As soon as I was able to attend to other matters, I found my books and papers in such confusion and so widely dispersed, many of them being still in New York, and in different hands there, that it was the work of much time to collect and arrange them. When I had got together the bigger part of your father's sermons, letters, etc., considering that everything of the kind must be peculiarly agreeable to the family, I meant to send them to you in New York, but, upon inquiry, was informed that you were gone into the country. Mr. Beach paid me a visit about the 10th of November, and then informed me that you were not in town. Since that time I have had the same answer to the same question, and did not know of your return, till I learned it from your letter. I shall now soon send you, to the care of Mr. Livingston, the various articles I have collected, they being, in my opinion, too bulky to go by post, unless divided into different parcels. Most of the Sermons and Letters I have found, and am not without hopes of finding the remainder. As to the "Memoir," I took it with me to England, imagining it would be safer with me, though subject to the perils of the sea, than if left behind, "in perils among false brethren." I brought it back with me in good preservation.

I have taken the liberty of inclosing a letter for Bishop Seabury, and must beg the favor of your passport for it. I now return the "Journal" of the Convention in Virginia. I had hardly time to read it in New York, and I brought it over with me, that I might be able to give a better account of the transactions to some people in England, in letters which I was a long time in writing. After making this use of it, I meant to send it with the other papers; and for the reasons assigned above, this part of my intention has not sooner been carried into execution. In the meanwhile, I hope you have not suffered greatly for want of this curious publication. A curiosity indeed it is for it exhibits such a motley mixture of Episcopacy, Presbytery and Ecclesiastical Republicanism as before was never brought together and incorporated, and must surprise the whole Christian world.

The proceedings of the Convention in Philadelphia, which is to be considered as a kind of *Œcumenical* Council, were much in the same style, though not so wild and intemperate. In their Address to the English Archbishops, they say that it is "their earnest desire and resolution to retain the venerable form of Episcopal government;" and yet they have placed their Church under a government that is evidently Presbyterian. Conventions, consisting of ministers and lay-elders, or messengers (no matter by what name they are called), are to meet without the call or license of the Bishop; it does not appear that he is to have any negative upon their proceedings, or even to *preside ex officio*; and, in case of his delinquency, he is to be arraigned before the tribunal of his own presbyters, etc., who have a power to displace him. They expect the Bishops in England to countenance this new-fangled Episcopate; but, from what I know of them, I can hardly believe that they will be aiding to a scheme formed with a design to degrade the Episcopal order by depriving it of that authority which it has ever claimed and exercised as an essential and unalienable right, since the time of the Apostles.

In Connecticut the Church has proceeded upon other maxims, and merits the approbation and applause of all the friends of genuine Episcopacy. I wish that so fair and proper an example may still, if possible, be followed in the other States. The more I consider the matter, the more I am pleased, that, as yet, you have made no alterations in the Liturgy, but such as are necessary to accommodate it to the change of Government.

You are pleased to intimate an inclination or wish to make me a visit. I should be extremely happy in seeing you here, and in giving you the best reception in my power; and I shall rejoice in every kind of opportunity of proving myself to be, with peculiar esteem and respect,

Your very affectionate humble servant,

T. B. Chandler.

Dr. W. S. Johnson.

INDEX.

A.

B.

K.

L.

BY THE SAME AUTHOR.

History of the Episcopal Church in Connecticut, from 1635 to 1865.

Two volumes, 8*vo,* $6.00.

www.ingramcontent.com/pod-product-compliance
Lightning Source LLC
LaVergne TN
LVHW020118110826
845151LV00001B/195

9781425542627